An Emergence Approach to Speech Acquisition

Doing and Knowing

Barbara L. Davis

and

Lisa M. Bedore

Ψ Psychology Press
Taylor & Francis Group
NEW YORK AND LONDON

First published 2013
by Psychology Press
711 Third Avenue, New York, NY 10017

Simultaneously published in the UK
by Psychology Press
27 Church Road, Hove, East Sussex BN3 2FA

Psychology Press is an imprint of the Taylor & Francis Group, an informa business

© 2013 Taylor & Francis

Library of Congress Cataloging in Publication Data
An emergence approach to speech acquisition : doing and knowing / edited by
Barbara L. Davis and Lisa M. Bedore.
    p. cm.
    Includes bibliographical references.
    1. Grammar, Comparative and general – Phonology. 2. Language acquisition.
    3. Speech. I. Davis, Barbara L. (Barbara Lockett) II. Bedore, Lisa M.
    P217.E44 2013
    414–dc23   2012034217

ISBN: 978-0-8058-4963-9 (hbk)
ISBN: 978-1-84872-654-3 (pbk)
ISBN: 978-0-203-37530-3 (ebk)

Typeset in Sabon
by HWA Text and Data Management, London

Contents

1 The Problem

OVERVIEW

The young child's ability to integrate physical speech perception and production capacities for building a neural cognitive knowledge base about her ambient language phonology is a uniquely human achievement. Between birth and four or five years of age, children's biologically based capacities, embodied in the production and perception systems, allow them to perceive, process, and produce a broadening array of ideas about their world. A growing phonological knowledge system grounded in neural structures and cognitive function provides the organizational means to interpret and express these increasingly complex messages. At the same time, the child's social environment expands from intimate parent–child interactions to links with an increasing diversity of communication partners. Children implement this heterogeneous and dynamically changing behavioral-cognitive-social system, driven by the functional goal of sending and receiving their broadening array of ideas about the world.

Theoretical perspectives about the nature of phonological acquisition abound. We will discuss them throughout this narrative. However, in a context of multiple competing options for understanding acquisition of phonology, our central goal is to evaluate the strength of an emergence perspective for this central component of spoken language. A primary question arises immediately: What is emergence? To start this discussion, we are going to propose a short working definition.

Phonological knowledge and organized behavioral patterns for coding that knowledge arise out of interactions among diverse physical, cognitive, and social systems that are accessible within the young child's world. The child's physical capacities include her abilities for processing perceptual input, neural-cognitive storage and retrieval capacities, and increasing ability to produce intelligible speech output. These physical or embodied capacities are used by the child to connect with the outside world through social capacities for sustaining interactions. Other people provide relevant social input for what and how to deploy components of the phonological system in communicating.

In an emergence view, all of these components are necessary to account for complex phonological capacities in young children that support growth toward intelligible speech patterns and comprehensive ambient language knowledge. Crucially, none of the components of this complex system is uniquely causal of the eventual product in an emergence view. While all may be necessary, none is sufficient to facilitate acquisition of the phonological component of language. We assert that available theoretical perspectives devoted to understanding acquisition of phonology are insufficient to model the overall process. An integrative view based on tenets of emergence can enable understanding the process of phonological acquisition comprehensively.

Interaction is a critical term that we employ throughout our narrative as a basic principle underlying our concept of emergence. Interaction refers to the kind of observable properties that occur based on the combined or reciprocal action of two or more physical systems. For example, perceptual and neural systems or individual children and caregiver social dyads may interrelate with one another. These physical systems and individuals within social relationships have an ongoing and reciprocal effect on one another.

The idea of a two-way effect is also essential to this concept of interaction. A one-way causal effect might be indicated if the perceptual system driving the neural encoding of knowledge had no interactions with the child's previous experience while she constructed an ambient language knowledge base. In social interactions, a one-way effect might be postulated if the child's maturation (e.g. Fodor and Katz, 1964) was the only factor seen as responsible for triggering of ambient language phonological knowledge. Two-way effects encompass diverse systems and their reciprocal interactions with each other across acquisition.

Interaction relates to the moment-by-moment experiences in the young child's life that evidence the working of the dynamic and complex system. A closely related term is interconnectivity. Interconnectivity implies that all the components of a complex system change and are changed by one another dynamically across acquisition. Interconnectivity is the result of the multiple interactions between the child and her environment that enable the emergence of phonological knowledge and behavioral patterns.

So what are the components that serve emergence? Several unique and interconnected strands compose our view of the acquisition of phonological knowledge. The first is the child's internal production, perception, and neural-cognitive capacities. These are the abilities that the child brings to the task of phonological acquisition. They can be seen as *embodied* in the sense that they are founded in the child's own bodily "equipment" for accomplishing this task. It is important to emphasize that "internal" refers to bodily abilities that grow and change with interactions of the child and the environment as well as with maturation. In an emergence view, they are not merely innate static properties that reveal phonological a priori phonological knowledge as the child matures. These capacities are critical and active components of the complex system.

Child internal capacities by themselves do not explain acquisition of phonology. A second factor is found in the child and adult's reliable capacities for social interaction. Capacities to initiate and sustain social interactions reflect a complementary and necessary set of factors for the child's internal physical capacities of perception, processing, and producing vocal output. These socially mediated links between the child's core physical capacities and available input from her environment drive incremental refinements in neural structure and function (Mareshal *et al.*, 2007) necessary to encode cognitively based phonological knowledge.

The social and cultural input from the environment illustrates a third dimension. The surrounding social environment refers to communication partners who employ the child's ambient language phonological code in culturally appropriate ways to produce relevant and salient messages for her. This external scaffolding also creates functional pressure on the young child for intelligible communication. Input regarding precision of the sound qualities the child needs to produce for intelligible communication is readily available in daily social interactions with familiar communication partners (Lee *et al.*, 2008). This rich matrix of environmental input sustains the young child's need to function for survival (Locke *et al.*, 1995). It also provides critical information to the child about learning to use the phonological component of language to code linguistically based communicative functions (e.g. to request or to refuse).

Critically, in an emergence perspective, these three components are not specific to language acquisition, or even to humans. In this regard, we will make the argument throughout that they are domain general rather than language dedicated. In addition, a single factor among these interconnected components of the system cannot be causal. Rather, the child's process of successful acquisition depends on the integrated whole interacting dynamically, and is reflected in emergence of behavioral expressions and growth in underlying knowledge (Thelen and Smith, 1994).

Increasingly complex behavioral output makes manifest the increasing efficiency of interconnections among these diverse strands across the acquisition process. Growth in diversity of goal-directed movements observable through the child's production of more types of sounds and sequences emerges in concert with the child's abilities to refine and replicate frequently available words perceived in ambient language input from communication partners. At the same time, an increase in the child's cognitive knowledge about the world, enabled via these social interactions, feeds into neural-cognitive storage of an expanding phonological knowledge base.

WHY CONSIDER EMERGENCE?

What might be our motivation for exploring an emergence conceptualization for the phonological component of language? One primary incentive springs from an intuition that phonological acquisition presents a fruitful area for thinking about complexity. Language is one of the most complex and unique capacities that humans possess. Mastery of the phonological knowledge component of language allows the speaker to coordinate the production of an ordered set of complex peripheral production system movements and perceptual capacities with a knowledge base of relevant sound patterns to respond to input or initiate linguistic output. Rather than describing phonological patterns using the frequency of language forms themselves as an explanation for proposed universal aspects of knowledge, emergence perspectives offer the option of considering diverse sources of evidence for the complex patterns observable in children and in adult speakers and listeners. In particular, the peripheral speech production and perception mechanisms are foundational to building an eventual long-term neural-cognitive phonological knowledge store.

As a second motivation, we also want to consider emergence as a perspective on acquisition to understand individual variation in children's pathways to achieving phonological knowledge and a behavioral repertoire (DePaolis *et al.*, 2008; Vihman, in press). This issue is relevant at the level of the individual child in considering the relationship between central tendencies for acquisition of sound patterns in languages and the potential range of unique child differences. Central tendencies reinforce a notion of universal patterns as an approach to understanding the emergence of phonological form. In an emergence perspective, the actions of the body, in particular the perception and production system, are common properties of children's biological makeup across all language communities. This common basis for observable vocal patterns implies that early periods of development may likely be similar across languages (Kern and Davis, in review, 2012).

Some classical phonological approaches have emphasized universal aspects of underlying grammar (UG) in the process of acquisition.

There the status of proposed UG knowledge rather than the observable behavioral repertoire based on common biological capacities is central to understanding the nature of acquisition. In contrast, cognitively oriented approaches emphasize individual differences in the path to acquiring phonological capacities (Vihman and Croft, 2007; Ferguson and Farwell, 1975). There, the emphasis is on the proposal that each child learner individualizes the status of underlying phonological knowledge in formative periods based on use. Emergence approaches can potentially encompass both central tendencies and individual variations into the complex system underlying acquisition. Neutralizing this dichotomy may potentially produce a more comprehensive picture of acquisition. Emergence perspectives can potentially accommodate this neutralization.

An additional motivation for our interest in relationships between individual variations and central tendencies in phonological acquisition comes from our clinical background in speech language pathology. Speech language pathologists deal with a range of speech production and/or phonological disorders. The origins of these disorders can be found in perceptual (e.g. hearing impairment), motor (e.g. cerebral palsy), structural (e.g. cleft palate), neural-cognitive (e.g. traumatic brain injuries, genetic syndromes, mental retardation), and social (e.g. autism) dimensions of development. As well, many developmental speech disorders are functional, or of unknown origin, potentially based on either immaturity of speech production and/or perception mechanisms, or in differences in a child's phonological knowledge base for the ambient language sound system.

Conceptualizing individual variability and central tendencies for clinical assessment and treatment is consistent with an emergent complexity perspective. Emergence offers a path to describing and understanding variations in starting points based on differences in perception, production, cognition, or social components of the child's capacities for developing intelligible speech. Outcomes of intervention logically related to differences in these capacities can characterize individual child profiles of developmental disorder or difference. Accounting for known variations in starting points for acquisition based on perceptual, production, cognitive, and social differences are the "meat and potatoes" of clinical assessment and intervention planning for children with developmental differences.

As an example, an emergence perspective can offer a way of explaining how interventions at a variety of time points in development can produce similar treatment outcomes. Sharma and colleagues' (e.g. Sharma *et al.*, 2007, 2009) exploration of the neural consequences of hearing loss provides an exemplar emphasizing the impact of perceptual differences from an emergence perspective. Issues surrounding repair for prenatally determined clefts of the palate provide another opportunity to consider the importance of differences in the structure of the production system on phonological acquisition. Both of these examples of internal differences in biological subsystems illustrate a view of multiple system components responsible for emergence of phonology. We will return to this issue in some detail in Chapter 4.

WHAT EMERGES?

Critical to evaluating an emergence perspective is a definition of the complex system that we propose. In the case of phonological acquisition, contemporary theories have centered on both structural properties of language (i.e. consonant and vowel phonemes and their rules for combination) and the process by which language structures are decoded and encoded (i.e. memory, storage, and retrieval processes for phonological structures). Fully developed phonological skills permit adult speakers and listeners to generate and understand a potentially infinite array of linguistic messages. That is the long-term outcome of acquisition for young humans. Accordingly, we will review contemporary definitions of language to generate a necessary set of background information for considering emergence proposals on acquisition.

STRUCTURAL DESCRIPTIONS

A general characterization of language is "the words, their pronunciation, and the methods of combination used and understood by a community" (Colman, 2001). This definition is particularly apt for our endeavor, because it emphasizes the role of pronunciation of words, which includes both phonetic implementation and phonological knowledge within a shared ambient language community.

Within the broader realm of language, phonology is the store of knowledge that a speaker/listener has about phonemes and the rules for combining them in linguistic communication. Phonemes are sound types used to contrast meaning in a language (e.g. pig and big). These contrastive entities and their combinations differ across the 7,000 or so languages that are spoken today. To make these contrastive sounds and patterns, speakers exploit biologically available sound-making capacities differently. For example, Arabic contains guttural phonemes and Xhosa speakers utilize clicks for making meaning distinctions. Both sound types are produced using contact very far back in the throat. Neither of these sound types is used to contrast meanings in English or Russian.

A phonological knowledge system provides the tools to generate unlimited mutually understandable and unique utterances (Hockett, 1960) in adult speakers. This phenomenon is termed "duality of patterning." That is, modern languages have both a meaningless level of structure composed of a finite list of sounds that combine in constrained ways to form words, and a meaningful level of structure in which those words combine to form sentences. Duality describes a fundamental property of languages whereby mature speakers can produce and understand a limitless array of meaningful words and utterances with a finite number of meaningless sound building blocks.

The phonetic and phonological systems interact with other levels of linguistic knowledge and production. Words code semantic conceptualizations for speakers. Words consist of sound sequences that a speaker must recognize in order to activate the corresponding meaning. Young children are more likely to remember and reproduce words with sounds and sound sequences that are within their productive repertoire (e.g. Storkel, 2006). Phonological working memory, or the ability to remember sound sequences, is associated with vocabulary learning throughout childhood and is a predictor of second language acquisition (Gathercole and Baddeley, 1993; Reuterskiold-Wagner et al., 2005; Santos and Bueno, 2003; Service, 1992).

Morphological knowledge is an additional aspect of linguistic form that is an aspect of mature language interacting with phonological knowledge for understanding and producing messages. Morphemes are the smallest units that delineate syntactic meaning in language (e.g. the plural marker -s on dots). Comparisons across structures and languages suggest that speakers are more easily able to learn and produce forms that are salient due to their stress or sentence position than forms that are more difficult to process (e.g. Slobin, 1985; Leonard, 1998).

Finally, at the level of discourse in which speakers organize sounds, words, and morphemes into multiword strings or utterances, it is challenging to communicate effectively unless these embedded forms can be produced in ways that are readily comprehensible to others in the speech community. Thus, phonology is integral to every level of linguistic knowledge and production. The mutual understanding of language-specific requirements for phonemic, semantic, syntactic and morphophonemic sequences is critical for successful communication among speakers of individual languages. These diverse areas of linguistic description interleave at the level of relationships between sounds and messages (Givon, 2009).

PROCESS DESCRIPTIONS

The process of generating linguistic communication needs to be incorporated into a full expression of speaker/listener capacities that children must master. With mastery, the child achieves a mature system that works successfully for language-based communication. This area of study has been termed psycholinguistics, referring to the cognitive processing required to understand, store, and produce ambient language phonological structures. Relative to the encoding and decoding of linguistic structures for listening and speaking, adult capacities provide a view of the destination for the child acquiring phonology. They do not specify the onset or nature of the acquisition process.

ENCODING

In adult speakers, speech encoding, or producing speech, encompasses the entire process from mental preparation and planning to actual execution. This process highlights the continuing central role of both phonetic capacities and phonological knowledge in fully intelligible linguistic communication. While these capacities are deployed in manual sign language systems (Goldin-Meadow, 2009), our focus in this work is on consideration of oral language acquisition.

Common components in diverse psycholinguistic models of mature speech production include conceptualization, lexical and phonological representation, and phonetic encoding for execution of overt speech forms. Some models focus on a linear relationship between components, from conceptualizing an idea, to generating and forming the words for that idea, to executing the needed utterance (Levelt and Meyer, 2000). Other models include the concept of spreading activation, centered on a process of weighting across and between semantic and phonological units as the individual speaker experiences repeated instances of input processing (Hanley *et al.*, 2004). Regardless of the scope and emphasis of various models, all agree on the necessity for the speaker to associate phonological information with semantic content and the necessity of rapidly coding messages with phonological forms.

Several models of adult speech production have outlined the sequence and components of speech encoding (e.g. Levelt, 1999; Bock, 1982; Hanley *et al.*, 2004; Gupta and MacWhinney, 1997). Consideration of these components and their associations provides a general picture of the acquisition task for the child. These models propose specific sequences of lexical and syntactic encoding prior to a phonological encoding stage.

Levelt and Meyer (2000), for example, propose that the speaker starts by selecting lexical items and their syntactic frames (i.e. verbs and their related arguments) necessary to express an idea from what the authors refer to as the rhetorical-semantic-syntactic system. Once retrieved, the phonetic and phonological representations of these elements are ready for motor encoding. At this level, a key aspect of Levelt and Meyer's scheme is the separation of morphological, phonological, and phonetic encoding. This separation allows the mature speaker to retrieve the precise morpho-phonological form required first to produce a sentence. For example, when encoding the concept of more than one, or plural, adult speakers retrieve an /ez/ for foxes, /–s/ for cats, and /–z/ for dogs.

Also of interest is the inclusion of a syllabary in which to translate phonological representations of syllables to phonetic syllables for output. Some modelers propose that syllabification does not take place online. Levelt and colleagues (Cholin *et al.*, 2006; Levelt and Meyer, 2000) suggest that speakers increase their efficiency by retrieving practiced syllables via the syllabary. Along similar lines, Hanley *et al.* (2004) propose, as part of their spreading activation model, that frequently practiced forms can be retrieved by speakers via a non-lexical route which permits imitation.

In these models, feedback loops exist at several points to ensure the fidelity of the speaker's message. Levelt and Meyer (2000) propose feedback links at the levels of the rhetorical-semantic-syntactic system for formulating the message as well as feedback links from the encoding and output phases of production. Bock (1982) suggests interconnections with working memory at the cognitive level, as well as during the phonetic and motor control phases.

Consideration of psycholinguistic models is paramount for understanding phonological development in the context of overall language acquisition. Models of oral language highlight the central role of phonetic capacities, phonological knowledge, and successful cognitively based retrieval mechanisms for linguistic encoding.

Speech encoding models rely on top–down processing from intent to utterance execution. Top–down processing here refers to the mental processes available to adult speakers with knowledge of the components of their ambient language system and the goal-directed praxis abilities to execute it rapidly and accurately. In contrast, in child speakers and listeners the process of acquiring the adult system is dynamic and changing rapidly in some phases. Sounds and their combinations, meanings, and the accompanying syntax and morphological requirements for utterance types gradually grow in diversity and complexity to match the adult speaker–listener decoding/encoding continuum. Inferences about phonological acquisition from models based on mature speakers are limited accordingly. The mature speaker begins with the generation of an idea or conceptualization. In contrast, children begin with the ability to produce speech-like vocal sequences without attached meaning during canonical babbling. Only towards the end of the first year or the beginning of the second year do they begin to link meaning with vocal forms in order to communicate socially (i.e. "milk" for requesting milk). Growth toward language mastery in both knowledge and behavior proceeds across a number of years.

The child may acquire output complexity to match mature speakers in two potentially overlapping stages. These stages include a bottom–up course of acquisition founded on biological production and perception capacities interacting with an emerging knowledge of the lexical, morphological, and syntactic aspects of language. We will refer to this early stage as *moving and sensing*. The young child uses simple forms like "mama" and learns that this vocalization can be used to get picked up by her mother. A longer stage that we term *refining pattern complexity* follows. In refining the complexity of phonological behavior, the child increasingly gains the ability to use top–down knowledge and goal-directed behaviors to encode more complex speech patterns. These increasingly complex knowledge and behavioral capacities enable the child to have increasing success in matching diverse language targets in social contexts. Growth in linguistic complexity reflects the child's growth in a suite of capacities for sustaining connections with people around her to get what she wants, effectively participating in social interactions while expressing increasingly diverse ideas. Use of knowledge about word types includes understanding when they are used to communicate messages. This last aspect encompasses the cultural dimension of message transmission.

DECODING

According to Cutler and Clifton, adult speech perception refers to a "device for conversion of acoustic input into meaning" (1999: 123). Sensing of the auditory signal by the peripheral hearing mechanisms indicates an initial psychoacoustic level of processing, termed auditory input. Decoding forms a second step in listening. Here the listener has to separate speech from other types of auditory input arriving simultaneously at the ear. The successful listener must exploit the periodic nature of speech signals as well as group mechanisms related to frequency of occurrence of sounds and sequences in input in order to successfully separate the acoustic signal of interest for actual speech processing from other sound patterns available at the same time.

Once the listener has effectively isolated speech input, he or she converts the code into more abstract levels of representation across a variety of sites for diversity, including differing utterance contexts and rates of speech as well as the age and gender of speakers. Segmentation of the acoustic signal permits the listener to recognize words and interpret utterances. Subsequent word recognition involves concurrent activation and competition within the lexicon available in the listener's long-term memory storage. Selection of the spoken word with accompanying morphological structure will constrain decoding relative to higher-level knowledge structures. This process of retrieval is termed *priming* in experimental paradigms. At a semantic level, the competition process may include simultaneous cross-modal priming of all ambiguous meanings regardless of word frequency (e.g. "weak"/"week" could trigger retrieval of both "strong" and "time") (Lucas, 1987). Utterance interpretation and integration includes dividing the sentence into components, determining the syntactic and semantic relationships of parts to the whole sentence, and placing them into the conversational discourse structure. Knowledge of language structure as well as the information provided by the particular words retrieved enables this part of the listener's task.

Models of the speech decoding process carry the same caveat as speech production models: A top–down emphasis assumes the presence of mature knowledge structures and processing strategies for perceiving, segmenting, and attaching meaning to language input. In contrast, the young child starts at the "bottom," with a wealth of domain-general biological and social capacities that can enable growth in knowledge structures about the phonological pattern regularities of her ambient language. Consideration of the speech decoding system in mature speakers gives a picture of the endpoint of the acquisition process. Importantly, an emergence view does not specify either the beginning child system or the qualitatively unique nature of the child's system throughout the acquisition process (although see Pinker, 1994, for an extended treatment of the opposing view within a continuity assumption).

HOW DOES EMERGENCE CONTRIBUTE TO UNDERSTANDING OF PHONOLOGICAL DEVELOPMENT?

In the context of a fully expressed definition of the phonological component of language in adult speakers and listeners, we want to set out a definition of emergence as a perspective on understanding the child's acquisition of this complex system. We want to investigate implications and presently available evidence that acquisition is both a reflection of the operation of a socially embedded biological system for gaining knowledge and a biologically based neural and output system observable in the child's behavioral repertoire for expressing knowledge. Phonological knowledge and behavior emerges from this complex and diverse human biological, cognitive, and social system.

Clearly, scholarly inquiry needs to move toward multidisciplinary attempts to formulate hypotheses that can test this assumption fully. Because phonological acquisition provides an example of emergent complexity, we hope to use it to tie child language development into the study of other natural phenomena, rather than keeping language conceptually separated from other complex systems in nature. As a corollary aspect of considering the relationship of emergence perspectives to phonological acquisition, we hope to spur the generation of research hypotheses to drive the interdisciplinary programs necessary for beginning to test hypotheses about emergence.

The biological sciences have long recognized the importance of interaction among and within organisms as being instrumental in emergence of functionally based complex behavioral repertoires. We suggest that dynamic social interaction capacities as well as abilities for mastery of complex input and output patterns underlies biological, cognitive, social, and cultural changes in young humans as well. In the case of language, the dynamic system that grows and changes across the acquisition timeline serves the child well. It helps her establish the social connections she needs to function optimally in her environment in a wide variety of dimensions. It also provides a potentially robust avenue to understanding the emergence of phonological knowledge and its expression in behavioral input and output processing by peripheral body systems.

Advances in contemporary scientific perspectives and paradigms in biological and physical sciences related to emergence of complex systems offer real hope for the realization of Lindblom's (2008) call for understanding of phonological systems from perspectives independent of the phenomenon of language itself. In short, how can we understand phonological systems in languages independent of frequency counts of components of those languages? Investigating the strength of independent explanatory principles is a critical aspect that suggests consideration of emergence.

Several contemporary theoretical perspectives are relevant to understanding the basic claims that follow from an emergence perspective on phonological acquisition. Complexity theory (Prigogine and Stengers, 1984), dynamic systems theory (Thelen and Smith, 1994), and embodiment theory (Clark, 1997) have been used to consider both biological and non-biologically based complex systems. None has been extensively linked with phonological acquisition (although, see Chirotan *et al.*, 2009 for reviews; Bybee, 2010). Complexity theory has been employed to characterize complex systems as diverse as weather systems, fluid motion, and population dynamics, phenomena that had long resisted linear explanations. Embodiment has been explored in construction of artificial intelligence systems (Boden, 2006) and in early cognitive-motor development (Smith and Gasser, 2005). It seems helpful to explore these theories as they may fruitfully apply to defining the nature and scope of emergence of phonological complexity in humans.

COMPLEXITY THEORY

Conceptualizations underlying complexity theory afford the most general theoretical framework for considering phonology as an exemplar of emergence. Studies of physics and geological sciences formed a first scholarly site for evaluation of contemporary complexity science assertions (e.g. Prigogine and Stengers, 1984; Haken, 1977). Observation of weather systems illustrates an early example of the application of complexity theory. These natural systems are composed of unique assemblies of separate components (e.g. clouds, air pressure, and moisture) that underlie observable phenomena (i.e. hurricanes, tornados). More recently, widely diverse disciplines, including developmental biology (Kauffman, 1995) and comparative studies of the biological structures and functions of diverse organisms (Camazine *et al.*, 2001) have utilized the explanatory power of complexity science. In comparative biology, complexity science is used to support understanding of structurally and functionally oriented behavioral patterns in groups of complex multi-cellular organisms as diverse as slime molds and fireflies, or the body markings of zebras.

The basic components of complexity science are consistent with the emergence view of phonological acquisition we are proposing. Complexity science refers to a view of complex phenomena where local components of a system interact and complex behavior emerges from those connections (Holland, 1998). Local interactions create interconnectivity in the sense that we have described it.

Applied to acquisition of the phonological component of language, phonological knowledge and behavioral patterns emerge from connections enabled by domain-general child capacities. As an example, local social interactions between mothers and children create mutually understood communications. These communications are coded with recognizable sounds as the child utilizes perception-cognition-production system links in the context of familiar social routines with her mother (e.g. the "peek-a-boo" routine). Child-internal interconnections between physical systems of the body and social interaction capacities tuned by input are all available to the child. These capacities enable her to differentiate between salient and non-essential incoming stimuli, gain and store increasingly precise phonological knowledge structures, and perform more diverse goal-directed movements related to her ambient language requirements. All of these strands cooperate in enabling the system to gain complexity. It is useful, therefore, to take into account some of the claims of complexity science as they fill out our definition of emergence of the phonological component of language across acquisition.

PATTERNS

A basic principle of complexity science across diverse scientific disciplines is the emergence of complex patterns. A pattern at the most general level is "a particular or organized arrangement of objects in space or time" (Camazine *et al.*, 2001). Within complexity science, pattern acquisition is the result of a continuous series of behavioral organizations and reorganizations. Gottlieb has proposed a psychobiological or developmental systems framework to characterize this non-linear process of organization and reorganization in human infants (see Gottlieb, 2001).

All of the components we propose as critical to emergence of patterns of phonological knowledge and behavior are seen as contributing to these types of patterns emerging from the complex system. Lower-level components of the system include both the child's active internal (biological) and external (social) capacities in addition to the widely attested passive processes of physical maturation. Continual interconnectivity between the internal and external parameters of the child's system creates and reinforces the foundation for emergence of phonological knowledge and goal-directed behavior. The child learns to produce a /b/ and to store and retrieve it for coding *ball*, *baby*, *cub*, and the myriad of other words that she is learning as she gains social competence and knowledge of her world.

CONTEXT DEPENDENCE

Context dependence is another essential principle underlying an emergence perspective on phonological pattern acquisition in young humans. Context dependence, at its most basic, implies that the intimate physical, social, and cognitive surroundings of the young child are relevant and critical to the types of patterns that emerge within the complex system. The operation of the child's internal capacities, readily available interaction capacities, and responsive adults who scaffold learning are necessary components of acquisition. Knowledge can be seen to emerge based on a context-bound set of interconnections between the child's physically available production, perception, and cognitive systems, abilities to maintain social interactions that incorporate phonological system refinements available from adults in the social environment.

GENERAL-PURPOSE SCAFFOLDING

One crucial aspect of a complex system infrastructure is found in general capacities not specific to language – or in some cases to human behavior. This infrastructure links the young child's core abilities with ambient language input–output properties. Speech production utilizes the respiratory (breathing), phonatory (airway protection, swallowing), and articulatory (chewing) subsystems. Speech perception exploits peripheral sensory and psychoacoustic (general knowledge gathering) subsystems. Processing and speech-related movements employ the child's neural, cognitive, and memory capacities for storing and retrieving all kinds of knowledge about her world. This neural-cognitive subsystem must acquire knowledge from experience across a broad range of life functions for humans.

Relative to communication, John Locke (2006) has suggested that the communicative function of vocal forms that emerge from this complex system is of adaptive significance for the young child's survival, indicating an essential purpose beyond the linguistic utility of the emerging vocal system. These survival strategies and functions share biological subsystems with those necessary for the child in acquiring the ability to execute speech patterns.

Over a number of years, there have been studies of general knowledge acquisition mechanisms in diverse complex living systems, both human and nonhuman. We suggest that these varied capacities also provide a rich resource for the young child in mastering phonological knowledge and behavioral patterns for mastery of her ambient language. These disparate capacities, important across a wide variety of domains of function for the young child, also can scaffold speaker–listener connections that are part of building a phonological system.

HETERARCHY

The biologically driven concept of a heterarchy (Wilson and Holldöbler, 1988) is integral to a complexity approach. Within a heterarchy, properties often considered to be at higher levels (i.e. neural and cognitive structures and functions) affect lower levels (i.e. production and perception). Concurrently, lower-level properties also effect higher-level properties of the system. In the terms we defined earlier, they are interactive systems that develop interconnectivity in support of growth in complexity of phonological knowledge and output patterns. As an example, the child's increasingly sophisticated movement capacities can affect her ability to explore the world and acquire cognitive knowledge more readily. The construct of heterarchy applied to phonological acquisition connotes mutual and dynamic interplay between the levels of the complex system underlying phonological acquisition in children.

A heterarchically based system of acquisition contrasts conceptually with hierarchical blueprint-driven ideas about the nature of development. Phonological concepts, including contemporary optimality theory approaches (Prince and Smolensky, 2004) exemplify an alternative hierarchical system concept. Phonological approaches require external top–down constraints to shape and reduce a pre-existing mental blueprint so that the child begins to match ambient language phonological forms as she matures. Lower-level peripheral or performance levels of behavior are seen as conceptually tangential to the progressive revelation of phonological knowledge that becomes evident with maturation.

FEEDBACK

Feedback within a complex system forms a corollary concept to context dependence in considering the philosophical claims of complexity science. Feedback connotes an influence of the child's past knowledge and behavioral capacities on emergence of more complex future knowledge and behavioral patterns. Emergence of a complex phonological system involves both internal (child) and external (environmental) feedback channels. These feedback channels serve the heterarchy through continuing and reciprocal interactions between lower and higher levels of the system. The individual child's biologically available capacities observable in verbal forms interact with input and feedback from diverse communication partners who provide language models. Social capacities, especially joint attention, provide the "glue" for these interactions. These external and internal feedback mechanisms produce confirming evidence that the vocalizations heard and vocalizations the child produces and perceives physiologically via internal feedback have important commonalities.

Internal feedback forms a special class whereby self-produced stimuli from the child's own production repertoire provide a benchmark for acquiring language forms (Davis and MacNeilage, 2000). Ongoing experience producing behavioral output in addition to processing perceptual input (see Smith and Katz, 1996) co-creates observable child speech production capacities. As an example, Vihman's (2004) articulatory filter model suggests that early in acquisition the young child's productions influence perceptual responses to salient sound types reliably attached to the early words the child wishes to say.

External ambient language models provide necessary input for increasing precision in the child's knowledge-based system. These external models "specify some of the initial conditions and positive feedback results in great sensitivity to those conditions" (Camazine *et al.*, 2001: 36). Children produce sound patterns in early words to get what they want (e.g. "milk") and accurate use of those patterns is rewarded by responsive adults in the environment who provide milk.

Bidirectional feedback with the external environment continually refines neural and cognitive subsystems. Neural pruning has been widely attested based on experiences in both moving and perceiving (Johnson, 1997). Pruning is a subtractive process. Neural structures are attenuated in number across acquisition in service of increasing the efficiency of message transmission. Efficiency increases through decrease in the number of unused pathways in the infant brain (Abitz *et al.*, 2007). Knowledge tuned by feedback within continuously occurring new experiences influences the child's understanding of concepts and corresponding language labels for them. These social interactions refine her increases in cognitive knowledge about her environment.

DYNAMIC SYSTEMS

Dynamic systems theory (Kelso *et al.*, 1986; Thelen, 1995; Thelen and Smith, 1994) incorporates the fundamental tenets of complexity science, including feedback, context dependence, and heterarchy as constructs operating within the system. Clearly complexity and dynamic systems are overlapping. How then are they unique? Complexity science is focused more on the nature of the system itself and the results of system operation. Dynamic systems theory, in contrast, emphasizes operation of the system over time and the process by which changes in complexity occur (Smith and Breazeal, 2007). Put another way, dynamic systems principles include relatively more emphasis on the time domain. In the time dimension, there are stable points where the child's system does not change (i.e. the child crawls for several months) and destabilization periods during which her system changes (i.e. she begins walking while also still crawling).

Researchers have employed dynamic systems to model early acquisition of complex action in the locomotor domain (Thelen, 1995; Thelen and Smith, 1994), in neuro-physiological structures, and in vocal tract biomechanics in neonates (Barlow, 1998). In particular, Thelen and Smith (1994) tested dynamic systems in the domain of infant acquisition of crawling and walking. Based on this body of work, they proposed that the infant's own system components for accomplishing diverse locomotion capacities, including walking, are mutually interactive across development. None of the components of the system can individually specify the locomotion outcome uniquely.

CHANGE OVER TIME

The unique focus of dynamic systems as a potentially valuable theoretical perspective for considering emergence is on the changing nature of a complex system across time. Diverse inputs from the child's environment interacting with child ability to organize locomotor movements create this change. Emphasis within dynamic systems theory is on qualitative changes over time in contrast with progressive revelation of child internal pre-existing, static knowledge structures about locomotion via maturation.

In the domain of phonological acquisition, components of the system operate in an interconnected way to co-create observable behavior patterns as well as an underlying knowledge base. Observable qualitative change in the complexity of behavioral expressions across acquisition is evidence of the state of the complex system (e.g. emergence of late acquired sounds such as /r/ or consonant clusters). The child's ability to deploy sounds that she can produce to match word targets illustrates a qualitative change from the early ability to produce those sounds without reference to their accuracy in word targets. These latter word-based patterns reflect increases in efficiency in interactions of perceptual, cognitive, and production system capacities. They signal the child's increasing ability to integrate aspects of the dynamic system to progressively achieve greater complexity.

Multi-causality

Dynamic systems theory implies multi-causality in acquisition, consistent with complexity science. The observable behavioral repertoire at any point in the acquisition process is an emergent product of multiple and heterogeneous sources of input into the complex system. Oyama (2000) has suggested the term "constructivist interaction" for this process. Constructivist interaction implies that interpenetration between organism and environment is integral to the acquisition of a complex behavioral and knowledge repertoire. Oyama's concept is consistent with our proposal that interactions between both physical internal systems within the child and the external social system surrounding the child enable interpenetration between components of the system supporting emergent phonological complexity.

Relative to speech acquisition, Thelen (1991) has asserted that perceptual-motor activities resulting in more diversity of vocal output require coordination of multiple subsystem elements. This coordination produces spatially and temporally organized behavior with a cohesive structure, the essential defining quality of observable speech-like behaviors. The operation of the elements of the production system and the observed perceptual biases toward sensitivity to salient acoustic and visual features embody two critical dimensions of this system. Thelen and colleagues envisioned neural and cognitive underpinnings for storage of knowledge about the locomotor system and its behavioral products. In the case of locomotion, the child learns to maneuver within the physical landscape. In the case of phonology, knowledge and behavioral diversity are gained from consistent connections within the social environment. The construct of multi-causality provides another critical piece of the puzzle in understanding of phonological acquisition (Smith and Gasser, 2005).

Open System

Thelen describes a dynamic system as an open system. An open system refers to one that is "stable, yet far from thermodynamic equilibrium" (Thelen and Smith, 1994: 53). Biological systems are prime examples of open systems. They maintain order and complexity over time. Phonological acquisition provides an example of an open system. Input to this system is continuous and dynamic and creates a unique output not specified by any of the components individually (Thelen and Smith, 1994). The status of the infant's production system, as well as sensory processes, externally available adult models, and the socio-cultural milieu are crucial inputs driving the nature of the overall system. The system is dynamically open to inputs from each of these subcomponents.

FUNCTION

In order for acquisition of phonological knowledge and goal-directed behavioral patterns to be viewed as a dynamic system, one also has to assume a functional origin for these outcome variables. Functionality can be seen as central in the language acquisition process in some conceptualizations (Budwig, 1995). Functional here refers to ways that early communicative vocalizations and eventually phonologically based linguistic capacities can help the child achieve diverse goals within her salient environment.

Goals for deployment of early vocal and later linguistic capacities in the vocal system include acquiring food, nurturing care, and support for exploration of the environment to gain relevant knowledge for survival and learning. The child's ambient language sound system grows in importance in this context as a vehicle for achieving these and other diverse functional goals. In each exemplar provided by child–environment social linkages, observable behaviors on the part of child and partner exist in real time. These interactively tuned behavioral patterns are functionally responsive to the nature of the communication task and the capacities of the participants, both child and adult.

Oyama's (2000) concept of "interpenetration between organism and environment" fits with considerations of function as well. Gibson has also emphasized the function of sensory systems for the young child. She proposed that "we don't simply see, we look" (Gibson, 1988: 5). In the same conceptual vein, we would assert that the young infant doesn't merely hear, but listen. Once again, however, the emphasis is on the overlapping and dynamic nature of perception supporting function within the environment for the young child acquiring a phonological system.

EMBODIMENT

Embodiment theory (e.g. Clark, 1997; Lakoff and Johnson, 1999; Port and van Gelder, 1995, for reviews) provides another foundational theoretical approach with potential for application to emergence of phonological knowledge and behavior. Prominent representatives of the embodiment perspective are found in philosophy (Johnson, 1987), linguistics (Lakoff and Johnson, 1999), cognitive science (Varela *et al.*, 1991), neuroscience (Damasio, 1994; Edelman, 1992), artificial intelligence (Clark, 1997), and developmental cognition (Smith and Breazeal, 2007). This perspective has arisen largely in reaction to the mind–body dichotomy of Cartesian philosophy. In the Platonic philosophical tradition, Cartesian philosophy emphasizes "essences" (Gelman, 2003) in understanding the origins of knowledge. Essences refer to static building blocks or units that are used to construct knowledge. A central aspect of Cartesian philosophy is an assumed disconnection between mind and body. Within psychology, one outgrowth of this perspective has been an emphasis on knowledge of the world being independent of an organism's actions in moving and perceiving information within diverse social-environmental contexts.

Embodiment theory characterizes the physical capacities of the body as a central component available to the child for building a complex action system "from scratch." Clark (1997) voiced the general thesis of embodiment approaches, noting that "mental activity and underlying brain activity cannot be understood outside the context of bodily activities" (p. 1). Clark also stated that "minds evolve to make things happen" and "minds make motions" (1997: 1).

Applied to phonological acquisition, embodiment approaches emphasize that the nature of the speech production and perception systems forms a primary limiting factor on the emergence of speech output as well as, potentially, the structure and processing of phonological knowledge. As a biological system, the speech production-perception apparatus actually operates to mold or sculpt the set of complex phonological patterns used for linguistic communication by humans. Sound patterns that utilize the optimal level of efficient operation of the human production and perception systems in achieving maximal perceptual distinctiveness for minimal production difficulty are valuable assets for efficient human communication. Those attributes spring from the tandem operation of the peripheral and physically embodied perception and production systems in speaking and listening.

Embodiment also incorporates the idea that the internal milieu of the body (e.g. homeostatic and hormonal states) heavily influences the higher cognitive processes in the brain, presumably via the emotional system (see e.g. Antonio Damasio's (1996) theory of somatic markers). To put it simply, the state of the young child's body has a direct impact on the kinds of cognitive processes that may arise and be coded as knowledge in the higher parts of her brain. Response to stimuli is accomplished from top–down cognitive processing of knowledge to plan for output, and by operation of bio-regulatory processes in processing input and output.

Embodied cognition, then, implies that a child's body, her world, and her brain are all parts of a complex and dynamically changing system. Together these system parts support emergence of intelligent behavior as a system property. Dynamic systems theory teams up quite naturally with the concepts of embodiment. These two perspectives are linked by the principle of a heterogeneously determined system that changes across time.

The embodiment piece of this proposal refers to the integral importance of peripheral body systems to construction of behavior and knowledge. Embodiment theory supports an assertion that action, perception, and neurological capacities scaffold the range of communicative functions observable in the child's growing vocal repertoire. Other embodied cognitive and social capacities that can be marshaled to increase phonological complexity include memory (Gathercole, 2001), imitation (Meltzoff and Prinz, 2002; Fadiga et al., 2002), joint-attention (Tomasello, 2003, 2008), and turn-taking skills (Oller, 2000).

To consider these capacities as embodied, one must assert that the observable outcomes of their use are based on operations of the body in support of goal-directed actions. Communicative interchanges provide a socially embedded means for the child to use her body to interface consistently with communication partners. As these interchanges occur, the child experiences, commits to memory, and neurally stores phonological properties associated with salient words and utterances. These stored phonological properties can then be deployed by the child to produce her own words and utterances. Over time, the child's physically embodied perception, storage, and production capacities are tuned by use in functional social situations.

AN INTERIM SUMMARY

The child's internally available biological capacities form a general-purpose skill set. This skill set is deployed for a variety of functions. One of those functions is to enable the child to interact within socially constructed communication experiences. Both biological and social capacities are found in the child-internal, interactional, and external environment we have used as a framework for describing the complex system underlying emergence of phonology. These areas reciprocally influence and are influenced by one another to build mature phonological knowledge and behavioral patterns in the young human. The child's pattern-building capacities are matched with the requirements of listeners and speakers in her surrounding ambient language community. The principles of complexity science, dynamic systems, and embodiment provide complementary theoretical perspectives to support these assertions. The present requirement for pursuing these ideas is rigorous testing by the scholarly community.

WHAT ARE SOME ALTERNATIVE HYPOTHESES ON ACQUISITION OF PHONOLOGY?

Consideration of the strength of emergence proposals on acquisition of phonology necessitates consideration of alternative hypotheses. We will address this issue in depth in Chapter 6. However, at this point, we wish to give dimensionality to an embodied emergence argument by considering how it relates to ideas about this issue that are already being explored. What does this perspective offer that these alternative theoretical perspectives do not, and where does it fall short?

STRUCTURAL HYPOTHESES

Most generally, contemporary phonological theory includes some sort of mental representation, in some treatments termed an underlying grammar (UG). UG is composed of a set of distinctive mentally available features for discriminating meanings in a language. In contemporary linguistic theory, a proposed UG underlies various types of proposed hierarchies containing mental units of differing sizes. Constraints on output guide the speaker's knowledge of possible combinations of sounds in words and utterances. During acquisition, the child parameterizes aspects of the ambient language by a process of feature subtraction from the proposed universal set of knowledge units in UG.

Contemporary phonological theories lie squarely within the nature side of the classic nature/nurture controversy. As an example, the seminal influence of Chomsky's UG formalism is manifest in contemporary optimality theory (OT) (McCarthy and Prince, 1993; Prince and Smolensky, 2004). OT approaches rely on the presence of a UG, but posit hierarchical rather than linear distinctive feature matrices underlying phonological competence. Overall, the idea of an internal–external brain-body-world as a single system implied by emergence contradicts the a priori form modular hypothesis driving structural approaches.

COGNITIVE HYPOTHESES

One of the problems with models that predict a universally invariable acquisition processes is accounting for individual variability. Proponents of cognitive models (e.g. Vihman and Croft, 2007) propose that the child selects sounds, generates a hypothesis, and attempts to use these sounds in words. In this process, she tests her own unique hypotheses for generating early language-based output. Thus, the child takes an active and cognitively mediated role in the acquisition process. Patterns of acquisition are seen as probabilistic, and the observable output of the child's acquisition process is potentially quite variable across children. Low-frequency sounds, which are presumably difficult to produce, could appear quite early in acquisition in an individual child's sound inventory. In available data on early acquisition, low-frequency sounds have been found to occur infrequently across languages (Kern *et al.*, 2010). However, the proposal of the child as an active problem solver to meet her own unique functional communication needs is quite congruent with an emergence proposal.

Newer psycholinguistically oriented models and paradigms, including neighborhood or competition models, focus on cognitive processing and output retrieval mechanisms (Luce and Pisoni, 1998; MacWhinney, 2004). These models place a stronger emphasis on memory storage, retrieval, and output planning for speech. There is far less modeling of the potential role of peripheral mechanisms (Kent, 2004) or the structure of underlying knowledge than is characteristic of classic early cognitive models (e.g. Kiparsky and Menn, 1977; Macken and Ferguson, 1983; Ferguson and Farwell, 1975).

PHONETIC HYPOTHESES

Contemporary function-based or nurture-oriented theories adhere to quite diverse conceptualizations. This heterogeneity of approach is counter to the relatively homogeneous pre-formationist hypotheses of modern linguistic theory. No single approach or paradigm represents phonetic approaches in the same way that Chomsky's original proposal as well as newer structuralist OT approaches represent the tenets of formalism.

A mosaic of data and information about phonetic aspects of acquisition of production and perception capacities best characterizes phonetic/functional approaches to understanding acquisition. Phonetic paradigms focusing on behavioral output across acquisition emphasize the production system (Davis and MacNeilage, 1995, 2000), production/perception links (Lindblom, 2004; Vihman, 2004), articulatory-modeling approaches (Ménard *et al.*, 2009), or perception-based hypotheses (Werker and Curtin, 2005; Dietrich *et al.*, 2007; Guenther and Gjaja, 1996).

Motor-speech-oriented kinematic paradigms attempt to link peripheral movement measurements of motor system function to the establishment of linguistic categories (Smith and Goffman, 1998; Green *et al.*, 2002). At present, this diversity of approaches may be a necessary step in the development of fruitful comprehensive hypotheses for acquisition of the phonological component of language. These perspectives are congruent with embodiment in emphasizing the integral importance of peripheral perception and production capacities. However, a necessary goal of phonetic perspectives must be to move toward considering more fully how the behavioral repertoire and perceptual capacities interface with increases in short- and long-term phonological knowledge, retrieval, and planning processes and what units of long-term knowledge might be.

BRAIN-BASED MACHINE MODELING

Contemporary neural net models (Elman, 2005; Elman *et al.*, 1996) are based on computer simulations of putative functional networks of neurons. These neural networks are used to model the functioning of human brain neurons. Artificial computer networks have been used to implement simulations of human learning (de Boer, 2001; Steeles, 2006; Westermann and Mareschal, 2002). The products and process of these simulations are proposed as being functionally analogous to how the human mind performs in acquiring new knowledge. Neural nets process input and generate output (i.e. in this case, speech output behaviors) based on internal information processing. The software (i.e. computational-representational capacities) interacts with the brain's hardware. The body is seen as an input-output device in service of the brain's knowledge acquisition. The world is the environment in which the cognitive agent acts in neural net models.

Computer modeling of emergent complexity via learning in these simulation paradigms relies heavily on the perceptual-neural-cognitive interface. These models are virtually silent on the potential role of the production system in effecting change in system properties. Present research programs do not incorporate a prominent role for self-produced patterns and feedback from those experiences. There is no direct modeling of the functional social environment. These types of inclusion await incorporation of a more inclusive role for production system and social factors at the level of theory with reference to the origins of knowledge. However, they contribute needed rigor to considerations of how the process of learning can progress in a functional neural network that models neural growth in phonological acquisition.

STRUCTURE OF THE NARRATIVE

What issues should be addressed in evaluating emergence as a proposition for understanding phonological acquisition? Most centrally, we would like to elaborate on what a model/theory of emergent phonological acquisition might look like. This aspect of our narrative will include outlining basic conceptual principles underlying emergence and how well they "fit" with human language, especially phonological acquisition. This exposition requires that we consider what the problems would be, what issues should be addressed, and how they might be worked out. It also requires that we consider whether postulating continuity between human language acquisition and other complex problems in nature is more scientifically valid and comprehensive than alternative explanations. Chapter 2 reviews potential enabling mechanisms within an emerging system conceptualization. We have included self-organization and learning as well as imitation and memory capacities. In Chapter 3, we will review an emergence model that includes core child intrinsic capacities as well as interactive and environmental input components as aspects of the complex system enabling phonological acquisition in humans.

Available acquisition data is one avenue to evaluating the strength of an emergence perspective for understanding acquisition of the phonological component of language. In Chapters 4 and 5, we will review data on typical and atypical acquisition milestones as they relate to considering the parameters of emergence we propose. Pertinent acquisition data include findings within cross-linguistic and bilingual areas of inquiry. These areas are relevant to a perspective that emphasizes universal aspects of language acquisition in the context of ambient language phonological and cultural differences across languages. Cross-linguistic studies challenge assertions about the course of acquisition of phonology made largely based on studies of English. In the case of bilingualism, the nature of learning and representation in the child acquiring two or more languages provides potential challenge to models based on monolingual phonological acquisition. It also helps to consider the amount of data on phonological properties that many children need to build mental representations.

Phonological disorders related to known etiologies within production, perception, neural-cognitive, and social components of the child's system can illuminate differences in outcomes. Differences can potentially be related to compromise in one or more of these critical dimensions supporting acquisition. Developmental differences in system components provide a test of their role in the acquisition process.

Chapters 6 and 7 provide the theoretical background and forward-looking pieces of our narrative. In Chapter 6, we review available theories and paradigms relative to consideration of emergence as a perspective on phonological acquisition. Here we suggest some needed syntheses for building a comprehensive emergence model for this process. Chapter 7 is a summary and evaluation of strengths and challenges for a comprehensive emergence perspective on phonological acquisition. We will also propose some research directions and paradigms that seem promising for testing an emergence hypothesis. We suggest applications of this perspective on phonological acquisition will include animal, machine, and genetics models, as well as evolutionary considerations on the emergence of complex knowledge. In addition, we will consider the potential for applications of this perspective to understanding the basis of disorders in children who do not acquire age-appropriate complexity to perceive and/or produce intelligible speech.

2 The Enabling Mechanisms

A critical dimension in outlining parameters of emergence concerns the enabling mechanisms underlying acquisition of phonological complexity. Here, we will emphasize the necessity of a comprehensive information processing view encompassing nonlinguistic cognitive machinery that facilitates the child's ability to acquire, store, organize, and use the components of phonology. Importantly, incorporation of mechanisms that facilitate these information processing capacities provides another example of the domain-general resources available for the child to solve the "problem" of phonological acquisition.

Mechanisms we propose include self-organization and learning. We will attempt to explicate these two constructs as they relate in particular to the emergence of complexity in phonological knowledge and behavioral patterns in young humans. The heterogeneity of child-internal factors and enabling mechanisms illustrates basic implications of complexity science and dynamic systems theoretical perspectives as these diverse components of the system operate together to co-create the knowledge and behavioral repertoires of phonology. Embodiment is also implicit in considering interfaces of the child's physical systems and cognitive information processing systems with the enabling mechanisms of self-organization and learning.

HOW DOES SELF-ORGANIZATION SUPPORT PHONOLOGICAL ACQUISITION?

Self-organization is a powerful mechanism underlying the emergence of patterned order in complex systems. It refers in the broadest sense to order emerging without a priori knowledge structures guiding the process. The structural and functional capacities of the system create patterned order. Kauffman (1995), in describing characteristics of molecular systems as well as utilizing macro-level applications to economic and cultural systems, characterizes self-organization as "order for free." He cites examples as diverse as oil droplets in water and snowflakes as simple physical systems that can exhibit spontaneous order based on their physical characteristics.

Esther Thelen explored the use of self-organization in considering early locomotor development (Thelen and Smith, 1994). In Thelen's terms, self-organizing systems are "fluid, context sensitive, nonlinear, and contingent" (1994: 320). Lindblom (2008) also employed self-organization mechanisms to characterize emergent knowledge in the early sound systems of human infants based on reuse in perceptual processing of input and in producing of vocal output to instantiate mental units of phonological knowledge across acquisition. Holt and colleagues have suggested, consistent with self-organization, that the general properties of the auditory system influence perception in ways important to eventual cognitive storage of phonological structures (e.g. Holt and Lotto, 2008; Holt, 2005).

An original locus for exploration of self-organization was in the physical sciences, first applied to the emergence of weather systems (Prigogine and Glandorf, 1971). Hurricane Katrina in the Gulf of Mexico in the southern United States illustrates a confluence of autonomous but linked influences where the component descriptors of the system do not specify the dynamic emergent phenomenon. When sufficient energy infuses a complex system, it self-organizes. For Katrina, local interactions produced observable weather system properties. Self-organization has also been used in contemporary biological science to describe a broad range of pattern-forming processes in physical (e.g. termite mound building) and biological systems (e.g. behavior of fish in schools) (Camazine et al., 2001).

Pattern formation in self-organizing systems occurs through connections internal to components of an overall system, without intervention by external directing influences based on explicit teaching (e.g. the tennis teacher), blueprints for what the patterns should be (e.g. the architectural drawing), or recipes for the patterns that should result (e.g. the cookie recipe). Local interconnectivity among system components creates the global properties of the system. As a result, complex patterning is seen as an emergent property of local connections. In this regard, Camazine has considered emergence of complex patterns in biologically based systems. He notes that "Emergent behavioral expressions differ from the elements that constitute the system, and these emergent patterns cannot be predicted solely from the characteristics of individual system elements" (Camazine et al., 2001: 33).

Relative to the acquisition of sound systems, self-organization describes the means by which order and structure are acquired and displayed in complex patterns of physical system function as well as observable behavioral patterns. An example of complex patterns of behavior is the onset of rhythmic speech-like vocal strings in canonical babbling (i.e. /dada/). The respiratory, phonatory, and articulatory components of the production mechanism of human infants converge in producing these observable patterns with largely consistent sound types and sequences within and across languages (Kern and Davis, 2009). Rhythmicity of early speech-like sound patterns reflects neural maturation as well. This rhythmicity is in common with other motor systems emerging into more mature phases of complex behavior (see Thelen and Smith's (1994) overview of large motor development). Infants produce a small and well-defined repertoire of vocal patterns that are available within production system capacities rather than the diverse range of potential sound types available to them in input. A "motor core" of cross-language similarities in phonetic output patterns in human infants precedes the earliest evidence of learning from the ambient language specific phonological properties (MacNeilage *et al.*, 2000a; Kern and Davis, 2009). These early sound properties are largely a result of self-organization exhibited in the operation of the peripheral physical speech production systems. Core vocal patterns available to the child based on the structure and function of this human vocal system appear in babbling and early word forms (Ménard *et al.*, 2009).

Critically, incorporating the conceptualization of self-organization suggests that the physical characteristics of components in a complex system coordinate uniquely based on their properties at a given point in the developmental time course. No a priori form is necessary for this mechanism to operate. The components of a complex system are qualitatively different from eventual observable behavioral products. Observable behaviors emerge through dynamic interplay among system components without blueprints, recipes, or explicit teaching.

HOW DOES LEARNING SUPPORT PHONOLOGICAL ACQUISITION?

Learning offers another powerful and undedicated mechanism available to the child for gathering information about the particular properties of behavior and knowledge required for linguistic communication. At the psychological level, *learning* is "the process by which an animal (human or non-human) interacts with its environment and becomes changed by this experience so that its subsequent behavior is modified" (Hall, 2005: 837). In integrating learning as a supporting mechanism, cognitive-neural capacities and information processing components become explicit aspects of the system. Physically sensing and decoding of relevant auditory input and encoding and physical implementation of speech output are also required. All of these dimensions are brought to bear on the child's learning of precise requirements of the ambient phonology available in input from communication partners.

It is sometimes difficult to disambiguate learning from physical maturation. In maturation, change over time occurs. In learning, change over time also occurs. However, learning-based change is induced through interactivity with external forces rather than being a manifestation of an already available blueprint, genetic or otherwise. This particular intricacy in defining learning is at the heart of Fodor's proposal (e.g. Fodor and Katz, 1964) that maturation reveals innate primitive concepts which the more competent (i.e. more mature) organism can then learn. In Fodor's view, the organism evinces quantitatively new knowledge based on the power conferred by maturation, but qualitatively new knowledge is not possible. Qualitative change is not necessary as knowledge structures are present in UG. Maturation enables expression of those a priori knowledge structures.

This difference in the proposed origins of complex knowledge reveals a crucial disparity between emergence and formalist perspectives. The core properties of production, perception, and cognition are diverse and undedicated to language in an emergence approach. Qualitative change occurs based on their unique interconnections rather than being excluded in the sense of Cartesian dualism. Qualitative change is termed a *phase shift* within the dynamic systems perspective (Thelen and Smith, 1994). General enabling mechanisms, including learning, afford the option for qualitative change without the need for innate pre-specified primitive units. In contrast, the basis of formalist perspectives is passive triggering of predetermined maturational sequences observable in the child's behavioral repertoire. The underlying drive enabling expression of phonological behavioral patterns is maturation, not the socially embedded functional consequences for the child using behavior to achieve needs. More contemporary formalist perspectives emphasize the role of statistical frequencies in language input, suggesting a role for the child's learning from perceptually available input in addition to the traditional central role assigned to maturational processes in development (Rose, 2009; Fikkert and Levelt, 2009).

Another dimension of learning new knowledge lies at the level of physical structures and neural tissue physiology. This dimension illustrates from another vantage point, the critical role of actions and capacities of the body in qualitative changes that underlie the child's knowledge and behavioral advances. Cellular-level changes in cortical and hippocampal tissue are the physical basis of learning, mediated by the emergence of long-term memory capacities. The synaptic junction is at the heart of the neural basis for learning. Previous activity modifies the efficiency of connection between cells. Short-term changes in neural structures rely on permeability for calcium ions at the synapse. NMDA receptors, a subtype of glutamate receptors, enhance this permeability. NMDA acts as a co-incidence detector and is the neural site of Hebbian learning mechanisms (Hebb, 1949).

At the behavioral level, learning mechanisms also come into play in qualitative changes during the last half of babbling and into the early word learning period. These changes occur at the interface between the child's internal production and perception capacities, interactive joint attention processes, and externally available sound system input. These qualitative changes are differently detectable depending on the paradigms employed. In laboratory studies, by about 10 months, young children show rapid learning capacities for pattern regularities in input where they did not show such capacities earlier in the first year of life (e.g. Saffran *et al.*, 1996b). They begin to demonstrate perceptual awareness of precise ambient language properties in the 12–18-month period (Fennell and Waxman, 2010) in laboratory paradigms, such as eye tracking studies, that were not shown before that time.

In the same period, evidence is less clear about the manifestation of ambient language regularities in children's output. Some studies of output phonology show little expression of the early learning capacities infants demonstrated perceptually in laboratory studies. For example, in spontaneously produced vocalizations, Davis, MacNeilage, and colleagues found continuity in the simple open syllable CVs produced in canonical babbling in the same children's early word-based output in a variety of languages (Davis and MacNeilage, 2002; Gildersleeve-Neumann *et al.*, 2013). However, Lee and colleagues (Lee *et al.*, 2010) found discontinuity in relative to within-syllable CV co-occurrence regularities between prelinguistic babbling and early word patterns in Korean-learning infants. CV co-occurrence regularities found across many languages were present during babbling of Korean infants. Importantly, the Korean language does not show predicted CV co-occurrence regularities, so they are not found in input to the Korean infants. By the first-word period, Korean infants were not producing the CV co-occurrences. This discontinuity in Korean infants indicates early similarities in babbling with children across many languages, and "loss" based on learning by the first-word period of within-syllable regularities from their own ambient language input regularities. Other studies (Majorano and D'Odorico, 2011; Vihman, 2004) have shown effects of ambient language learning in children's reproduction of syllable-level phonotactic regularities relative to number of syllables and syllable-level stress patterns in French, English, and Italian in this same period (Majorano and D'Odorico, 2011). Understanding the types and timing of young children's beginning to reproduce ambient language regularities provides a fertile site for understanding the role of child-internal production capacities that are shown in broad similarities across languages, as well as perception and learning as children begin to reproduce their own language unique patterns. Production system capacities in late babbling and early in the single-word period of development (roughly 10–18 months) reflect early implicit learning that may occur without the child's conscious meta-awareness. However, when they are apparent, the appearance of ambient language patterns characteristic of individual languages reflects input to the young child from frequent social links with familiar communication partners. Ortega-Llebaria *et al.* (in review) showed early indications of tonal regularities in output of Mandarin infants relative to English-learning infants in the same period.

These studies of the spontaneous vocal repertoire provide evidence that children may start to detect and consistently reproduce vocal patterns and sound qualities specific to their linguistic environment late in the second half of the first year of life before they produce meaningful words. The presence of regularity in sequences of input sound patterns indicates that learning can occur during this early period within spontaneous communication contexts on some dimensions of phonological regularity that infants must master.

As communicative demands increase and production system abilities mature, the importance of learning mechanisms in induction of phonological knowledge from the child's core capacities increases. Explicit learning, where the child begins to show some meta-awareness of the task, may emerge in this period. Studies of older children demonstrate learning of phonotactic sequences (Munson, 2001) as well as relationships between the familiarity of phonetic sequences and their presence in lexical targets (Storkel, 2002). In fast-mapping paradigms, children show abilities to quickly form a basic representation of a sound sequence (e.g. the sounds in *chromium*), and a concept (a particular color or material) (Carey and Bartlett, 1978; Merriman and Schuster, 1991). Learning and memory mechanisms enable such growth in phonological knowledge based on both pattern recognition and growth production system capacities. We will consider the role of memory later in this chapter.

Diverse dimensions of learning seem relevant when considering mechanisms underlying the emergence of complex knowledge and behavior. *Observational learning*, a type of socially mediated mechanism, occurs when the child produces the same behavior as an adult following observation, even though the form of the child's behavior differs from that of the adult. An example of this emulation is congruent with the limited accuracy seen in children's renditions of adult models across acquisition, as when the child produces /lello/ for the adult's "yellow" (Vihman, 1996).

Inductive learning mechanisms also facilitate an increase in the precision of perceptual capacities as they relate to speech acquisition. Here the child has to discover the general rule or pattern when exposed to a series of events. Pattern recognition using rapid learning is observable when an infant detects patterns and learns novel phonetic sequences matching ambient language patterns with minimal exposure as early as eight months in laboratory settings (Aslin *et al.*, 1998) or in Bayesian modeling paradigms (Tenenbaum *et al.*, 2006).

Learning mechanisms also provide a means for maintaining reliable links with the environment. Daily and repeated social connections between the child and communication partners enable social learning. At the most general level, an adult's behavior will consistently draw a child's attention to a location or object (i.e. triadic joint-attention, Moore and Dunham, 1995). Powerful domain-general linking mechanisms allow the child to interface internal capacities with external models through learning in joint attention episodes. The child learns which objects deserve attention more explicitly from an adult model, and the child's response is contingent on the adult's actions. As an example, Baldwin and Markman (1989) looked at 10- to 14-month-old infants' visual attention to objects in the context of an adult's naming of an object while looking at the infant, talking to another adult, or pointing to the object. Infants showed more responsiveness and more efficient learning when the adult was both looking at and verbalizing about a lexical item in the shared environment, indicating the facilitating role of both visual- and language-based adult input.

Reciprocal influences of the child on the environment occur in adult modifications of behavior only in the presence of the child. Infant-directed speech (IDS), or motherese (Newport, 1976; Snow and Ferguson, 1977), with its well-described patterns of simplification and modification for the purposes of talking to children, represents a consistent strand of external modeling enabling implicit learning by the young child. Phonetic modifications in IDS input are related to child-specific phonetic patterns of output that occur in babbling in English and across languages (e.g. Bernstein-Ratner, 1984, 1986; Lee, 2003; Malsheen, 1980; Lee and Davis, 2010).

Consideration of learning as a critical mechanism supporting phonological emergence suggests that the young child possesses powerful capacities with multidimensional applications. These mechanisms make possible the acquisition of knowledge via processing and reproducing precise perceptual and behavioral properties and their usage within the social environment. No evidence is presently available that these mechanisms are dependent on a priori internal knowledge structures. Learning is enabled by interactive capacities of the child in connections with communication partners that achieve socially relevant functions (e.g. learning about bouncing a ball). These communication partners demonstrate the precise and general requirements of the ambient language and provide feedback on the child's deployment of those properties in word forms that support learning by the child: "Why don't you bounce the ball, Tom?"

In a two-phase process, self-organization is available based on a principle of initial optimization of body structures and their functions. It is observable in the earliest motor core of vocal behavioral patterns produced by young children, characterized by a limited repertoire of sound types and sequences across languages in canonical babbling (Kern and Davis, in review, 2012). This general-purpose mechanism underlies the initial emergence of phonetic properties before the young child begins to link capacities for perceiving, storing, and reproducing sound properties with early meanings. In a second phase, general learning mechanisms available for gaining a wide variety of needed knowledge about the world contribute to the child's acquisition of ambient language precision.

WHAT IS THE ROLE OF IMITATION IN PHONOLOGICAL ACQUISITION?

Studies of imitation have a prolonged history as they relate to understanding the child's acquisition of knowledge about the world. Investigations in the mid-19th century carried the implication that imitation was a low-level capacity observed in immature individuals, rather than behavior that met the higher standard of trial and error. Thorndike's (1911) demonstrations that animals who could learn through trial and error could not imitate turned the issue around to show that imitation was, in fact, more cognitively demanding and potentially unique to humans.

A base-level definition of imitation is copying (Hurley and Chater, 2002). Contemporary study of imitation has enjoyed a renaissance with the discovery of mirror neurons (Rizzolatti *et al.*, 1996), indicating supra-modal neural links between production and perception processes. Contemporary understanding of imitation indicates a comprehensive capacity, implying that the infant or young child can take in environmental input via perceptual mechanisms, process the input at some level, and reproduce it with her own movements. Tomasello and Carpenter (2005: 146) note that "human children are the planet's most skillful imitators."

Terminological disputes abound in contemporary understanding of the boundaries of imitation in young humans. Tomasello (2003) identifies intentional understanding of the mental states of others as a necessary boundary condition on imitation. In contrast, Meltzoff and Prinz (2002) suggest that the basic components of the imitative process are in place at birth, and are not dependent on intention-reading of others. In the area of phonological learning, the young child hears multiple exemplars of relevant sound categories in the language provided by communication partners in the social environment beginning at birth (e.g. Davis and Lindblom, 2000). What the child hears and what she can do with her own body serve to link basic early categories in the performance-imitative sense proposed by Meltzoff and Prinz (2002).

This contrast in boundary values for defining imitation may relate to a difference between *imitation as performance*, where bodily movements replicate environmental models but may not be stored for later uses, and *imitation learning*, where imitation may play a role in building up of knowledge and skills in a social context. Both sensory-motor-based bodily imitation and imitation-based long-term learning may be logically included as factors in a dynamic and complex system.

Perceiving, representing, and reproducing external action system models provide a general-purpose enabling mechanism for the emergence of phonological knowledge. Early on, a capacity for performance-level imitation is available to newborns. Neonates have been shown to possess the ability to imitate events and behaviors accessible to the visual perceptual and production system, such as tongue protrusion and mouth opening (Meltzoff and Moore, 1989; Meltzoff and Prinz, 2002). Throughout childhood, children imitate behaviors including speech and language at least part of the time as a means of practicing behaviors that are more complex. In representational play, children imitate events that they have observed directly (i.e. household activities) or indirectly (i.e. the actions of a firefighter in a book). Imitation is a crucially important mechanism in these activities, as it allows the child to observe events and connect the relevant vocal behaviors to language forms within her social environment. Using their perception-cognitive-production system capacities, young children very soon begin to tune word output performance toward accuracy for salient ambient language targets. Relative to the course of acquisition of language-based vocal output, this tuning is especially evident in word-initial position, as young children produce mostly CV forms in early words, consistent with language input properties (Davis *et al.*, 2002).

HOW DOES MEMORY SUPPORT PHONOLOGICAL ACQUISITION?

The development of memory functions, neurally instantiated in the hippocampus, is involved in phonological acquisition as well as in diverse achievements of early childhood across knowledge and action domains. Memory is clearly an internal mechanism underlying complexity of function that is not dedicated to phonology or even to language. It consists of several processes which serve distinct functions and work differently in child acquisition (for a review, see Davis *et al.*, 2002). Procedural or non-declarative memory is the mechanism used to develop specific skills or habits. In contrast, declarative or explicit memory designates the ability to recall episodes or events. This second aspect is termed semantic memory.

Short- and long-term memory capacities indicate another general-purpose dimension of the young child's suite of capacities in service of the acquisition of complex knowledge and goal-directed actions related to phonology. Short-term memory is the temporary storage bin for perceptually and behaviorally produced material. Long-term memory enables more permanent storage of information, coded as knowledge about what phonological structures are relevant.

Short- and long-term memory capacities play a critical role in the development of phonological working memory and in building of adult-like representation of the phonological form of words across acquisition. In Gathercole and Baddeley's (1993) model of phonological working memory, the "phonological loop," a short-term memory store, captures and rehearses information. The individual must compare information in this phonological loop to memory traces in his or her long-term store. Familiar information is processed differently than new information. For example, an unrecognized phonological trace may act as a signal that the word is new (Gathercole and Baddeley, 1993). The child listener might then attempt to deduce the meaning of the new word using cues available in the physical, social, and linguistic context. Well-represented words will have more rapid processing (Gathercole and Baddeley, 1993). Thus, phonological and semantic information ultimately interact with the development of traces in short- and long-term memory to build a phonological store based on experience.

Procedural memory is responsible for learned patterns of behavior and leads to a very durable memory trace. Bicycle riding and playing musical instruments are examples of behaviors related to procedural memory. In the realm of phonological acquisition, procedural memory can be seen as playing a role in constructs such as the syllabary, a mental store of frequent syllables (Levelt, 1993). At the production level, the early CV co-occurrences based on rhythmic jaw oscillation proposed by MacNeilage and Davis (1990) could be seen as basic movement patterns that underlie later diversification. McCune and Vihman's practiced syllables (McCune and Vihman, 2001) present another candidate for procedural memory where early and frequent speech-related behaviors provide a template for later diversification in words. However, speech production does fall into the genre of learned motor patterns of behavior that become automatic and efficient in adult speakers. As such, production of speech output is quite relevant to considerations of the scope of procedural memory in phonological emergence.

Episodic memory contributes to language development by creating memory traces of events. Semantic memory forms over time by overlaying memories of one event upon memories of similar events. This aspect of memory is important relative to exemplar-based models of acquisition (Lindblom, 2008). As a general example, a young child may hear the word airplane while seeing a jet flying overhead in the distance making a loud, scary noise (an episodic memory). Through experiences with multiple airplanes flying and landing and with different kinds of airplanes (military jets, bi-wing planes), the child forms a category for airplanes. When the child rides in a plane and sees that riding in a plane is somewhat like riding in a car or bus, he may progressively form a category for transportation. To express these ideas and to recognize new instances of these words, the child must link the concept to the phonological form of the coherent word expressing this diversity.

Phonological working memory skill and vocabulary development are closely related in preschool children. Two aspects of working memory that change significantly by early school age are speed of processing and the memory span (Hitch and Towse, 1995). The more effectively children process, the more rapidly they can access words. Having strong phonological as well as semantic traces of the words will also influence how effectively the communicator is able to access this knowledge. This scenario with memory as one critical enabling mechanism is consistent with a complex embodied dynamic system.

WHAT ARE GENERAL-PURPOSE SCAFFOLDING MECHANISMS SUPPORTING PHONOLOGICAL ACQUISITION?

In addition to imitation and memory, two general-purpose domains of child development, genetic capacities and maturation, form the backdrop to the emergence process. Genetics provide the basic human endowment underlying biological structures in humans. One of the central contemporary issues being addressed about the origins of complex knowledge and behavioral expressions is the degree to which these human abilities may be a result of specialized, genetically encoded structures and predispositions. The implications of emergence suggest that biological structures provide a genetically determined experience dependent set of capacities for constructing phonological knowledge and behavior. These general-purpose scaffolding mechanisms rely on "interpenetration between individual and environment" (Oyama, 2000), or experience, for supporting acquisition, however.

GENETICS

Some studies have investigated genetic capacities for speech in order to calculate children's risk for developing speech and language disorder (Rice, 1996; Stromswold, 2001). As many as 15 percent of children demonstrate delays in speech development, but about 75 percent of these children will have normalized speech development by the age of 6 years (Shriberg et al., 1999). Studies of family histories of children with persistent speech disorders reveal that these disorders tend to aggregate in families (Bishop et al., 2006; Felsenfeld, 2002; Lewis et al., 2004). Recent work by Shriberg et al. (2005) points to omissions and distortions in the late-eight consonants (i.e. the last eight consonants sounds to emerge in English) as a clinical marker of speech disorder that reliably distinguishes these children from those with typical speech development.

Oral apraxia, a relatively severe type of speech disorder, has also been studied to consider genetic bases of speech acquisition. Investigation of one family with inherited speech and language impairment has focused on identifying a genetically based lower-level disorder resulting in oral apraxia. Relative to control individuals with normal speech development, members of the affected family exhibited difficulties producing simple and complex oral movements, such as sticking out their tongue or repeatedly tapping their teeth together, as well as in speech production. Their production was described as being most like that of the control participants with left-hemisphere brain lesions (Alcock et al., 2000).

These difficulties have been linked to damage to the FOXP2 gene which results in protein binding (Lai *et al.*, 2001). To date, a precise speech or language gene has not been located, however. In another line of research, a gene near FOXP2 that may play a role in language development has been described (O'Brien *et al.*, 2003), although the assertion has not been widely tested.

The Human Genome Project provides one contemporary general perspective on the nature of human genetic makeup. Funded by both government and private sources, this large-scale project was initiated in 1990 to map the genetic makeup of the human species. Researchers on this project are identifying all genes within the human genome as well as mapping the sequencing of individual genes. One outcome of the Genome Project cogent to considering the question of the genetic basis of human language capacities is the concept of genetic distance. Genetic distance measures the similarity of genetic material between members of the same species as well as across different species. It can build comparative family trees for humans and other close species. At present, evidence shows that the genetic distance between chimpanzees and human beings is only 1.6 percent (i.e. about 98.4 percent identical). This level of identical material leaves little leftover unique human genetic heritage for a proposed modular and unique human language capacity. Instead, it strongly suggests that general-purpose genes shared with other living organisms may play a part, along with a diverse group of other genetically endowed capacities, in emergence of language abilities in young humans.

Though these genetic studies may show promise for increasing our understanding of speech disorders, it is important to keep in mind that one predominant mechanism for the process of the emergence of phonology is the feedback between the biological components of the child system and the external world (Gottlieb, 1998, 2001). Interactive feedback represents an overlay on both the genetic substrate and the biological maturation process. The external environment becomes a key extension for the child's system, an external scaffolding in the psychological sense of Vygotsky's (1962) zone of proximal development. The zone of proximal development refers, in Vygotsky's perspective, to "the distance between the actual developmental level as determined by independent problem solving and the level of potential development as determined through problem solving under adult guidance, or in collaboration with more capable peers" (Vygotsky, 1978: 86). Thus, genetic capacity may provide one impetus for speech acquisition, but is not fully predictive of emergence of phonological knowledge in a complexly determined and dynamic system.

MATURATION

Maturation can be described as the unfolding of structural and functional capacities of a living organism over time. These capacities are directed toward more developed levels of anatomical and physiological function based on natural biological processes. It refers broadly to a biologically determined unfolding of events where a young organism changes from a simple to a complex level on a defined variable or variables. Early proponents of maturation as the single mechanism underlying a relatively passive unfolding of biological capacities evidenced in behavioral complexity included Gesell (1946), Waddington (1962), and Kagan (1994).

Maturation includes two dimensions. Altricial (later emerging) capacities in development include motor system function that enables the child to produce goal-directed behaviors for speech production. Many children take until 4 or 5 years of age to achieve accurate reproduction of all the components of their ambient language phonology in output. Precocial or early emerging capacities, such as the auditory and visual sensory systems responsible for input processing, are largely adult-like within the first six months of life. These asymmetries in maturation underlie biological aspects of emergent complexity. They introduce a non-linear component to the process as they unfold on differing developmental timetables.

In our case, maturation relates to biologically motivated growth in the complexity of production, perception, and neural capacities and supporting mechanisms that enable the emergence of phonological knowledge and behavior. As we have pointed out, however, biological maturation is only one component of a heterogeneously determined system: necessary but not sufficient. Connectivity with interaction capacities and external components that serve the social function of providing "glue" for the system also fall into the category of necessary, but not sufficient, components in this model of emergent complexity.

SUMMARY

Emergence principles suggest the need for general-purpose mechanisms to enable the factors within the system to interact. Self-organization and learning mechanisms provide "glue" for the heterogeneous factors within the child's dynamically changing and embodied system. These mechanisms facilitate operation of a cooperative system that undergirds acquisition of phonological complexity. Imitation and memory capacities are another form of "glue" for this dynamic system. These capacities operate from early within the first year of life and grow in complexity across acquisition to enable processing and storage of phonological knowledge and oral praxis requirements for producing output. Child internal capacities are seated within neural tissue as well as within peripheral body systems that perceive and produce the behaviors necessary to build a phonological system. The child deploys these embodied components of the dynamic system in functional social experiences to code ideas and needs she wishes to express. Scaffolding mechanisms common to all children include physical maturation of bodily systems and the genetic endowment that enables human development. Maturation and genetics serve as a needed backdrop for growth in the dynamic and complex system. The resulting knowledge and goal-directed behavioral repertoire is reflective of the emergent nature of this system.

3 The Model

OVERVIEW

In Chapter 2 we enumerated general mechanisms for acquiring and organizing behavior and knowledge that are compatible with an emergence viewpoint. These support mechanisms are general-purpose in the sense that they serve a variety of non-language domains in a number of dimensions of behavior and knowledge necessary for the young child to function independently within her environment. Beyond these general-purpose mechanisms, what capacities underlie the young child's increasing ability to store knowledge and generate phonologically directed actions that serve diverse communication functions? We propose multifaceted answers spanning the biological, social, and psychological domains. At its most basic, our answer is that phonological complexity arises from the interactions and subsequent tight interconnectivity of biologically motivated child-internal and socially motivated interaction capacities with environmental input from communication partners. Figure 3.1 illustrates the three core facets of this complex system. These facets, as well as the supporting mechanisms we have reviewed, outline basic parameters of an emergence perspective for the phonological component of language.

In Figure 3.1, the first factor is termed *child-internal* capacities. These include production, perception, and cognition. The overlapping inner circles illustrate the physical capacities involved in acquisition of knowledge structures that form the basis of a fully realized phonological system. Each relies on an overall general capability for pattern formation. The production and perception systems include peripheral structures and functions. Cognition includes the neutrally instantiated processing capacities for the decoding and encoding of linguistic messages.

As with the supporting mechanisms reviewed in Chapter 2, these factors serve the emergence of complexity across diverse domains of knowledge and behavior. The young child actively implements each of these internal components in acquiring progressively independent function within the environment for both linguistic and nonlinguistic purposes. As noted, a corollary principle of emergence is that more complex knowledge and behavior is not blueprint-driven but dependent on dynamic interplay among biological, cognitive, and social system dimensions.

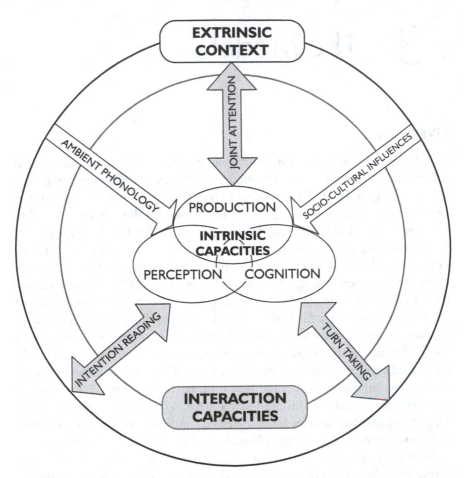

FIGURE 3.1   Schematic of Intrinsic and Interactive Capacities and Extrinsic Context Effects

The middle circle in Figure 3.1 represents the second factor in the system, *social interaction* capacities. The bidirectional arrows indicate links between the child's capacities, and capacities for interactions of people in her social environment. Capacities for social interaction include joint-attention and turn-taking, as well as intention-reading. These interactive abilities extend beyond their importance for phonological acquisition. They constitute, in addition, a potential axis of difference between human infants and other species relative to learning and socialization. Research has revealed that joint-attention, turn-taking, and intention-reading may be a potential boundary value on the capacity to acquire a generative linguistic system within an emergence viewpoint (Tomasello, 2003).

Our outer circle represents the important aspect of input from speakers in the child's external environment. This external context is integral to emergent complexity. The concept of function implies that early communication vocalizations and later linguistic forms are useful for the human child in getting what she needs from those around her, as well as for learning about the world to communicate ideas. This third aspect of the phonological system supporting emergence develops with consistent exposure to communication partners who are in the child's environment. Two major factors define this context related to phonological emergence.

The first factor defining the external context as it relates to phonological emergence is of integral importance. Multiple input exemplars of ambient language phonological forms (Davis and Lindblom, 2000) are provided for the child across naturally occurring social interactions. These exemplars give the child information about sound–meaning correspondences to build an ambient language system of phonemes and rules for phonemic combination. As children engage in multiple socially embedded communicative experiences containing rich phonological raw materials, they employ internal perception, production, and cognitive capacities. Using these capacities, they can respond to, store knowledge about, and behaviorally reproduce incoming ambient phonological models with increasing precision.

This concept of a rich source of function-driven external input connotes an antithesis of "poverty of the stimulus" (Chomsky and Halle, 1968) in the child's input. As Smith and Thelen (1994) have noted, solutions to the emergence of complexity and change depend on the relations among system components, not on pre-specified design. Smith and Katz (1996: 421) further proposed that "causality between internal and external events is mutual, complexly interdependent, and continuous." In the case of phonological acquisition, the association between child output and infant-directed speech input containing higher frequencies of sounds tuned to the child's level of production ability (Lee *et al.*, 2008) provides a salient example of this mutual, complexly interdependent, and continuous type of connection between the child and the environment.

The socio-cultural milieu provides another critical aspect of the external environment encouraging growth in message intelligibility across acquisition. Positive pressure comes from diverse functional experiences during which the child employs the auditory-vocal channel to get what he or she needs from the environment. This aspect of the child's communication context helps to tune both knowledge and the behavioral repertoire toward intelligibility of speech forms over the course of acquisition for function. Cultural pressures also exert a more global influence in showing the child the community rules for deployment of phonological forms. These relate to both social rules and culturally constructed patterns of speech that dictate sound–meaning correspondences for words and idioms of the group.

Figure 3.1 also illustrates the major components of our emergence view from the vantage point of complexity science. The parameters of the complex and dynamic system that enable a coherent theoretical framework for emergence include the interconnectivity between children's internal capacities during social communication with input from the environment. The bidirectional arrows within the interactive component illustrate the concept of a feedback-based heterarchy whereby these diverse components operate interactively rather than hierarchically. The child acts on the environment by employing available capacities. At the same time, mature models influence and help the child to refine her vocal output. Communication partners adjust their level of input to the growing abilities of the child partner in communicative exchanges. Child and adult influence one another. Bidirectional connections across the course of acquisition are essential to the emergence view of phonological knowledge. These exchanges are necessary critical determinates of phonological acquisition rather than incidental aspects of development unrelated to passive triggering of innately available phonological knowledge. They are embodied in the sense that they are intimately dependent on internal biological capacities, not autonomous from them.

WHAT ARE THE CHILD'S INTRINSIC CAPACITIES?

Figure 3.1 illustrates that a child's biological capacities include perception, production, and cognition components. Their reciprocity in function results in the emergence of the phonological knowledge base studied in psycholinguistic models of encoding and decoding speech (Levelt, 1999), in classic and contemporary linguistic theory (Chomsky and Halle, 1968; Prince and Smolensky, 2004), in biologically based theories (Lindblom, 1992; MacNeilage and Davis, 1990), and in perception-based computational systems (Guenther, 1995). Growth in phonological knowledge as well as increasingly intelligible expressions of that knowledge in diversified input and output processing are evidence of the convergence of the emerging capacities of these three systems across the acquisition process. We want to focus on each of these to fill out the picture of their role in the emergence process.

As we consider each of these systems from an emergence view, we will utilize the construct of developmental stages. While the concept of stages can imply a non-overlapping linear process of development, as in Piaget's well-defined stages (e.g. Piaget and Inhelder, 1958) or Jakobson's theory asserting universal stages of perceptual contrast development (1968), we emphasize the overlapping and non-linear nature of stages of emergence. Stages are helpful descriptive tools to capture stable patterns of connections between the child's internal capacities and the external environment. As an example, at the output level of description, canonical babbling (Davis and MacNeilage, 1995; Nathani *et al.*, 2006) provides an exemplar of such a stage. In canonical babbling, an infant produces rhythmic syllable-like output with no meaning attached. However, babbling persists far into the single-word period. Children continue to produce babbling concurrently with their first words (Davis and MacNeilage, 1990). Strictly speaking, the two stages merge. However, there is descriptive power in discussing prelinguistic babbling patterns uniquely, and that is the sense in which we employ the concept of stages.

THE PRODUCTION SYSTEM

The production system is a necessary but not sufficient principal factor in the emergence of an orally specified phonological system. We can observe peripheral production system capacities in a growing and changing set of vocal behaviors based on the child's growing and changing physical structures. These structures include the respiratory, phonatory, and articulatory systems. Production system development relative to respiratory, phonatory, and articulatory function has been widely explored using a variety of paradigms. Both the respiratory and phonation subsystems change rapidly in the first half of the infant's first year to support crying and vocalizing of varied types (Nathani *et al.*, 2006; Oller and Griebel, 2008a). A wide diversity of vocal signals can be observed in young human infants based on the operation of these two subsystems. Increasing organization in the interactive operations of the three systems, especially the emerging control within the articulatory system, is evident at around 7 or 8 months. This maturing organization is evidenced by the attachment of infant phonation and respiratory vocal capacities to more mature articulatory capacities for producing rhythmic syllable-like output. These rhythmic syllables are based first on jaw movements without much independent movement of other articulators (e.g. Davis and MacNeilage, 1995; Kern and Davis, 2009).

We have termed a first stage in the young child's acquisition of output behaviors based on production system operations as *vocalize*. Vocalize refers to the stage of acquisition in the first year of life where biological capacities of the young human mature and begin to be tuned by input/ experience. Here we see, as we will describe in Chapter 4, evidence of self-organization mechanisms in the common patterns frequently described during the first year of life (Oller, 2000; Kern and Davis, 2009). Self-organization, or *order for free* (Kauffman, 1995), indicates optimization of the child's biological systems for processing input and producing output. This use of unfolding biological capacities serves an ongoing social adaptive function for the young child. Along with those observable patterns of the biological sub-subsystems based on self-organization comes early evidences of learning in infants' perceptual abilities to refine and focus output in the presence of adult models, even in the first six months (Kuhl, 2009, in press). This refinement provides early evidence of interactions between the production and perception subsystems.

A second period is termed *increase and refine output complexity*. In later periods of acquisition after the first year, the young child learns to attach the speech-like vocal sequences observable in babbling to early word meanings (Vihman *et al.*, 2009) and eventually to utterances. This sound–meaning link has its origins in children's emerging use of vocalization to express communicative intents to request, comment on, or reject people, objects, and activities in their immediate environment.

The status of the production system capacities also includes pre-motor planning as a necessary component to the encoding of ideas in the auditory-vocal channel in the *increase and refine output complexity* period. We can also observe output patterns as evidence of emerging cognitively instantiated phonological knowledge. Forms coded for communication express an increasingly complex knowledge of ambient language properties and rules for employing them in linguistic communication. In the *increase and refine output complexity* stage, which extends over a long period of development, learning mechanisms enable growth toward a linguistically based phonological knowledge system and goal-directed patterns. Across a prolonged period, the physically based components of the production system continue to mature for support of this increasing precision, even up to the age of 16 in typically developing children (Kent and Vorperian, 1995b).

THE PERCEPTION SYSTEM

Perceptual sensation and processing form a second strand of the child's internal biological makeup. Perception underlies the input dimension of linguistic communication in the auditory-vocal channel (see overlapping circles in Figure 3.1). Dual biological and psycholinguistic capacities describe sensation, perception, and decoding processes. This dual conceptual foundation is analogous to the central encoding and peripheral output capacities of the young child described for the production system.

Biologically based perception system capacities include auditory sensation and auditory discrimination. Initial stages of processing input rely on the function of the external and middle ear structures. Inner ear connections with the auditory nerve enable sensation of relevant auditory signals. Subsequent signal decoding includes discrimination at a psychoacoustic level. Perception is the metaphorical doorway to the decoding/encoding continuum.

Cognitive decoding capacities leading to storage and retrieval mechanisms for linguistic knowledge rely on segmentation and memory processes. Ultimately, perceptual processing provides the means for segmentation at a phonemic level as well as word recognition and utterance integration for decoding the child's ambient phonology. The concept of general and overlapping periods can be helpful in considering the acquisition of complex knowledge interactive with functioning of peripheral perceptual structures to sense and discriminate auditory input. We have designated these two stages in emergence of perceptual capacities as *pattern detection* and *pattern refining and complexity*. We emphasize their conceptual congruence with the stages proposed for the production system.

Pattern detection skills enable children to form perceptual categories. Existence of categories implies signal changes and recognizable boundaries on input phenomena from the child's environment. Infants respond to novelty and can detect boundaries in the incoming auditory stream at birth. Pattern-finding skills rely on multiple exemplars of input to children from the environment across acquisition in building an eventual ambient language knowledge base. Clark (1997: 24) proposes a process of "niche dependent sensing" or "Umweldt," implying that infants inhabit affective environments selectively, perceiving the parameters that matter to them in functional behavior. In the larger sense, what is sensed is focused by what matters in the environment. Clarke's perspective is an echo of the classic Gibsonian ecological model (Gibson, 1966). Gibson proposed that the sensory and action systems as well as the motivation to engage in exploration guide the young child, leading to an "ever spiraling path of discovery" (Gibson, 1988: 37). The importance of both environment and child to this process provides another example of a heterarchy. Child-internal capacities and environmental partners both change and are changed by one another dynamically. These components are equally important to the emergence of phonological knowledge.

Pattern refining and complexity occurs as the young child moves toward a phonetic level of processing. At 10 months, infants have shown the ability to respond differentially to native and non-native language contrasts. In the earliest word period, aspects of phonological structure that are accessed perceptually such as onsets and codas begin to be represented by young children and can be accessed with visual fixation tasks (e.g. Swingley, 2009b). Edwards and Beckman's cross-linguistic studies of phonological accuracy in the vocabulary growth period after 2 years of age indicate a number of language-specific accuracy patterns indicating growth in sophistication of perceptual access, cognitive access, and production system reproduction (Edwards and Beckman, 2008). Edwards *et al.* (2004) have also proposed that vocabulary development may drive phonological representation in this period. They have found that there is an interaction effect of vocabulary size and accuracy. Children with larger vocabulary sizes show a smaller effect of ambient language word frequency on accuracy (Edwards *et al.*, 2004).

In later periods of acquisition, Storkel explored the size of lexical neighborhoods, which contain target words differing by only one sound, as a component of retrieval and accuracy of phonological forms when children are acquiring more complex language forms (Storkel, 2002). Her findings showed that the number of phonologically similar words a child knows, as well as their input frequency, influences patterns of generalization for learning accurate production (Gierut and Storkel, 2002). The patterns of words in the child's process of syntactic learning can be abstracted (Bannard *et al.*, 2009; Tomasello, 2003). Similar strategies can be marshaled for abstracting the phonological patterns needed to comprehend and produce words and sentences across the acquisition process. These increasingly cognitively mediated uses of perceptually available phonological input provide ongoing illustrations of across system interconnections.

THE COGNITIVE SYSTEM

The cognitive system is the locus of neural and memory capacities as well as psychologically describable processes such as lexical retrieval (Luce and Pisoni, 1998). This system enables the long-term storage of the child's increasing knowledge about phonological properties and their implementation across diverse communicative interchanges. Social links with significant persons in the child's environment intimately tie to growth in neural-cognitive knowledge about an ambient language phonological system. Pre-motor retrieval and planning operations for producing output are vital to the progressive emergence of this cognitively instantiated phonological knowledge. The social impetus to communicate ideas intelligible to listeners creates functional pressure on the child to store vocal system properties for efficient use.

The cognitive journey for the child is from the early sensori-motor and non-intentional levels of processing and acting in the world toward the emergence of permanent knowledge structures and intentional communication. More efficient organization of neural connections enables her to increase the precision of knowledge storage. Co-temporally, short- and long-term memory mechanisms enable gradual increase in abilities for the mental manipulation of stored knowledge about ambient language patterns of sounds and sequences (Gathercole and Baddeley, 1993). As cognitive scaffolding for ambient language phonology grows, enabled by these short- and long-term memory increases, the child can increasingly rely on learning as a primary mechanism to accomplish the emergence of refined cognitive capacities (see Chapter 2).

A broad-spectrum definition of cognition (Colman, 2001) emphasizes a general body of knowledge and/or the mental activities involved in acquiring and processing information. Cognition scaffolds both ideas about the world that the child wishes to express behaviorally and a phonological knowledge base to code, categorize, and manipulate those ideas for functional use. This code-categorize-manipulate continuum within the cognitive subsystem is conceptually congruent with the early and growing pattern categorization capacities of the perceptual system. As evidenced by increasing phonetic precision, the child's production system is first producing sound qualities that are relevant from the universe of sounds available to the production system without conscious awareness of their communicative properties (Lindblom, 1992; Oller and Griebel, 2008a). At the onset of canonical babbling, the categorization of sound qualities into rhythmic consonant-vowel sequences such as /bababa/ occurs via close–open jaw cycles resulting in listener perceptions of speech-like CV syllables (Davis and MacNeilage, 1995). Over time, cognitively mediated organization and manipulation of production system capacities emerges so that young learners can produce contrastive phonemic units (i.e. "mit" versus "sit") recognizable as contrastive lexical items.

Growth in long-term cognitive storage is intimately interconnected with perception and production capacities, consistent with the construct of a heterarchy. Cognitive capacities are intimately linked to changes in precision of production system capacities, perceptual refinements for processing ambient language regularities and general world knowledge the child is acquiring in the same period. In each of these three systems, patterning forms a prominent conceptual theme for the process of acquisition: linguistic input patterns, patterns in knowledge schema and neural structures, and goal-directed output patterns. Like the production and perception system dimensions of the young child's suite of internal raw materials, cognitive capacities apply to widely varied dimensions of the acquisition of complex knowledge and behavioral capacities. Their application extends beyond phonology.

NEURAL COGNITION

Emergence of cognition includes both biologically instantiated neural structures and functions and psychological descriptions of the cognitive bases of phonological knowledge. Biological cognition is in the domain of neural cognition (see Brown and Hagoort, 1999; Mareshal *et al.*, 2007, for further discussion of this relationship). Neural cognition refers to the physical instantiation in neural tissue of cognitive or psychologically available knowledge.

Models of adult neural organization for speech production have a long history in scientific inquiry, beginning with Broca in 1861 (in Penfield and Roberts, 1959; see Hickok and Poeppel, 2004; Indefrey and Levelt, 2004, for contemporary reviews) and have produced some well-defined principles for the understanding of neural structures and functions underlying language capacities in adults with acquired cerebral insult.

Conceptualizations of neural development encompass structural changes in neurons and their resulting networks for precise connections, as well as metabolic changes in neurotransmitters to facilitate message transmission (see Johnson *et al.*, 2002, for a contemporary review of these issues). In particular, two structural growth processes are especially critical examples of an experience-embedded view of neural development supporting emergence: arborization and myelination.

Arborization refers to the growth and refinement of synaptic connections between individual neurons and their diverse connections, based on experiences with the environment (Singer, 1995). PDP networks (Rumelhart and McClelland, 1986) that simulate the refinement process via node weights have been used to model arborization. Conceptually, the neurons that are used become stronger, and those that are not do not survive: "Neurons that fire together wire together" (Hebb, 1949).

Myelination is a parallel structural development crucial to increasing precision of cognitive capacities across development (Paus *et al.*, 1999).

Myelination refers to the thickening of the special insulation (myelin) around axons. These axons are the connecting fibers between synapses. In myelination, the growth of external insulation on neurons increases the velocity and efficiency of information transmission. This type of neural change across the acquisition process increases precision in the young child's coding, categorization, and manipulation of emerging knowledge. Myelin sheaths undergo conspicuous growth during the first two years of life. However, myelination may not be fully complete by adolescence or even early adulthood.

One way of characterizing arborization and myelination in young organisms is termed "experience-expectant" and "experience-dependent" processes (Greenough and Black, 1992). Experience-expectant processes are common to all members of a species. An example is the early presence, then disappearance, of neurologically based reflexes in typically developing human infants. Experience-dependent processes are the large number of unique and active links with the environment that characterize the functional environment of the young child. Coexistence of experience-expectant and experience-dependent functions within neural development is consistent with an emergence perspective because of the importance of both physical internal capacities and consistent links with environmental input for building complexity in the young human's repertoire. Both species-typical biological maturation and individual levels of experience with the environment establish the neural structures and functions to build phonological knowledge and a complex behavioral repertoire.

Relative to early periods of infant development, processing of experience by subcortical structures gives way to the onset of experience-based cortical differentiation by 6 months (Price and Willshaw, 2000). Cortical structures underlying memory enable integration of coding and categorization for speech-specific information in long-term neural storage beginning in the first year of life.

At the onset of subcortical to cortical connectivity, overproduced synapses cross the cerebral cortex, and characteristically random connections across neurons (termed reticular organization) exist. This diffuse organization gives way over time to more orderly transitions of neurally coded information across neuron networks and is termed phasic organization. The child's diverse and unique experiences with the environment enable arborization since there are reliable cortical connections and the child can begin to pay attention and store memories from the world around her. Arborization is in harmony with an emergence view in portraying a developmental process in neural tissue precisely shaped by a child's varied and often repeated experiences with the social environment. Experience-expectant neural structuring interfaces with experience-dependent changes to refine neural circuitry for scaffolding the child's growth in efficient use of knowledge and behavioral decoding and encoding.

Seminal work on mirror neurons (Rizzolatti *et al.*, 1996; Rizzolatti and Arbib, 1998) and their implications for links between perception and production is cogent to considering the neural bases of cognition supporting phonological acquisition. Rizzolatti and colleagues (e.g. Rizzolatti and Arbib, 1998) have described an observation/execution neural matching system based on studies of mirror neurons in Area 5 in the pre-motor monkey cortex. These neural structures provide an interesting platform indicating the importance of studying the range of relationships between perception and production in human infants during the acquisition of speech. In Rizzolatti's experiments (e.g. Rizzolatti *et al.*, 1996), identical neurons fire both when the monkey acts to grasp food and when the animal observes an experimenter grasping food in the same manner. This finding suggests a tight linkage between action and perception whereby motor-based perception and representation emerge from the actions of the individual on the environment.

Researchers have also found that the monkey homolog of Broca's area, mostly involved with ingestion of food and oral-facial communication, houses oral mirror neurons (Ferrari *et al.*, 2003). This type of neural link between oral-facial perception and action operates at a level closer to the human auditory-vocal system and suggests promising avenues for exploration of perception–production relationships underlying knowledge acquisition in human infants. In the same monkey species, electrical stimulation of an adjacent area (F6) has produced rhythmic jaw movement similar to ingestive movements (Petrides *et al.*, 2005), a fundamental property underlying early vocalization patterns in human infants (Davis and MacNeilage, 1995).

From age 2 to 5 years, maturation of axonal neuron connections into deep cortex layers (Moore and Guan, 2001) with accompanying myelination until age 6 (Conel, 1963, 1967) is found. These advances correspond with the explosion in comprehension and use of speech forms and accompanying emergence of a phonological knowledge base. Between 6 and 12 years of age, maturation of axons moves into superficial cortical layers (Moore and Guan, 2001). This final phase of physiological maturation corresponds to increase in abilities for finely grained speech discrimination in degraded listening conditions (e.g. Eisenberg *et al.*, 2000). Here the emergence of phonological knowledge capacities is tied to ongoing altricial time-course events in the connection of peripheral and central structures and their mutuality of function.

As is characteristic of other aspects of the developmental process, coding, categorizing, and storage of phonological information is only one aspect of the function of this neural system in processing information. Domain-generality, feedback, and heterarchy concepts apply once again to a critical aspect of this heterogeneous and dynamic system.

SOCIAL COGNITION

The socio-cultural basis underlying increase in cognitive knowledge is termed social cognition (e.g. Snow and Ferguson, 1977; Tomasello, 2003). In considering an emergence perspective, this dimension is especially relevant. Social cognition binds tightly to the functional nature of child–caretaker associations within socially salient interchanges. The social-cultural milieu provides both inputs about what ideas to communicate and how to communicate those ideas, and functional social pressure to code ideas vocally using precise ambient language requirements.

Locke (2006) and Oller (2000) have considered the importance and power of the social-cultural milieu for an emergence view of phonological knowledge and behavioral implementation. In their view, communication partners model semantic, pragmatic, and discourse variables coded via ambient language phonology. The young child manages these dimensions of language use concurrently with production of early prelinguistic vocalizations and later phonologically based word forms. All these aspects of language are critical to achieving intelligible communication. Phonological forms provide the vehicle for accomplishing social-cultural meaning exchanges. These exchanges of meaning about functional experiences in the environment produce pressure for the acquisition of more complex and more accurate vocal forms. They nurture newly emerging production and perception capacities. Social cognition is reflective of the young child's growing understanding of functional communication and of the value of intelligible communication within it.

We have termed the two stages in cognitive development as *sensing and moving* and *refining and increasing complexity*. As in the production and perception systems, patterns are ubiquitous in the sensing and moving stage of cognitive development. From the earliest periods of post-natal life, the initial emergence of cognitive capacities relies on perceptual abilities for extracting patterns from the environment. Before 6 months of age, during the sensing and moving phase, neural connections between lower brain structures as well as within the cortex that house memory and representation capacities are not yet available for laying down permanent knowledge stores (Johnson, 1997). The period before cortical-level neural processing is the sensori-motor period. In the cognitive sense, much of the very young child's moving and sensing in the immediate context is neither directing the processing of information nor moving in goal-directed ways. However, even in this early period, children show the capacity to recreate patterns of organized actions with their bodies that they can perceive (Kuhl and Meltzoff, 1996; Meltzoff and Moore, 1977).

In the early phases of refining and increasing complexity, children begin moving beyond a pre-representational system, dependent on perceptual processing and production capacities occurring within the immediate social context. Bruner, an early proponent of goal-directed actions as a crucial component to acquiring cognitive capacities for intentionality, suggested three central themes: "intention, feedback, and the patterns of action that mediate between them" (Bruner, 1973: 1). In his schema, growing capacities for anticipation of outcomes control goal-directed actions. Bruner's work represents an early conceptual precursor to the dynamic system perspective of Thelen and colleagues (e.g. Thelen, 1984). It provides a scaffold for phonological emergence by linking perception and action with increasing cognitive storage of knowledge and neural efficiency.

Early systematic links of sound production capacities with words illustrate Bruner's intention, feedback, and action triad. Patterns of vocalization in the prelinguistic period, produced by infants across languages, show strong similarities in consonant and vowel inventories (Gildersleeve-Neumann, 2001; Locke, 1983; Oller and Eilers, 1982; Roug et al., 1989; Kern and Davis, 2009), as well as within and across syllable patterns (Davis et al., 2002; MacNeilage and Davis, 2002). Subsequent learning based on feedback from the environment forges links between these forms and salient word meanings (Vihman, in press). In later stages, vocabulary growth facilitates phonological organization and accuracy (Edwards et al., 2004). Feedback tunes intention toward increasingly intelligible and complex goal-directed action consistent with Bruner's conceptualization.

A picture of emerging cognition intimately interactive with perception and action capacities is consistent with Gibson's ecologically embedded notion of *affordances*, linking perception, action, and meaning in children with reference to both the environment and the child (Gibson, 1979). Gibson notes that the idea of affordances "implies the complementarity of the animal and the environment" (Gibson, 1979: 127). The scaffolding afforded by social interaction capacities and environmental input is the basis for this complementary relationship. As all are equally necessary and mutually interrelated, one can view these as existing within a heterarchical system. A heterarchy emphasizes the unique and necessary contributions of varied internal components of the complex system linked to one another by feedback. Externally available feedback occurring between the child and diverse caregivers operates as well to co-create recognition and modification of pattern complexity in language-based social exchanges.

WHAT IS THE ROLE OF SOCIAL INTERACTION CAPACITIES IN PHONOLOGICAL ACQUISITION?

We have employed *interaction* to describe the child's capacities for maintaining frequent and consistent links with an increasingly wide circle of diverse communication partners. In these daily experiences between the child and others, reliable bonds with both familiar and novel partners are forged. These bonds enable refinement in the child's social capacities through bidirectional feedback. Initially, feedback moves from adult to child in caretaking and in early play routines (Bruner, 1983). The child takes an increasingly active role in refining and diversifying her social roles as her production, perception, and cognition capacities grow in precision in both knowledge stores and physical implementation with her body. Core internal perceptual capacities are receiving and processing input. Core internal production capacities are enabling initiation and response with the vocal system. Both perception and production system refinements are honed via interaction capacities that maintain social links.

Figure 3.1 indicates interactive capacities available to the human child. They include *joint-attention*, *turn-taking*, and *intention-reading*. These interactive abilities are neither particular to phonological acquisition nor completely confined to human children. Early in acquisition, these linking mechanisms enable the neotenous human to access the environment dependably for meeting biological demands in caretaking (Locke, 2006). Reliable connections between infants and caregivers, based on robust dyadic joint-attention mechanisms, occur from birth. Early capacities for eye contact served by infant preferences for human faces over other input stimuli (Locke, 2006) attract adults to the helpless infant. Facial preference provides a fertile ground for the infant to begin the process of sensing, recognizing, and categorizing environmental input related to vocalizations occurring within a functional social network.

Later in acquisition, reliable patterns of social-cultural experience enable the young child to meet diverse and intentional communication needs within the child–adult dyad. Subsequent triadic social connections including child, adult, and environment enable the child to connect concepts from the widening environment with vocal forms. Communication partners provide important feedback on the phonological accuracy of the word forms employed by the child in triadic joint attention contexts. Adult communication partners provide a social impetus for connecting effectively. The child maintains connections enabled by his increasingly complex cognitive capacities.

These interaction capacities reflect another aspect of the dynamic system underlying phonological emergence. Their inclusion in an emergence model is congruent with embodiment notions, whereby capacities for joint-attention, turn-taking, and intention-reading enable the child to maintain consistent connections with her environment. These links enable growth in complexity of phonological capacities. Both the child and her communication partners tune the system using feedback managed through these general capacities. This tuning between the child's expressions and the partner's adjustments to those expressions within communicative exchanges reflects embodiment.

JOINT-ATTENTION

Joint-attention is a powerful and ongoing general-purpose mechanism. It refers to the infant's ability to maintain mutual attention with a communication partner. At birth, joint-attention is dyadic in nature, including only the child and another person in close visual proximity. Dyadic joint-attention is evident in episodes where infants prefer faces to other objects or aspects of their perceptually accessible environment (Morton, 1993) and make consistent eye contact with caregivers (Butterworth, 1995). Young infants respond with diffuse whole body responses or reflex behaviors when caregivers stimulate them with talking, eye contact, and/or touching. Later in the first year and into the second year, joint-attention episodes become triadic when children attend to communication partners concurrently with salient objects, actions, and persons in the immediate context.

To characterize emergence of triadic joint-attention, modelers have emphasized diverse aspects of the young child's suite of capacities. Bates and colleagues (1978) suggested that joint-attention is primarily an expression of general aspects of cognitive development, seeking continuity between early joint-attention capacities and later language outcomes. In contrast, Tomasello and Carpenter (2005) emphasize social cognition in a stronger emphasis on the social linkages of infants and partners in the emergence of triadic joint-attention. Some examples of triadic joint-attention behaviors include the infant's use of gaze-and-point to indicate objects or events of interest to an adult, imitation of instrumental or arbitrary acts, and the use of declarative and imperative gestures (Carpenter *et al.*, 1998).

Joint-attention is a critical capacity (see Figure 3.1) in the acquisition of phonology as well as for language acquisition more generally. It provides the child with a basic mechanism needed to achieve consistent relationships with persons and environmental events (Baldwin, 1995). This mechanism is critical because the focus of the child's attention is accompanied by linguistic input from communication partners. Linking linguistic input with multiple meaningful experiences provides the child with a way to experience varied exemplars of relevant phonological input attached to salient word forms and utterance types as linguistic capacities expand. Joint-attention forms a basic building block for a phonological system as children begin to overlay vocal output on the early use of pointing and other gestures as mechanisms for the expression of meaning. It continues to provide social binding within the complex system as the child acquires precision for the full repertoire of phonemes and sequences of phonemes in her ambient language.

TURN-TAKING

Turn-taking is a second general-purpose interaction capacity that can be marshaled for growth in phonological complexity. It provides the basic scaffolding for communication interchanges. In adult conversations, turn-taking requires that adults talk and listen to one another alternately. Recent cross-linguistic work on diverse language types has indicated a universal timing of turn-taking in conversational exchanges across languages (Stivers *et al.*, 2009). In acquisition, this rhythmic alternation gives structure to functional interchanges between children and their communication partners (Bruner, 1983; Trevarthen, 1998). Lamb and colleagues (2002: 375) have noted that the adult use of turn-taking alerts the infant to the "basic principle of reciprocity." We would merely refine this principle to include the consistent presence of vocalizations within this reciprocal relationship.

This fundamental capacity for reciprocity is present in early post-natal life, within infant caregiver routines related to feeding and mutual-gaze episodes. Keller and Scholmerich (1987) suggest that, by 4 months, parents tend to respond to positive infant vocalizations with verbal reactions and to negative infant vocalizations with lower use of vocalizations and more touch or movement. In a series of studies of infants in the first six months of life, Bloom *et al.* (1987, 1993) have found that infant vocal turns were perceived as more speech-like when adults used speech-like responses. When adults responded with means other than vocalizations, infant responses were less speech-like. Oller (2000) has noted the social implementation of vocal "gooing" in turn-taking exchanges when infants are between 4 and 7 months. He proposes that this capacity enables the infant to act as both initiator and responder in proto-conversational interchange. Thus, infants and caregivers are mutually responsive, tuning in to one another's quality of input very early in life at the onset of intentionality in the period before language emerges.

Turn-taking also enables the emergence of content in interchanges and provides temporal structure for communication exchanges. Bornstein and Tamis-LeMonda (1990) found that social content, related to infant preferences for social connection, characterizes early vocal exchanges in the first six months. Later, turn-taking episodes scaffold didactic interchanges as the infant turns her attention to objects in the environment (triadic joint-attention), and the caregiver responds verbally in turn-taking episodes to code relevant actions, persons, and objects in the shared social environment.

Across phonological acquisition, increasingly complex behavioral routines scaffold, in Bruner's (1983) sense, the child's phonological knowledge and the social-cultural context for employing that knowledge in goal-directed behaviors. The early and reliable presence of dyadic and later triadic joint-attention on objects and actions interleaves with turn-taking capacities. Oller has noted that "any topic of mutual interest or imagination or any conceivable circumstance of social function can create the frame around which turn-taking vocalizations can be elaborated by humans" (2000: 255).

INTENTION-READING

Tomasello (2008) has emphasized the important contribution of intention-reading to development of linguistic competence. Intention-reading occurs during speech or other joint-attention-based episodes (Tomasello, 2003). It is the last to develop of the three social capacities we have indicated in Figure 3.1. Intention-reading provides an integral link between the child and other speakers. It permits the child to recognize intentions inherent in the phonologically coded words he or she hears within social contexts.

Intention-reading is a motivator for intelligible communication. Through this capacity, the child understands that others have a perspective and needs within the communication dyad. In this regard, message intelligibility is an aspect of the suite of capacities the child must marshal to make his message understandable to communication partners.

Intention-reading builds on joint-attention, as it requires a shared focus. At the same time, it goes beyond joint-attention in requiring a collaborative engagement to reach a common or shared goal regarding the object of interest (Tomasello and Carpenter, 2005). Thus, intention-reading necessitates sufficient world knowledge to represent a mutual problem between two or more persons. There must be sufficient cultural knowledge to implement possible solutions. In our model, the sources of this knowledge come from the child's communication context (see Figure 3.1). Socio-cultural influences, the macro-dimension of environmental input, provide language learners with information about the use of language in context, and language input comes in the form of the ambient language phonology.

WHAT IS THE ROLE OF EXTRINSIC MODELS IN PHONOLOGICAL ACQUISITION?

Extrinsic models are the third dimension of integral importance to a system-based emergence view for phonological complexity. Emergence perspectives include function in reliable links between the child and communication partners. In this regard, input from models provides information to the child about the phonological characteristics of salient language targets. Input from more competent partners also illustrates the semantic and pragmatic function of those words and rules for their position within utterances the child hears and experiences. Factors within this aspect of the complex system include the nature of the ambient language phonology, illustrated via both child- and adult-directed speech styles (Lee *et al.*, 2008). Socio-cultural expectations for use of word forms and utterance types conveyed by communication partners account for the second aspect integral to growth in characterizing emergence of phonological complexity.

Implicit to both of these aspects of the environment is the general concept of intelligibility. Intelligibility is a perceptual judgment made by a listener about how well a person can be understood (Kent, 1992). Listener judgment deeply implicates the environment in the emergence of fully adult-like phonology. Direct measurement of speech intelligibility in acquisition relates to the accuracy with which a child reproduces the ambient sound system relative to chronological age expectations.

A number of broader factors in the personal-social environment are important to intelligibility judgments as well: listener familiarity with the child speaker and the topic, the linguistic experience of the listener, and the variety of additional communication cues available to the listener. Characteristics of the environment (e.g. noise level) potentially influence overall message intelligibility as well. Mastery of this broader requirement of message intelligibility is an implicit aspect of speaker–listener communication in the auditory-vocal channel. To achieve intelligible speech, the young child must learn to navigate these issues flexibly and to reproduce needed phonological characteristics of linguistic targets in varied speaking and listening contexts.

Integration of intelligibility into considerations of successful linguistic communication requires consideration of the entire spectrum of biological child-internal, social interaction, and external variables. These aspects interact in dynamic and flexible ways for the successful emergence of phonology. The narrow definition of phonology as knowledge of the sound system is inadequate to this larger task. The construct of emergence as we have described it broadly can encompass this broader spectrum definition of intelligibility as phonology is deployed in myriad daily speaking and listening experiences.

Ambient Language Phonology

Input about ambient phonological target forms is the most obvious aspect of the external communication environment. Diverse examples of ambient language goals illustrate that the challenge of matching precise aspects of phonology is learning how to appropriately perceive, segment, and reproduce forms to link with meanings. This process is supported by increasingly complex knowledge of those patterns. Language form (e.g. phonology, morphology, and syntax) and linguistic functions map onto one another in different ways across languages (Croft, 2003; Comrie, 1989; Peters, 1985). These differences lead to varied patterns of trade-off in linguistic complexity and may potentially influence the rate and order of acquisition.

One example of different patterns of complexity that may potentially trade off in different ways is the relationship between morpho-phonological forms in English and Spanish. English and Spanish are both subject-verb-object (SVO) languages, but English word order is relatively invariant, while Spanish word order may be changed (or subjects may be dropped) to indicate a change in focus (Maddieson, 1984). In this regard, the regularity of English places less memory demand on the speaker than does Spanish. However, in English, speakers must produce two- and three-element consonant clusters (i.e. *stop* and *strong*) in initial, medial, and final positions of words. English grammatical marking often takes the form of word final consonant clusters with unstressed elements such as /s, z/ or /d, t/ (i.e. the past tense form of "walk" is "walked" /wakt/). In contrast, Spanish uses relatively fewer consonant clusters than English, and morphological markers are more readily perceived, given that they take the form of full syllables and can be stressed (i.e. *caminó*, or *He walked*). Differing patterns of form and function mapping can be found in Korean, where word order is free and grammatical roles carry postpositional case markers (Kim, 1997). Thus, the child acquiring the Korean phonological system must closely attend to the final portion of the utterance. These patterns of relative ease and challenge for processing may facilitate some acquisition processes but slow others. More cross-language research is necessary to validate this trade-off assumption and the ways that it influences the development of phonological knowledge. This issue illustrates, however, the importance of relevant input for the child in gaining knowledge to coordinate ambient language phonological and later acquired morpho-syntactic regularities.

Socio-cultural Influences

Socio-cultural influences include the ways in which communication partners simplify speech input for children, the expectations for child output, and the reinforcement of aspects of this output. This acculturation process begins early in life. Researchers have consistently documented the use of infant directed speech (IDS) (Fernald *et al.*, 1989). This unique speech register is also termed *motherese* across languages and cultures. Across the early period of phonological acquisition, functions of IDS facilitate infant attention to patterns in the linguistically accessible and relevant language input that they will eventually reproduce to communicate. IDS includes exaggeration of pitch contours. In addition, adults simplify the semantic and syntactic level of their input to children relative to that of the language directed to adults. Comparable modifications exist in speech directed to infants across cultures (Lee and Davis, 2010). Potentially drawn by the prosodic qualities, infants listen longer to IDS than to adult-directed speech styles in input (e.g. Jusczyk, 1997). Recent research emphasizes the generalized nature of IDS. Studies indicate that IDS style of input is present in early sign and gesture communication in infant–parent pairs (Iverson and Goldin-Meadow, 2005; Ozcaliskan and Goldin-Meadow, 2009).

Young children engage in a variety of culturally unique social routines across acquisition. Social routines grow in complexity and increasingly demand more active participation and higher levels of output skill from children. In many Western cultures, adults and other caregivers often speak directly to children (vanKleeck, 1994). A child in a middle-class American family might initially engage in a play sequence, such as pointing to body parts, at around 8 to 12 months. By 15–20 months, the child can engage in naming games in which the parent or the child names objects in triadic joint-attention episodes, characterized by shifts in attention between child, communication partner, and object. This responsiveness forms an important set of expectations of child input. In contrast, in non-mainstream cultures such as the Inuit in Alaska, young children spend more time observing, and adults less often speak directly to children (Crago, 1992). Kwarea'ae parents in the Solomon Islands provide "calling-out" routines (communicative frames that speakers employ when working in the bush when others are not in the visible range) for their infants to imitate. Parents emphasize certain parts of the routine and provide feedback until children are able to reproduce them (Watson-Gegeo and Gegeo, 1986). In Equadorean-Quichua environments, adults do not respond to young children's vocalizations as meaningful words until later in development, past the single-word period of development in English learning children (Gildersleeve-Neumann, 2001).

These different patterns of parent–child communication styles illustrate the diversity of decoding and encoding demands that the child must master in processing input and deploying output within their own cultural context. Socio-cultural experiences that include both adults and children help them to refine the requirements for intelligible communication. This pressure, applied through multiple functional interactions, reinforces the need to progress toward the acquisition of intelligible speech forms used in culturally acceptable ways. Increasingly, the child begins to understand the need for intelligible speech as she perceives and stores more information about language and grows in production system capacities for matching ambient language phonology. The external context noted in Figure 3.1 interacts with both the child's biological capacities and consistent use of culturally tuned social interaction capacities with communication partners.

SUMMARY

Each of these three main aspects of the complex system is necessary, and none is sufficient to drive the process of phonological acquisition.

A dynamic and multiple component conceptualization is consistent with complexity theory. Of necessity, the multiple component notion integrates the concepts of heterarchy and feedback as the "glue" binding the complex system together. Mutual interactive influences, whereby both child and environment affect and are affected by one another, suggests a richly endowed system. This rich system uses general-purpose capacities and mechanisms. They are not specifically dedicated to phonology or even to language in achieving phonological complexity.

If the processes and products of phonological knowledge and behavioral acquisition in the young child are emergent properties of a complex and embodied dynamic system, some interesting ramifications arise. Importantly, this complex system is rooted in a core of non-language dedicated factors, which include biologically embodied production, perception, and cognition systems. General-purpose enabling mechanisms, including self-organization, learning, memory, and imitation provide means for the child's deployment of those systems. Additional general social interaction abilities consisting of joint-attention, intention-reading, and turn-taking enable reliable connections with the social environment. Readily available input contains the raw materials needed for the young child to tune phonological knowledge and behavior toward culturally tuned deployment of ambient language patterns. Function drives the emergence of the phonological system. Function describes the need for intelligibility between the child and communication partners as they serve diverse mutual requirements that arise and are met in daily social experiences.

4 Vocalization and Pattern Detection Through Moving and Sensing

We have proposed that the young human child has diverse and heterogeneous enabling mechanisms and system components to facilitate emergence of complex phonological knowledge and behavioral patterns. Here, we examine developmental data for the earliest stage of acquisition, which we refer to as *vocalizing* and *pattern detection through sensing and moving*. We evaluate whether this data can be interpreted fruitfully as support for an emergence perspective for the phonological component of language. The following period (discussed in Chapter 5) is one we have termed *refinement*. There, we will track the acquisition story as the prelinguistic behaviors observable in these domains are implemented as a knowledge-based system of goal-directed behaviors for linguistic communication.

In Chapter 1 we reviewed requirements for linguistic communication. We concluded that for a child's verbal output to be considered linguistic, she needs to send and receive messages that demonstrate the symbolic, arbitrary, rule-based nature of language. Current psycholinguistic conceptualizations propose a largely top–down model of mature speakers' encoding and decoding capacities (Levelt, 1999). In contrast, processing accounts suggest a bottom–up option (McClelland *et al.*, 2010). Here, we examine available data on the earliest period of acquisition to consider how young humans begin the process of constructing the mature system envisioned in contemporary models of the adult speaking and listening process. We propose a synthesis based on new theoretical perspectives relative to consideration of phonological acquisition. Accordingly, our long-term goal is to consider what we need to know to support an emergence perspective. We will focus on key changes in the developmental period from birth through the first 50 words period, extending to approximately 18 months of age.

To evaluate an emergence position, we consider how available research on this period indicates that the child's intrinsic perception, production, and cognitive capacities interact with extrinsic socially mediated input as cooperative aspects of a complex system. In this regard, cross-domain and cross-species studies are relevant to demonstrate general appearance of early capacities for learning, particularly perceptual capacities. This body of research indicates that the shift to greater complexity is not uniquely characteristic of human language, including phonology, but a general feature of systems and skill domains across species. We will also detail how differences due to deficits and/or delays in age-appropriate abilities to perceive, store, and produce speech early in children's development result in differing trajectories for acquisition. These developmental differences can be helpful in revealing the importance of interaction across components of a complex system. Differences in developmental trajectories illustrate the potential for lack of convergence of intrinsic, interaction, and extrinsic factors in supporting successful acquisition of phonological knowledge and behavior.

In Figure 4.1 these diverse strands of the complex system are represented as factors that pull production and perception closer together into an efficiently integrated heterarchical system. This system supports emergence of the full spectrum of linguistic requirements for mastery of the phonological component of the child's ambient language.

As shown in Figure 4.1, the production and perception systems are drawn closer across the earliest periods of acquisition. Ambient phonology input and the socio-cultural influences of caregiver–child interactions (as discussed in Chapter 3) provide one important impetus for qualitative change in the interactions of these two systems. Child-internal capacities reflected in motor system and memory development support increases in knowledge and in the ability to reproduce more complex behavioral patterns based on ambient language input. Self-organization and learning mechanisms are essential to the "pulling together" of these two systems.

Integration of cognitive processing, production, and perceptual operations results from heterarchical interactions between bottom–up processes (ability to produce syllables and sounds, ability to recognize sound sequences) and top–down information (production of phonetically consistent forms to obtain desired objects or events; recognition of speech in context). Ambient phonological input shapes children's language experience to help define the precise types of sounds and combinations they need for intelligible linguistic communication. At the same time, the broader socio-cultural context of communication influences the kinds of learning experiences within which they interact. The socio-cultural context also influences the prelinguistic and early language-based behaviors reinforced by the child's family as well as the extended community of speakers who use the ambient language for

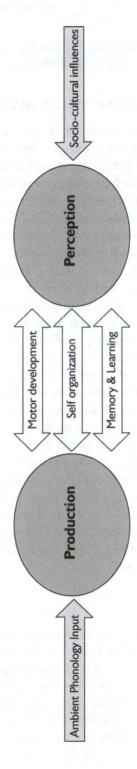

FIGURE 4.1 Child-internal and Child-external Factors Interact to Support the Emergence of Phonological Knowledge.

communicating ideas. As illustrated earlier in Figure 3.1, child-intrinsic and child-extrinsic pressures facilitate this integration.

WHAT ARE THE EARLY STAGES OF VOCAL DEVELOPMENT?

Evaluating the strength of available data on acquisition begins at birth. Newborns have only general sensory and movement capacities to move and perceive input within their social environment as they are nurtured by caregivers. They produce vocalizations in the form of cries (e.g. Stark, 1989). Recent research indicates that these early cries may reflect language-specific prosodic qualities (Mampe *et al.*, 2009). Perceptual experiments in laboratory environments have shown that infants recognize recurrent speech patterns such as their mother's voice (DeCasper and Spence, 1986), their maternal language (Mehler *et al.*, 1988), or a nursery rhyme repeated by their mother (DeCasper *et al.*, 1994). These capacities may imply linguistic competence. But from an emergence perspective, they can be seen as preliminary steps along the young child's general path toward processing input relevant for the later developmental period where they perceive, store, and produce linguistically based phonological material. Some of these early abilities are also observed in birds or other mammals (e.g. Kuhl and Miller, 1975; Kluender *et al.*, 1987; Tyack, 2008; MacDougall-Shackleton, 2009).

As we noted earlier, we have conceptualized vocal development as occurring in two overlapping phases rather than in sharply autonomous and qualitatively different stages. In the first period between birth and about 18 months, we propose that *vocalizing* and *pattern detecting through moving and sensing* are general capacities. These early capacities provide perceptual and vocal foundations for eventual linguistic communication by around 12 to 18 months of age. During this early period, a number of interdependent systems lay the earliest foundation for children's later language-based use of sound patterns.

VOCALIZE

Physical maturation of production system structures and their interactive functioning is widely acknowledged to be a "bottleneck" impeding the child's speech output capacities over a prolonged period, extending to 16 or more years of age (see Kent and Vorperian, 1995b, for a review of development of peripheral production system capacities). We have noted that this prolonged period of development has been termed *altricial* to indicate complex capacities that emerge over a longer time course.

Both development of physiological structures and their implementation in goal-directed speech motor control impede the young child's full expression of emerging long-term knowledge during the first years of phonological development.

The vocalize stage begins at birth with the infant's ability to produce cry. Phonatory control of the larynx precedes articulatory control for syllabic output (Koopmans-van Beinum and van der Stelt, 1986; Oller, 1980; Stark, 1980, 1981). Control is evidenced by changes in pitch and intensity of sounds, based on airflow and laryngeal operations before children start to produce syllables based on rhythmic articulatory jaw movements. These early speech-like movements of the jaw, accompanied by phonation produced at the level of the vocal folds, are observed from 4 to 8 months of age. The perceptual regularity of these movements is guided by the prototypical movements of the articulators and the spatial restrictions placed on movements by the early configuration of the oral cavity (Kent and Vorperian, 1995b).

The period before cortical-level neural processing has been termed the sensori-motor period. In the cognitive sense, much of the very young child's moving and sensing in the immediate context is neither intentionally processing information nor moving in goal-directed ways. Newborns show the capacity to recreate patterns of organized actions with their bodies that they can perceive through the visual and/or auditory systems (Kuhl, 2004; Kuhl et al., 1988). Reproducing oral movements in the presence of a model supports the suggestion that the capacity of linking adult input to their own output exists very early in infant development. Proto-representation of the links between auditory and visual input and self-produced output increases across this period in the presence of relevant environmental experiences. The infant's capacities for sensing and reproducing patterns supported by environmental models within dyadic interactions with caregivers are early precursors to construction of a long-term cognitive knowledge base in an emergence view.

The developmental trajectory of output patterns in the early vocal period is constrained by maturity in peripheral motor subsystems enabled by maturation of neural structures and functions. By 7 to 8 months, typically developing infants produce rhythmic, perceptually speech-like syllables (Oller, 2000; Davis and MacNeilage, 1995). Rhythmic vocalizations that sound to listeners like speech are termed canonical babbling. They constitute a seminal step toward the emergence of phonologically based speech forms. These readily observable coordinated oral behaviors are based on mutual organization across the peripheral respiratory, phonatory, and articulatory subsystems. Babbling emerges reliably in children who have sufficient auditory access, even in very impoverished environmental circumstances (Oller, 2000). The developmental trajectory toward rhythmic speech-like output in the prelinguistic period is consistent with rhythmic behaviors observable in other motor systems during this early period (Thelen and Smith, 1994).

While canonical babbling signals a substantial level of neural organization in support of organized speech movements, these utterances that sound speech-like to listeners are not yet linguistically intentional. Only by approximately 12 months of age do children start to intentionally use the vocal system to code meaning. In this early phase, infants cannot represent their wants, needs, or knowledge via recognizable vocalizations that follow linguistic conventions. They can only simulate the language patterns around them through vocalizing of basic syllable forms containing a limited repertoire of sounds and syllable types.

The most sophisticated vocal production skills reported are the production of phonetically consistent forms with practiced sounds (Vihman, 1996). Early vocal forms are characterized by a common core of sounds and sound patterns that share the characteristics of the ambient language in infants in a variety of language communities (Kern and Davis, 2009). Both of these achievements are critical because they increase the likelihood that caregivers reliably interpret the child's utterances as communicating meaning and respond accordingly. Thus a caregiver is more likely to respond to a request for a cookie if the child consistently produces /tuti/ for *cookie* than if a child just says /di/, for example. As in earlier periods we have described, the child and adult accomplish these interactions through reliable capacities for joint attention, now clearly triadic in nature.

Important to considering an emergence interpretation, the adult may be interpreting the young child's meanings in this early period. The child's oral output may not actually match the entire word target (e.g. /ba/ for *ball*). The adult, familiar with her child's sound patterns, provides the interpretation. However, response to young children's vocalizations is an area of cultural difference. Adults in some language communities do not attribute meaning to children's vocalizations in the same way as adults in mainstream US culture (Gildersleeve-Neumann, 2001). Gildersleeve-Neumann (2001) found that Quichua-speaking adults in Highland Ecuador do not respond to children's vocal output and interpret it as meaningful in this early period. Quichua-learning children are not given credit for language-based skills until after the single-word period.

Pattern Detecting

Like the physical systems supporting vocalization, pattern detection builds on basic biological functions of the auditory and perceptual systems. The ability to detect regularities in sound input relevant to constructing phonological knowledge is another general capacity in support of phonological acquisition. Perceptual capacities are used by young infants to gather myriad types of world knowledge important for functioning in their environment that are not limited to language knowledge.

The timing of maturation of relevant physical structures relative to perception system operations is quite different than those in the production system. In contrast to the altricial developmental timetable described for production system capacities, early response to sound in the environment is designated as precocial, designating the infant's early maturation to adult-like response patterns. Maturation of peripheral auditory structures supporting sensation and psychoacoustic processing occur within the first six months of life in infants with normal hearing sensitivity (see Moore and Linthicum, 2007, for a review of pre- and peri-natal auditory system maturation). As examples, earliest fetal response to womb-external sounds has been noted by the 28th to 29th week (Kuhlman *et al.*, 1998). Full cochlear maturity is reached in the period before birth (Eggermont *et al.*, 1996). Axonal myelin density in the cochlear nerve and brainstem paths becomes adult-like by 6–12 months of age (Moore *et al.*, 1995). These precocious events in the auditory perception system are in accord with early discrimination abilities in newborns established in classic laboratory speech–sound discrimination studies.

The biological structures and function of the peripheral auditory system are largely in place by birth (Steinberg and Knightly, 1997), although the presence of amniotic fluid may depress middle ear function. The human infant's biologically based auditory capacities are evident in early post-natal abilities to attend to auditory features critical for differentiating the phonemes of the ambient language. Studies of early categorical perception show that neonates and infants up to about 6 months of age readily respond to differences between a variety of features critical in speech perception, including voice onset time (e.g. /p/ versus /b/) and place/manner characteristics (for /t/ versus /k/, and /d/ versus /s/) (Eimas *et al.*, 1971).

Neonates respond differentially at birth to stories read to them in utero by their mother (Moon *et al.*, 1993; DeCasper *et al.*, 1994). Their mother's voice is a familiar auditory input. This seemingly precocious pattern of response is based on early maturation of auditory sensitivity to the vocal spectrum of the human voice by six months gestation. Maturation of the auditory cortex to support auditory responsiveness is in place by the third trimester (Moore, 2002). Even when stories are read by another female, infants still prefer material they have already been exposed to, suggesting a preference for familiar acoustic patterns. In the same developmental period, very young infants also respond differentially to syllabic- and prosodic-level properties of syllable sequences that they have experienced previously (Mehler *et al.*, 1988; Moon *et al.*, 1993).

The linking theme of available general auditory system capacities with experience in early pattern detection illustrates the infant's capacities for discrimination of relevant differences in the incoming sound stream. These auditory patterns reflect the differences necessary for later language learning that adult human listeners and speakers exploit in differentiating linguistic messages via phonological properties. However, unlike adults, infants attend only to auditory patterns and do not yet extract linguistic meanings. What they attend to has little obvious influence on what they produce in their first six months of life. This early capacity for attending to relevant distinctions highlights the general nature of auditory system processing as well as the lack of coordination between the perception and production systems in earliest phases of development.

Reliable evidence from laboratory-based studies indicates that infants are capable of recognizing patterns of their ambient language from 6 months of age. One important aspect of these pattern-recognition capacities is the infant's dependence on input from their environment as well as increases in short- and long-term memory. During this developmental period, infants also begin to utilize converging cues to recognize diverse patterns of ambient language regularity. Some examples include development of preference for the stress patterns of their ambient language (Jusczyk *et al.*, 1993), preferences for pauses in expected locations in utterances and clauses (Jusczyk, 1992), and recognition of words in some constrained contexts (Vihman *et al.*, 2004).

Maturation of connections to higher cortical structures, as well as increase in maturation of those structures themselves by around 6 months of age, accompanies an increasing ability to focus on the phonetic structure of the ambient language (e.g. Werker and Tees, 1984). The shift suggests an emerging awareness of the sound patterns they will ultimately use in the comprehension of socially relevant ambient phonological input. The shift is gradual but critical to tuning of the auditory system toward specific ambient language patterns for speaking and listening successfully. Some important examples include findings that infants no longer respond to non-ambient language vowels starting at about 6 months of age (Polka and Werker, 1994). The timing of refinement in responses to ambient and non-ambient or non-native sounds corresponds temporally with increase in ability to treat groups of vowel exemplars as equivalent (Kuhl et al., 1992).

This increasingly complex skill set of auditory perceptual abilities permits infants to respond differentially to repeated words or familiar monosyllabic words (Saffran et al., 1996a; Jusczyk and Aslin, 1995) and to learn minimal pairs with relatively few exposures (Saffran et al., 1996a) in the second half of their first year. In experimental tasks, infants recognize words faster. These results suggest greater efficiency in the processing of words, in that infants can successfully recognize words based on less phonological information. They also indicate a richer representation of the sound patterns of the native language by typically developing infants. Infant responses to non-ambient language consonants also change between 8 and 10 months (Best et al., 1988, 1995). By around 9 months of age, children demonstrate expectations about regularly co-occurring segments (Gerken, 2004, 2006). However, the ability to attend to differences between consonants does not change at the same rate. The earliest consonant contrasts that give evidence of the infant's sharpening awareness of ambient language contrasts are those that can be assimilated into native language categories, such as the stops with different aspiration values than those observed in English (Best, 1993). During this period, infants continue to respond differentially to consonants that cannot be assimilated to ambient language categories (Best et al., 1995). A particularly clear example is the click. Clicks are phonemes in some languages (e.g. Xhosa), but in English they are non-phonemic (i.e. not used to discriminate word meanings). At some level, this change represents a loss of perceptual skill. At this same age, infants have been shown to learn the sound units and words of a foreign language through personal interaction but not with television input, implicating the importance of social interaction in learning (Kuhl et al., 2003).

Taken together, these results suggest that infants in this period are encoding increasingly greater amounts of detail about the patterns of their ambient language, even while they are still unable to marshal their production system capacities to reproduce these patterns. All of these emerging talents for focus on relevant ambient language properties indicate a critical role for experience with sound input. Perceptual abilities do not readily map onto the child's major task at this period, which is making sound–meaning correspondences to code relevant aspects of her social environment. Infants must begin to learn to produce these sound contrasts for sound–meaning correspondences using their production system capacities (Vihman, in press), generally at around 12–18 months of age.

HOW DOES SENSING AND MOVING SUPPORT EMERGENCE OF PHONOLOGY?

The first 12 months of vocal and perceptual development lays the groundwork for the emergence of sound system links with socially salient meanings for young children. Typically developing children produce early word forms using the substrate of babbling vocalizations they have been producing already (Davis *et al.*, 2002). The speech production and perception systems are gradually integrated over the course of the first 12 to 18 months in support of these observable vocal behaviors. Some recent research suggests the presence of an auditory filter, whereby young children's attention to detail in incoming words is shaped by their own production preferences in the formative period of word learning (Vihman *et al.*, 2009). Cognitive, motor, and social/interaction development across this same period are additional key dimensions of the complex system that enables perceptual and production capacities systems to function effectively in support of growth in early phonological raw materials for constructing phonological knowledge and behaviors.

Critical skills in the domains of cognition and processing, motor development, and social interaction each play a unique role in emergence of speech production skills applied to early word forms. In this section, we will review available research on these behavioral capacities that are necessary for supporting integration of speech production and perception. We will consider evidence to suggest that they may contribute to the process of integration, and why these data support a complex system view of general capacities supporting emergence of the phonological component of language.

HOW DOES COGNITION AND PROCESSING SUPPORT EMERGENCE OF PHONOLOGY?

Memory for speech sounds and sequences and representation of events is logically related to the ability to link sound patterns with meanings. Contemporary speech perception findings indicate that speech input is especially salient even to neonates. As we noted earlier, infants show the ability to respond to salient properties of speech sounds that will later begin to signal linguistic meaning differences. Importantly for development of the neural substrate supporting emergence of phonology, the human brain shows greater activity in areas of specialization for speech in the left hemisphere by about 3 months of age. Brain maturation processes are largely responsible for increases in processing speed and coordination of the multiple brain structures that support the behaviors. These structures undergird the development of speech and communication (Kuhl and Rivera-Gaxiola, 2008; Grossmann and Johnson, 2007; Paterson *et al.*, 2006). These underlying neural correlates enhance the efficiency of production and perceptual systems working together. After about 6 months, young children have developed the neural wiring that allows connections between lower brain structures and the cortex (Johnson, 1997). Maturation of these neural structures (e.g. myelination) increases the precision of movements, including those involved in speech production, although increases in speed and precision continue to develop up until the teenage years (Kent and Vorperian, 1995b).

Available data on maturation of the supporting brain structures and their increasing precision in guiding peripheral function support the assertion that during infancy children are developing key capacities to support the approximation of speech output, consistent with an emergence perspective. The first is memory. Short- and long-term memory capacities allow children to build and store knowledge about speech-related input. Neurally instantiated storage and retrieval capacities support emergence of a growing knowledge base. This knowledge serves the young child as a resource in understanding and using speech-related information. A second capacity is oral motor coordination and its neural correlates. The ability to manipulate the oral motor mechanism is one key to reproducing speech-related patterns in the communication environment. Finally, the child's functional ability to engage in sustained social interactions, using capacities that include joint-attention, turn-taking, and intention-reading, provides the context in which children begin to understand the need to use and practice speech for communication. We will explore available data on these capacities below.

HOW DOES ORAL MOTOR DEVELOPMENT SUPPORT EMERGENCE OF PHONOLOGY?

Oral motor development is another key for the young child in reproducing ambient speech patterns and using them to engage in social interactions. Growth and coordination of respiratory capacities (Boliek *et al.*, 1996) underlie the transition from low-volume cries at birth to a fully functional respiratory capacity for support of rhythmic syllables by 7–9 months.

Phonatory capacities for producing sound, based on the respiratory system energy source, provide the sound source for cries at birth. Control over phonation for precise regularities relevant to phonatory function in support of phonological patterns develops over an extended period, extending into the fifth year of life in some instances. As an example, the voicing distinction for phonemes (i.e. /t/ and /d/ distinctions) requiring phonatory and articulatory system coordination is one of the last sound properties mastered by young children.

At birth, the articulatory system is structured to facilitate feeding and protection of the airway. As the infant grows, the tongue drops. More space is available between the jaw and velum (Ménard *et al.*, 2004). This change is important at the onset of canonical babbling because it allows the child to begin to produce the vertical open–close jaw movements required for perceptually rhythmic speech-like babbling vocalizations. Growth of the oral motor mechanism results in change in the spatial relationship between the articulators and oral cavity by putting them into an adult-like alignment (Vorperian *et al.*, 2005; Ménard *et al.*, 2004).

Growth and change in inter-oral relationships in turn enhance the capacities of the biomechanically based speech production system, allowing the child to produce a greater variety of vocal forms (Menard *et al.*, 2009). These are the same forms that predominate in languages (Maddieson, 1984). Continued growth permits additional freedom of movement in this biomechanically based mechanism. Importantly, development of oral motor skills serves general biological functions, including breathing and eating. Implementation and coordination of these systems for speech production directed to linguistic message forms is an overlaid function, marshaled by humans uniquely among living species.

HOW DO SOCIAL INTERACTIONS SUPPORT EMERGENCE OF PHONOLOGY?

Social interactions provide another critical element that contributes to drawing together perception and production capacities for efficient use in acquiring a phonological system in this early period. Social interactions throughout the first year of life shape infant behaviors in ways that facilitate speech acquisition. The earliest observable behaviors in this domain are not clearly social in nature. But these domain-general capacities support the infant in attending to communication partners in her immediate social environment, forming the first foundation for the child's engagement in interactive social experiences using language.

Preference for and attention to faces (Frank *et al.*, 2009; Gliga *et al.*, 2009) and face recognition in dyadic joint-attention episodes (Striano and Stahl, 2005; Tremblay and Rovira, 2007) are among the striking early preferences demonstrated by infants related to social linkages, illustrating how readily young human infants orient toward other humans.

Early dyadic joint-attention episodes beginning at birth include reliable eye contact between mother and child. This orientation is reciprocated by caregivers who accompany the interaction with language input (Goldstein and Schwade, 2008; Bloom *et al.*, 1987). In the first six months of life, infants are entirely dependent on caregivers as they engage in daily feeding, bathing, or play routines. When caregivers are highly attuned, infants demonstrate joint-attention at younger ages (Tremblay and Rovira, 2007). Attunement is defined by the mother noticing and commenting on the infant's focus of attention or other non-verbal behavior, indicating she has registered the infant's attention. Some of the kinds of behaviors that mothers attune to include motoric behaviors by which infants initiate behaviors such as throwing objects, focusing, loss of balance, uncontrolled behaviors, and displeasure (Jonsson and Clinton, 2006). In these interactions the infant's gaze monitoring or attention to the mother's gaze can be observed.

In another critical functional domain available from the first days of life, feeding routines provide a regular opportunity for infants to see and imitate adult facial expressions (Field *et al.*, 2010). Here, infants show capacities to imitate oral motor and facial movements from the first days of life (Meltzoff and Goswami, 2002). Feeding is also an important general social context since it continues to provide a context for routine use of communicative behavior, as infants have regular ongoing face-to-face contact with caregivers. Feeding routines are especially structured, regular, and offer consistent opportunities to move from use of eye contact and dyadic joint-attention to use of gesture and later to phonetically consistent forms and recognizable words. This progression provides a lovely example of heterarchical linkages across domains that grow in complexity with social functional impetus.

At around 8 months, infants have been shown to increase the maturity of vocal types toward more mature syllable types, including faster consonant–vowel transitions, when they are engaged in contingent caregiver social interactions (Goldstein and Schwade, 2009). Further, infants who are vocalizing relative to objects show differentially positive readiness to learn during babbling (Goldstein *et al.*, 2010). Earlier in the infant's first year, mothers have been shown to provide differential feedback to their 5-month-old infants' sound pattern output

(Gros-Louis *et al.*, 2006), reinforcing more mature vocalizations differentially in spontaneous interchanges. Overall, Goldstein and colleagues' body of work indicates a strong influence of social contingency within the first year of life on infant's movement toward more mature speech-like vocalizations. This social milieu involves both parent teaching through use of more mature vocalization patterns and infant responses as they gain the maturity to code more mature vocalizations consistently in canonical babbling.

Following a communication partner's gaze in triadic joint-attention episodes (Legerstee *et al.*, 2007) is another prominent example that begins to occur late in the first year and into the early months of the second year of life. In triadic joint-attention episodes, infants and partners focus mutually on external objects or events. By this time, infants are engaging intentionally on a consistent basis in social interactions that help them to learn about their world through social scaffolding. Emergence of triadic joint-attention may be a key achievement in social scaffolding of phonological acquisition. At least one study indicates that later vocabulary learning is predicted by infant abilities for utilizing eye gaze in triadic joint-attention episodes; infants who looked longer showed higher productive vocabularies tracked as late as 2 years (Brooks and Meltzoff, 2008). Social awareness is a critical key for children to begin to use their vocal capacities within socially relevant experiences to get attention from others.

Initially, joint-attention episodes are infrequent and brief in duration (Carpenter *et al.*, 1998). Following infants across development shows that the frequency and the duration of these interactions increase across development. By 15 months, children show dramatically enhanced ability to engage with more communication partners in triadic attention episodes and to sustain interactions over several turns in play episodes. These qualitative shifts in interactions, and importantly, the child's awareness of intentionality, reinforce the idea that children are coming to relate in more mature ways to others during the second half of their first year as they move toward the early period of word use.

Another behavioral change illustrates how infants are becoming more intentionally social across this same period in interactions with others. Pointing to objects reliably emerges around 9 months of age for "requesting" (Butterworth, 1995). Emergence of gestures and vocalizations as proto-imperatives and proto-declaratives occurs reliably between 9 and 12 months of age (Bates *et al.*, 1975). The use of gestures to capture attention and control the actions of others provides an overt behavioral sign in a parallel domain to the vocal output system that children are relating to those around them as social beings (Tomasello *et al.*, 2007). Pointing is an invaluable tool to help the child leverage herself into vocal communication. It indicates awareness of the intentionality of communication and the mental state of others, but does not require the ability to produce specific phonological or word forms to convey this intent.

In a developmental progression from early attunement in the first days and months of life, by 10 months of age infants whose mothers show higher levels of attunement earlier in development also show higher levels of coordinated attention (Legerstee *et al.*, 2007). In contrast, depressed mothers tend to show less affect with their infants. Infants of depressed mothers attend to their mother's gaze as do the infants of non-depressed mothers, but are less responsive to voices and faces around them (Field *et al.*, 2009). Low levels of infant responsiveness have been associated with higher levels of arousal and delayed attention or slower processing of stimuli (Field *et al.*, 2009).

Later in the first year, games, such as "peek-a-boo" and ball tossing, illustrate a social context that supports communicative interactions as infants become more independent. Rome-Flanders and colleagues (1995) followed mother–child play in young children between 6 and 24 months. Mothers played an active role in scaffolding child participation throughout. Infants demonstrated an increasing understanding of the rules by following established patterns in the games and gradually aligned the time of their turns to those of their mother. Simple play routines provide a rich and repeated source of experiential input for infants to understand words associated with their needs in familiar contexts. In turn, adults understand and reinforce the infant's use of relevant word forms. Just as infants (and their caregivers) build up expectations about what will happen in the game, expectations are gradually built up about the vocalization patterns and the phonetically consistent forms or words that are used within these routines. These vocal expectancies within routines provide a rich source of ambient language input for young children to begin the process of extracting phoneme and sequence regularities.

HOW DO EARLY IMITATION AND MEMORY SKILLS SUPPORT EMERGENCE OF PHONOLOGY?

As we have noted, the child's increasing access to memory for storage and retrieval is critical to the acquisition of the phonological component of language. Memory allows children to build representations of the social exchanges within events and attach them to perceptions and actions that are salient within these events. At birth, children can imitate motor movements such as a mouthing gesture (Meltzoff and Kuhl, 1994). This ability to reproduce with her body what she has seen is enabled via the action of mirror neurons. Mirror neurons allow the neonate to imitate specific mouth movements (Ferrari *et al.*, 2003; Westerman and Miranda, 2002). At this early period, neither short- nor long-term higher-level memory processes seem to be involved; sensori-motor reproduction of environmental events produced by another person is implicated. This early capacity, like categorical perception, forms a building block for later language-based complexity. Importantly, this type of see-and-reproduce sequence occurs within the infant's social environment, scaffolded by joint-attention and preference for faces.

Declarative memory refers to the system that stores facts. It can be used to support emergence of the child's representation of knowledge and procedures. The simplest explanation of procedures is that they are "how to do things." In order to plan and organize socially relevant output in actions, young children must start with a foundation of knowing about how to sequence motor movements to accomplish particular goals. Holding a spoon to eat yogurt is a goal-directed sequence of movements, for example. Early procedures are embedded in goal-directed movements. Repetition of events (in daily routines) provides a context for building representation of sequences of events. Speech output and the motor sequences related to speech production itself will be employed to implement the stored memory of declarative memory procedures. In both cases, repetition and use of motor behaviors support recall as well as continued expansion of the schema.

Experiments in the first six months of life illustrate the infant's earliest implementation of memory capacities. Change in the ability to hold on to visual experience and reproduce it is indicative of the emergence of declarative memory. By 6 months of age, children can reproduce motor sequences (using a puppet to ring a bell) with a delay, when they have merely observed the two repetitions of the sequence two days apart, or when they were actively encouraged to repeat the sequence in the same time interval (Barr *et al.*, 2005). In these experiments, both observer and the actively participating infant demonstrated deferred imitation up to 10 days later. Infants who imitated the sequence were likely to continue to be able to imitate it up to 2.5 months later, suggesting that the opportunity to use the behavior supports its later recall.

Relative to an emergence perspective, this type of experiment illustrates the importance of the social dyad for providing the infant with models of behaviors that she can reproduce. This same type of external model/child reproduction template can be proposed as characterizing later growth in attunement of vocalizations toward language-relevant patterns. Infants are likely to increase the amount of babbling they produce when social partners reinforce the pattern (Dodd, 1972). Furthermore, when the amount and timing of input is controlled, infants come to match their mother's vocalization patterns (vowels or words) more under contingent conditions than yoked conditions (Goldstein and Schwade, 2008). The infant's reproduction of environmental movements, produced by persons they see and hear make those movements in daily routines (e.g. "pat-a-cake"), provides evidence of the connection of perception, movement, and social bonding. These interactions lay a critical foundation for later acquisition of both knowledge and goal-directed actions. Children's early comprehension of words and production of phonetically consistent forms and words tend to organize around these daily routines.

By about 11 or 12 months of age, children are more likely to demonstrate the comprehension of words in the context of commonly recurring events than in isolation, or in less-familiar events (Swingley, 2008; Fernald and Hurtado, 2006). Long-term memory in this early period is still maturing relative to the child's ability to set down permanent knowledge stores, although short-term memory allows retention of learning over a few days (Jones and Carr, 2004; Klein and Meltzoff, 1999; Learmonth *et al.*, 2005; Lukowski *et al.*, 2005; Markova and Legerstee, 2006; Heimann *et al.*, 2006; Nielsen, 2006). Children need capacities of this type to accumulate permanent representations of vocabulary knowledge and to eventually demonstrate decontextualized comprehension of words and simple utterances. The ability to comprehend language out of context emerges gradually in the period during which children are refining patterns and developing greater complexity (to be discussed in Chapter 5). In this early period, context is completely necessary to emergence of more refined patterns. Input enables tuning in concert with the child's growing intrinsic capacities.

HOW DOES THE EXTRINSIC ENVIRONMENT SUPPORT EMERGENCE OF PHONOLOGY?

We have asserted that child-internal capacities enable increasingly efficient coordination of early output-based vocalizations and input-based pattern-detecting abilities. This increase in coordination supports growth in goal-directed use of the vocal system for communication. To support this process, environmental input scaffolds and guides qualitative change in the young child toward use of vocalizations and pattern-detecting abilities for coding precise ambient language patterns. We have proposed that two child-extrinsic variables also serve as scaffolds. These variables are found in the nature of precise ambient language phonological input to the child, and cultural socialization practices in which uses of these forms are embedded.

Available data on this period illustrate how parent and caregiver input provide needed information about the child's ambient phonology. Children gradually shape their own vocal output to match ambient language input regularities over their first 4–5 years. Processing studies indicate that by around 10 months of age, children are sensitive to the statistical properties of the language input in learning experiments based on random strings of sounds (Saffran, 2003; Saffran *et al.*, 2009; Gerken, 2004, 2006). This rich daily source of input from parents and caregivers helps to shape children's construction of a mental knowledge base, as well as their understanding of how to produce sounds and sequences that replicate their growing store of ideas in new words.

Simulation of the rich daily input from communication partners illustrates how children may use this available raw material to construct a mental knowledge base. In the natural learning environment, multiple repetitions of salient word forms from familiar communication partners shapes children's expectations of what sounds and sequences make up familiar words and how these patterns cohere in the connected speech they hear every day. Routines such as bathing, eating, sleeping, and toileting provide multiple daily experiences with word forms and their deployment in familiar and salient contexts. As the child grows, play with objects and later symbolic play provide repetitive and highly salient episodes, as well as multiple repetitions of content-specific vocabulary.

Caregivers, who are often mothers, specifically shape their input through the production of "motherese," or infant-directed speech (IDS) (Fernald, 1989). Common characteristics of IDS include shorter than average utterances with exaggerated pitch contours and frequent repetition of words and sentence types. IDS speech style is manifested in similar ways across diverse languages studied to date (Lee *et al.*, 2008; Vihman *et al.*, 1994; Zamuner, 2003). IDS is produced more frequently by some cultural groups than others. Mothers in the United States, for example, use different input characteristics than Japanese mothers (Toda *et al.*, 1990; Fernald and Morikawa, 1993).

IDS contains different phonological properties than adult-directed speech (ADS). Lee *et al.* (2008) found that Korean IDS speakers showed significant differences in consonant and vowel frequencies compared to speakers using Korean ADS. Patterns observed in IDS were consistent with speech sounds described for early infant speech output in English and across languages (Kern and Davis, 2009). A follow-up study of English (Lee and Davis, 2010) matched the results for Korean, indicating that American English-speaking mothers also used a more simplified phonological inventory in their IDS than in their ADS. These comparisons of IDS and ADS within the same language and across languages supports an argument that ambient language input in IDS is tailored to children's capacities in this early period (Sachs, 1977; Cross, 1977), indicating a critical role of experience in emergence of precise ambient language mastery.

WHAT DOES PHONOLOGICAL ACQUISITION IN DIVERSE EARLY DEVELOPMENTAL CIRCUMSTANCES REVEAL ABOUT AN EMERGENCE PERSPECTIVE?

Breakdowns in communication development as a result of developmental differences provide another source of evidence for the role of intrinsic physical capacities and the supporting mechanisms of self-organization and learning in emergence of phonology. Here the child's capacities are different, the nature of interactions may change, and the extrinsic input from communication partners may be quite qualitatively different. Outcomes may illustrate the effects of missing components of the system.

HEARING IMPAIRMENT

Hearing impairment is a well-documented cause of early childhood communication disorders, especially as related to successful emergence of speech perception capacities and speech intelligibility. Evaluating consequences for speech perception and production as well as developmental change in children with significant hearing impairment can provide insight into the patterns of interaction between production and perception system capacities for producing age-appropriate speech output and detecting speech-relevant patterns.

The growing population of infants identified with hearing loss at birth who may receive hearing aids by 3–6 months and/or cochlear implants by 10–12 months offers a naturally occurring opportunity to observe the emergence of speech production and perception capacities as they mutually influence one another. Based on their lack of auditory access to the speech input signal in daily life, these children show consistent patterns of nasal consonants (i.e., /m/, /n/, and /ŋ/) and neutral vowels (i.e., /ə/) predominantly, with very rudimentary production of canonical CV syllables (i.e. *baba*) (Moeller *et al.*, 2007a).

Studies of children between 3 and 18 months with varying degrees of loss (mild to severe levels) who are in early stages of development after receiving hearing instrumentation can illustrate the role of sufficient auditory input on vocal development. Emergence of rhythmic syllables, reduction in nasal consonant use, and vowel space diversification have been observed at a group level within 6–8 months of auditory experience with hearing instrumentation (i.e. hearing aids), comparable to age of syllable emergence in children with typical hearing profiles. In addition, auditory capacity has been significantly associated with number of utterances containing syllables, and number of rhythmic canonical syllables versus less mature vocalization types, use of oral consonants, and vowel space diversification (Davis et al., 2004; Davis et al., 2005; von Hapsburg et al., 2008; von Hapsburg and Davis, 2006). Children with moderate losses showed more variable and less predictable outcomes, but a higher proportion of nasals, neutral vowels, and pre-canonical syllables than hearing children overall. As degree of hearing loss increases, children with more severe to profound hearing loss show overall lower frequency of speech-like syllables, more use of nasals, and frequent use of neutral vowels. This decrease in sound patterns characteristic of hearing children with increase in hearing deficit indicates a clear influence of auditory access on speech patterns observed. This is not a new finding. However, the relatively rapid response to sound observable (i.e. within 6 months or so) is supportive of suggestions of a dynamic and embodied complex system.

CLEFT LIP/PALATE

Cleft lip/palate (CLP) is the most common congenital craniofacial malformation. It is defined as a congenital malformation of the face in which the lip, primary palate, or secondary palate are not fused, resulting in an open space or cleft (Peterson-Falzone et al., 2001). Surgical repair of the cleft cannot be accomplished at birth. However, the structural malformations of an unrepaired cleft may lead to complications in early speech development and production (Chapman et al., 2008). Since the cleft palate impacts the structures involved in speech production, there are particular areas of logical vulnerability relative to the course of typical speech development. These differences illustrate the impact of structural integrity on emergence of an age-appropriate speech output repertoire. In addition, this disorder category illustrates the positive effects of repair of speech production structures on outcomes for intelligible speech acquisition.

Although there is a variety of cleft types, cleft palate involves a lack of distinction between the oral and nasal cavity prior to surgical repair of the palate. Deficiencies in velo-pharyngeal functioning may persist following initial surgery, preventing adequate velar closure to produce distinctions between oral and nasal sounds (Wyatt et al., 1996). The result of these structural deviations is altered vocal resonance. Speech may be hyper-nasal, and audible or inaudible nasal turbulence may be present (Harding and Grunwell, 1998; Wyatt et al., 1996). Nasal resonance and/or turbulence continue if structural deviations persist after surgical repair procedures. Production of consonants requiring intraoral pressure (e.g. stops, fricatives, and affricates) is negatively impacted by emission of air through the nasal cavity based on lack of ability to build intraoral pressure due to the cleft. Children with clefts may attempt to compensate to achieve the closure of the vocal tract necessary to produce stops and fricatives by producing consonants in posterior places of articulation (e.g. glottal or pharyngeal), before the air has reached the nasal and oral cavities (Wyatt et al., 1996). These sound substitutions are referred to as compensatory articulation patterns (Trost, 1981).

Chapman et al. (2001) compared the prelinguistic vocal development of thirty 9-month-old infants with unrepaired cleft palate to fifteen age-matched peers without CLP. The infants with clefts had a tendency to vocalize less, although the differences between the children with and without cleft palates did not reach statistical significance. The authors also measured canonical babbling ratios (number of true canonical syllables/number of total syllables) and the percentage of infants that had reached the canonical babbling stage. Only 57 percent of children with CLP had reached the canonical babbling stage, compared to 93 percent of children in the typically developing group, as determined by achieving a canonical babbling ratio of 0.15 or higher. Consonant inventories for the 9-month-old infants with intact articulatory mechanisms were on average twice as large as the infants with clefts. Alveolar consonants are favored in the babbling of typically developing children (Davis and MacNeilage, 1995), while they are not favored in speech produced by children with cleft palate (Chapman et al., 2001).

In a follow up study at 21 months, Chapman et al. (2003) compared speech characteristics of fifteen children with CLP and fifteen typically developing peers. Children with CLP produced a significantly smaller consonant inventory in both total utterances and in lexically based utterances only. Number of emerging consonants and number of stable consonants were also smaller than typically developing peers.

Scherer and colleagues (2008) compared the vocalizations of 26 children (13 with clefts and 13 with intact oral structures) to describe vocalizations at 6 and 12 months of age, and to investigate the relationship between early vocalizations, speech, and lexical development at 30 months of age. No significant difference in the frequency of vocalizations between the two groups was present at 6 months, however significant differences were observed at 12 months. Each utterance was assigned a babbling level of 1–3 based on Stoel-Gammon's mean babbling level (MBL) (Stoel-Gammon, 1989). Utterances composed of a vowel, voiced syllabic consonant, or CV syllable in which the consonant was a glide or glottal stops were assigned a Level 1. Level 2 utterances contained a VC or CV syllable, or a CVC syllable with a single consonant type, while Level 3 utterances were representative of variegated babbling. They were composed of syllables with two or more different consonant types. Children with CLP produced significantly lower mean babbling levels at 6 and 12 months, indicating that their utterances were less complex in both syllable structure and phonetic content. At 12 months, consonant inventories of 50 percent of children with CLP consisted of /w/, /m/, /n/, and /h/, and /ʔ/, while the inventories of 50 percent of typically developing peers consisted of /p/, /b/, /w/, /m/, /t/, /d/, /k/, /g/, /n/, /l/, and /j/. At 30 months, children with CLP produced a variety of stops, nasals, glides, and laterals, but produced significantly fewer fricatives than typically developing peers.

Hardin-Jones and Jones (2005) subsequently investigated the speech of 212 preschoolers with CLP ranging in age from 2 years 10 months to 5 years 6 months of age. The percentages of children requiring speech therapy, the presence of moderate to severe hyper-nasality, and glottal/pharyngeal substitutions were reported, with cleft type and age of surgical intervention taken into consideration. Sixty-eight percent of the participants were currently enrolled or had been enrolled in speech therapy, and 37 percent demonstrated moderate to severe hyper-nasality and/or glottal/pharyngeal substitutions (Hardin-Jones and Jones, 2005). Persistence of compromise in acquisition of age-appropriate speech output capacities indicates the potential for persistent effects of early differences in structural integrity of the speech mechanism on output patterns in the face of some age-appropriate development of sound system patterns.

Bilingualism

Data from bilingual children provide a useful example indicating that differences in input patterning make a difference in children's knowledge about their ambient language. Bilingual infants are of interest since they hear a greater variety of consonants and vowels in their language input by virtue of their dual (or more) ambient language inputs. Work with bilingual infants suggests that children exposed to two languages are able to learn to recognize the sound patterns of their languages early (Bosch and Sebastián-Galles, 1997). They develop the ability to differentiate language-specific contrasts in each of their languages within the same time frame as monolingual infants develop categories (Sundara *et al.*, 2008; Burns *et al.*, 2007), and are flexible in their ability to classify the patterns of both of their languages (Kovacs and Mehler, 2009).

Much of this work has been focused on infants whose languages differ in prosody and phonetic inventory and are thus readily distinguishable. An interesting exception is when the representation of two languages may compete, as is in the case of the Catalán and Spanish monolingual and bilingual child. In Catalán the /e/-/ɛ/ distinction is contrastive. It is not contrastive in Spanish (Bosch and Sebastián-Galles, 2003). Bilingual infants go through a period of treating the sounds as equivalent around 8 months of age until they are able to differentiate them at later test periods. On the whole, infants are able to accommodate as much linguistic experience as they receive. Bilingual infants may start to incur a cost of separating the two systems in early word recognition. In several cases, investigators have documented the emergence of word recognition to be somewhat later in bilingual infants than their monolingual peers, such as when words are similar-sounding across language or are more phonologically complex (Vihman *et al.*, 2007; Fennell *et al.*, 2007).

In cross-linguistic studies focused on listener perceptions of infant vocal patterns, monolingual listeners identify monolingual infants who are babbling in their own language. Adult listeners can do this more reliably when they judge long samples with prosodic cues than short samples without cues. However, when untrained Spanish bilingual listeners were asked to identify the language of Spanish and English babbled sequences they did not do so reliably (Thevenin *et al.*, 1985).

In contrast to studies of perception in bilingual infants, there are relatively few studies on output patterns. Children from bilingual environments are constrained by their motor development just like monolingual infants. Zlatic *et al.* (1997) showed that twins growing up in an English Serbian environment demonstrated the same within-syllable CV co-occurrence patterns as have been documented for monolingual children (Kern and Davis, 2009). Oller *et al.* (1997) compared a group of seventeen infants growing up in a bilingual environment to their monolingual peers. Both groups began to produce canonical babbling at about the same time.

Social interaction in the language the child is learning guides the child toward communication rather than language-specific skills. These findings highlight the assertion that importance of the maturation of the oral motor mechanism is setting the pace for speech output acquisition in the face of input from varied languages in earliest periods of speech-like vocal development.

WHAT DO EARLY INFANT CAPACITIES HAVE IN COMMON WITH NON-HUMAN SYSTEMS?

Mature ambient language knowledge and a full repertoire of speech pattern recognition and linguistic output capacities illustrate a uniquely human achievement. However, the precursors that enable emergence of this system are general. They can be seen as general capacities marshaled for this goal rather than dedicated only to human language. In this section, we want to explore what early infant behaviors have in common with non-humans as diverse as primates, birds, and dolphins. All of these species develop elaborate calls and social interactions that function to support their survival through food gathering and procreation, as well as protection from predators. We will also consider the ways in which pre-speech achievements of infant humans are general and can be considered similar to achievements in other aspects of infant human development, underscoring the generality of complex intra-human behaviors.

VOCALIZATIONS IN OTHER SPECIES

Many animal species use vocal calls, or songs, to convey messages to members of their community (e.g. dolphins, Pack and Herman, 2004; birds, MacDougall-Shackleton, 2009; and primates, Arnold and Zuberbuhler, 2006). This commonality is referred to as call convergence (Tyack, 2008). Shared calls become more similar as demonstrated by social ties among groups (e.g. animals in captivity versus animals in the wild, Noad et al., 2000; Tyack, 2008; Mitani and Nishida, 1993).

Two species stand out in their vocal learning as points of reference for considering an emergence perspective on infant speech development: songbirds and dolphins. Songbirds learn to produce vocal sequences based on perceptually based learning from tutors, or other members of their species (Helekar et al., 2003). Like the babbled sequences produced by infants, these vocal sequences consist of repeated syllables and phrases (Helekar et al., 2003).

There are qualitative differences between early- and late-learned songs (Holveck *et al.*, 2008). In the early sensori-motor period, songs are simple motor repetitions. Later, more complex songs are produced by adult members of the species. Not all birds learn these more complex patterns; learning in part depends on having a tutor to model these forms (Helekar *et al.*, 2003; Burt *et al.*, 2007). One difference in these two song types is that the brain regions activated during early and late songs are different (Bolhuis and Gahr, 2006). Qualitative changes across development in other species suggests the possibility that early babbling may be based on qualitatively different brain mechanisms than babbling occurring after human infants start to convey meaning. Brain damage, specifically lesions to the basal ganglia circuits of birds, prevents them from producing the context-dependent changes in song variations needed for communicative purposes (Kao and Brainard, 2006). This type of issue represents an empirical question that should be addressed in evaluating the domain-general notion central to an emergence perspective.

Dolphin learning also offers interesting insights to understanding of the general nature of early human infant production and perception abilities. Dolphins, like young language learners, can imitate or mimic the cries of other animals in their pack (Tyack, 2008). In one experimental study, two mothers and their male offspring were taught to use a keyboard that emitted signals sounding like dolphin cries. The young dolphins mimicked these cries more than their mothers' vocal patterns (Reiss and McCowan, 1993). However, only the young dolphins produced these cries spontaneously. Their rate of production increased after they had been hearing and mimicking them for about one year (McCowan and Reiss, 1993). This finding, too, suggests qualitative differences between the sophistication of babble and calls and words for communicative purposes. It also highlights the conceptualization that not only the amount of time spent using these signals, but the opportunity for learning and practicing in early development is important to making the qualitative shift from producing rhythmic speech-like vocalizations that sound like speech to intentionally using sound sequences for communicative purposes.

PERCEPTION IN OTHER SPECIES

Speech perception abilities also display general properties in common with other species. Early auditory system capacities or perception behaviors that on the surface seem like sophisticated precursors of human language capacities are also present in non-humans. Non-human species demonstrate categorical perception skills and sensitivity to the auditory characteristics of speech sounds, such as voice onset time, that are associated with voicing across place of articulation (Kluender et al., 1987; Kluender and Walsh, 1992; Kuhl and Miller, 1975). Recent work suggests that cotton-top tamarind monkeys show language-discrimination abilities similar to those of the human infant (Ramus et al., 2000). Unlike human infants, other animals are not able to form language-relevant phonetic categories (Kuhl et al., 1992). They have not yet demonstrated the ability to learn grammatical rules based on the statistic properties of speech input (Saffran et al., 2008).

Infants demonstrate similarly complex patterns of processing in music and visual stimuli. This general capacity provides another reason for arguing that early achievements in speech processing are non-linguistic. Around 6 months of age, infants respond differentially to distinct rhythmic patterns in music (Trehub and Shenfield, 2007). With repeated exposure to melodies, children respond to structural violations (Hannon and Johnson, 2005) and start to develop preferences for new (i.e. higher- versus lower-pitched) variants of melodies they are unlikely to have heard outside the experimental sessions. In the visual domain, infants can detect regularities as well. Baldwin and colleagues have shown that infants use the regularities in dynamic action sequences to parse action sequences (Baldwin et al., 2008).

SOCIAL AWARENESS IN OTHER SPECIES

Awareness of others, leading to social interaction within communities, is also well represented in non-humans. Attention in primates, gaze in dolphins, and ability to use gestures in bonobos provide examples that social awareness is not unique to humans. Dolphins have been shown to respond to human gaze direction and gestures (Pack and Herman, 2004). Primates not only respond to gestures but can use their hands and feet to produce gestures understood by others within their communities. Female gorillas have been observed in wild communities (as opposed to captive communities) to use two hand claps to maintain group cohesiveness (Kalan and Rainey, 2009). In experimental contexts, great apes have been shown to use begging gestures to initiate food exchanges (Pele et al., 2009).

In sum, like vocalization and pattern detection capacities, social interaction capacities at this general level are found across species. Their use is not confined to human language acquisition. At least one difference in developmental patterns between humans and other animals is the time course of development. Human infant development is protracted relative to other species. The protracted course of maturational development of human biological capacities, termed neotony, provides critical opportunities for human infants to develop breadth and depth of repertoire that is simply not observed in animal behavioral patterns. Repeated participation in familiar events over the course of development gives rise to opportunities for use of biological capacities to practice perception and production of language forms.

WHAT IS THE ROLE OF SUPPORTING MECHANISMS IN THIS EARLY PERIOD?

Self-organization is a facilitating mechanism. The child's optimal utilization of her physically embodied production and perception systems enables her to perceive and produce behavioral patterns used to connect with others in her environment. These patterns, based on self-organization of the child's bodily systems, are tuned by frequent social experiences in which she hears relevant sound patterns. This embodied system propels her from general, non-linguistic sensing and moving within her environment, toward marshaling her perception and production capacities for comprehending and producing linguistic messages in communication interactions. Critically, these operations are embedded within the child's capacities for maintaining interaction that are concurrently developing.

Learning skills are also necessary in enabling the child to build and store a knowledge base for understanding messages and producing relevant responses. Maturation of short- and long-term memory capacities and their deployment in myriad experiences operate in concert with learning mechanisms. These capacities permit the neural/cognitive instantiation in long-term knowledge of increasingly complex ambient language behavioral patterns. In short, memory is critical to the storage of a broader and deeper world knowledge base that forms the foundation of word learning and linguistic creativity through the vehicle of phonology. These foundations scaffold the later stages in acquisition of phonological complexity.

Embodiment has been described in Chapter 1 as the child's use of the biological capacities of her body to gather and incorporate knowledge of the world. Through embodiment across this early period of speech acquisition, children situate their capacities for speech-oriented motor movements within their growing internal fund of world knowledge. They repeatedly experience the consequences of their own bodies operating to produce and perceive their own vocalizations. This internal feedback occurs in the context of events in which adults are also using a verbal code containing ambient language patterns to share relevant social experiences. The result is an embodied cognitive representation of events shared by the child and the adults in her environment. The system is heterarchical in the sense that the child's growing knowledge base and her growing behavioral repertoire provide mutual feedback, tuned by adult phonological models deployed in culturally appropriate ways.

This heterarchical development can start within hours of birth (Meltzoff & Moore, 1977), when neonates imitate oral gestures such as tongue protrusion, a skill attributed to the actions of mirror neurons (Rizzolatti and Arbib, 1998). With reference to speech-related vocalizations, Kuhl and Meltzoff (1996) have illustrated an early capacity in infants between 12 and 20 weeks to show progressive differentiation of vowel productions when presented with an adult model to imitate in laboratory conditions.

In the second half of the first year, young infants begin to engage in speech games by taking turns babbling with caregivers. Embodiment in this phase situates the child's intentional speech-related movements in the context of emerging social interaction skills facilitated by joint-attention capacities. By about 10 months, children may begin the process of producing phonetically consistent forms in social interactions. Speech movements without communicative intent shift to being used for proto-communicative intentions (i.e. consistent forms that are not accurate relative to word targets, such as /dae/ for "I want something"). These proto-forms may not resemble actual words but are produced consistently in familiar social contexts with communication partners. Adults interpret these unique forms to have meaning based on their reliable appearance with games and routines in familiar contexts. At this point, infants are using organized speech-like movements. They are beginning the long process of pairing vocalizations with meanings, a crucial cornerstone for mature linguistic communication. Very soon, by the end of the first year or early in the second year of life, infants begin to associate the names of familiar objects or events with their own ability to reproduce a particular sequence of speech movements linked with that object or event. /ba/ becomes reliably associated with *ball*.

As indicated in Chapter 1, self-organization accounts for the emergence of speech-like behaviors, wherein qualitatively distinct, rhythmic, speech-like "syllables" emerge from the less organized vocalizations that preceded them. They emerge as the child's perception, production, and neural-cognitive subsystems converge on an optimization of interactions accompanied by those observable speech-like rhythmic vocalizations.

Children produce a variety of consonant–vowel combinations primarily based on the rhythmic open-and-close movements of the vocal tract (Davis and MacNeilage, 1995). As they learn to produce their first words, they rely on practiced consonant–vowel combinations from their earlier babbling repertoire that may effectively appear to reduce the complexity of their output (Vihman and McCune, 1994). Importantly, the capacities of these subsystems that underlie emergence of organized rhythmic vocalizations are general in nature. Rhythmic and organized vocal behaviors are also produced by non-humans. They are consistent with organized rhythmic behaviors in other body systems, termed "rhythmic stereotypies," in young infants (Thelen and Smith, 1994). These rhythmic behaviors precede the period in which the actions are used for goal-directed behaviors.

Oral motor change occurs in the context of the child's general motor development. Thelen's classic work on motor development shows that children refine coordinated motor skill through repetitive movements (e.g. leg kicking or hand banging) that are ultimately combined into qualitatively different and more advanced motor movements. For example, prior to learning to walk, children produce rhythmically organized, repetitive leg kicking movements, examples of the rhythmic stereotypies. This large motor system process of acquisition of movement complexity is relevant to emergence of organized and rhythmic speech syllables. Canonical babbling vocalizations provide a prominent and consistent example of a rhythmic repetitive movement that precedes use of the vocal system for speech production related to language use (Oller, 2000). Both are qualitatively more advanced behaviors than their predecessors.

Entrainment is the process by which two patterns become more similar to one another (Thelen and Smith, 1994). Young children may match the rhythm of speech patterns to the adults around them. In this way, infants can start the process of sounding more adult-like. As infants' productions sound increasingly more speech-like, they are recognized and reinforced as speech attempts by supportive adults in most, though not all, cultures (for an exception, see Gildersleeve-Neumann, 2001, with a description of infant speech development in Quichua).

Self-organization is evident in the qualitative changes in production abilities of young children as they marshal the use of rhythmically organized vocalizations, already available to their production system in canonical babbling, for communicative intentions. From a dynamic systems perspective, children move from states of disequilibrium or dynamic states to states of equilibrium or attractor states (Thelen, 1991).

When attractor states are achieved, qualitative shifts in the behavioral repertoire emerge.

On the production side, qualitative shifts are evident in the use of more labials in the first-word period when there is a higher frequency of coronal consonants during canonical timing. The babbling frequencies match the most frequently occurring consonant phonemes across languages for consonant place (Maddieson, 1984). The labial regression in first words has been termed a reorganization relative to the functional load of pairing sounds and meanings (Davis *et al.*, 2002). Children regress to a less-complex sound pattern in the face of the need to actually use their production system for word forms.

Qualitative shifts in perceptual skills can be observed in the loss of non-native contrasts. This perceptually driven loss provides evidence for tuning of the perception system to focus on native language phonemic categories. There are corresponding qualitative shifts in children's linguistic knowledge base. And as children's comprehension of incoming messages increases, there is another shift toward the production of true communicative intents. Qualitative shifts in speech perception capacities and language knowledge create instabilities in the complex system. Thus, as children move from a general representation of speech (babbling, pattern detection) to a linguistic representation in which they are attempting to use words and comprehension of increased numbers of words, their system destabilizes. In production, this shift is observed in a reliance on a reduced set of sounds and sequences of sounds available to produce words. In perception, this is observed in the reliance on contextual cues to interpret sound sequences that on their own may have been well represented earlier.

From the perspective of speech production models such as Levelt and Meyer (2000), infants in the vocalize stage function at the *articulation* level. However, at this level of the model, children's peripheral structures execute speech-related movements but meaning is conveyed without the adult-like syllabic organization required for linguistic interchanges. As a prominent example, prelinguistic infants use /ə/ in concert with a pointing gesture to request actions or objects from communication partners by 9–10 months. As will be seen in the discussion of pattern detecting that follows, children's vocalizations do not yet reflect details in input patterns they have been shown to detect experimentally in laboratory settings. It is only at the end of this period that children's production skills begin to converge with their emerging ability to comprehend language based on processing of refined patterns in input.

Language learners are resolving the speech puzzle from birth onwards at multiple levels. On one hand, children hear far more input than they understand from birth until well past the end of the vocalization and pattern detection stage we have described here. They produce chunks that do not necessarily correspond directly to the production of actual words starting as early as 10 to 12 months (Peters, 1985). These forms may actually connote a kind of top–down processing as children approximate meanings based on cognitive knowledge with holistic protoword forms that are consistent but not accurate, as related to their word targets. In the same period, children are actively engaging in the process of cracking the code of their ambient phonology and the ways that it can be used to produce meaningful linguistic productions. In the beginning, they match parts of words (i.e. the first consonant in *ball*) or put on final consonants (i.e. the /t/ sound for words such as *hat* or *cat*). Perceptually, they learn to recognize words in context, related to their frequent repetition accompanying games and routines, conveyed in IDS by familiar adult partners.

The process of acquisition cannot be fully understood unless the heterarchical nature of simultaneous bottom–up and top–down learning processes is taken into account. From a top–down perspective, children's perceptual representation of patterns within larger events shapes their knowledge of concepts and words (Baldwin *et al.*, 2008; Walley *et al.*, 2001; Swingley, 2005). On the production side, children's early attempts to produce words may be viewed as holistic movement patterns rather than deliberate attempts to produce word forms based on a fully specified representation of ambient language phonology.

From a bottom–up perspective, maturation of the oral motor system and the ability to produce a greater variety of syllable types (e.g. final consonants, such as the /t/ in *bat,* and clusters, such as the /bl/ in *blue*) allows the child to produce increasingly more accurate approximations of the ambient phonology in socially salient word forms as they begin to emerge. Both are needed for the child to make the qualitative shift to use of production, cognitive, and perception capacities for linguistic ends.

WHAT IS THE OUTCOME OF THE COMPLEX SYSTEM AT THE END OF THIS PERIOD?

Available data on earliest periods of infant development in the first and second years of life strongly support the assertion that general moving and sensing experiences can support young children in acquiring increasing complexity relative to the phonological component of language. These early embodied experiences enable the child to move toward gradual instantiation of long-term cognitive storage for decoding and encoding via memory and attention processes as well as growth toward refining goal-directed behaviors relative to ambient language phonology. The extrinsic environment supports the child's growth in complexity as she is guided by socially embedded input from communication partners enabling her to recognize the need for increasing precision in knowledge and in goal-directed behavior to support message intelligibility. In the next section, we will explore how data on the *refinement* period of acquisition continues to provide support for an emergence model.

5 Refining Patterns of Complexity

Toward the end of what we have termed the *moving and sensing* period, the young child begins the process of *refining* her abilities for producing the sounds of her ambient language. Her ability to remember and store speech sounds for understanding and speaking about a broadening array of topics is growing at the same time. These refinements in "knowing" and "doing" support her building of a long-term phonological knowledge base. Her growth in the two areas of knowledge and behavioral capacities is based on emergence of increasing complexity in ability levels in the areas of speech production, perception, and neural-cognitive knowledge. Growth is also based on weaving together of these capacities for efficient use in learning how to rapidly deploy her behavioral repertoire and phonological knowledge in social communication contexts. In concert with phonological growth, she is rapidly adding vocabulary and building longer sentences. These corollary achievements require overlaying of use of her phonological abilities on diverse layers of complexity in other dimensions of language.

The next few years of the child's life are devoted to building on these early capacities that have been supported to the level of word use by her interaction abilities, including joint-attention, turn-taking, and intention reading. Abilities for interaction using phonological tools are deployed in social situations that meet the young child's functional daily needs. In these interactions, social input from communication partners "tunes" growth in accuracy for perceiving, storing, and reproducing ambient language phonological target behaviors in words and utterances.

In Chapter 4, we emphasized that the child's internal capacities in the areas of cognition, production, and perception must be integrated so that her ability to recognize speech in context and reproduce salient word forms based on phonological patterns can begin to emerge reliably. These patterns cannot be drilled and practiced but must be learned in accordance with linguistic conventions in functional social situations where they are used to communicate. The goal of this review is to demonstrate how these aspects of the complex system continue to enable the child to master needed elements of her ambient language phonology for fully intelligible speech within increasingly complex utterances and ideas.

Here we argue that there is continuity in emergence of more complex levels of neural-cognitive knowledge, perception of language input, and production of language forms from the elements that begin to be produced, perceived, and stored earlier in acquisition. Thus, the child's dynamically changing achievements during this refining period should be seen as continuous with the achievements of the earlier *moving and sensing* period. Refinements can be observed in these three critical areas as increases in phonological knowledge and output intelligibility become apparent to listeners. There is also a growing external pressure from an increasing number of listeners to be understood in social situations. As the child gains new ideas to express and the complexity of her utterances increases, she moves from interacting primarily with her nuclear family and caregivers to an ever-increasing circle of teachers, peers, and other unfamiliar adults. This expansion can be viewed as growth in external complexity in the social realm that occurs in interaction with growth in child-internal complexity.

CONTINUITY OF PRINCIPLES

The same principles that motivate development at the moving and sensing stage support continued growth in speech production, perception, and cognitive processes throughout the refining phase. The motor skills required to produce rhythmic vocalizations based on coordination of articulatory movements with respiration and phonation are observable at the onset of canonical babbling around 7–8 months. However, across the *refining patterns* period, children gain the ability to coordinate production of later acquired sound types (Shriberg *et al.*, 1997; Smit *et al.*, 1990) and more complex phonotactic structures, including consonant clusters such as /bl/ in *black* (Smit *et al.*, 1990), final consonants like /t/ in *mat*, and multisyllabic words like elephant (Hodson and Paden, 1991). Perceptual categorization capacities available early in life that are refined to focus on the child's ambient language by 10 months become reliably linked to phonetic categories relevant for coding even more diverse and salient word forms (Best and McRoberts, 2003). Cognitive development supports the broad representation of speech events as well as attention to and memory for the ambient language phonemes and sequences that must be reproduced accurately to enable their use in producing intelligible words and phrases.

CONTINUITY AND CHANGE IN SUPPORTING MECHANISMS

Embodiment continues in importance across the *refining patterns* period. Growth in efficiency of perception, neural-cognitive storage and retrieval, and reproduction of intelligible speech forms relies on the repetitive use of goal-directed body actions in daily life events. These events, where the child uses her perception and production capacities, are organized around dynamically changing experiences in which she participates socially and uses phonological forms to communicate in meeting her functional goals. We have noted that earliest word productions are more likely to contain highly practiced sounds and sound sequences that children can perceive and reproduce with their bodies (Vihman, 1993; McCune and Vihman, 2001). In addition, these early experiences are likely to be repeated in familiar games and routines and socially focused on present events. Across the *refining patterns* period, children perceive, store, and reproduce an increasing array of language forms that combine ambient language phonological components in diverse ways through the vehicle of goal-directed speech action patterns. This process enables the child to connect behaviors and ideas as she participates in embodied communicative experiences. The eventual outcome of this period is a stored knowledge base for ambient language phonology action patterns. This knowledge base can be perceived by the child listener, retrieved, and produced flexibly to convey messages on myriad topics in her role as speaker.

Self-organization, evident in the *moving and sensing* stage, is gradually replaced by learning as a dominant mechanism underlying acquisition of more complex speech behaviors and knowledge. As we noted in Chapter 4, early self-organization within this complex system yields transformative shifts in the organization of behavior in the first year of life. Learning mechanisms build on the child's embodied capacities through gradual and systemic changes in speech-related behaviors within functional interactions. Other speakers provide the critical component to enable the child's learning: ongoing models of the child's ambient language that are functionally relevant within the cultural norms for communicating ideas and thoughts.

Learning is evident as children increasingly demonstrate awareness and use of the rule-based nature of phonological interfaces with lexical and morphemic dimensions of language. Learning is primarily marked by changes toward the goal of intelligible production and perception of salient language forms, but may be accompanied by declines in related behaviors as children shift their efforts towards more complex phonological targets within more complex linguistic contexts. As children master the task of employing speech production for an arbitrary linguistic system that can be employed generatively, qualitative reorganization of the representations that the infant learner employed during the earlier moving and sensing period occurs. Early holistic or word-based representations give way increasingly to phoneme-based representations that guide the child's journey to complex generative language capacities based on more finely grained units (Pierrehumbert, 2012; Swingley, 2009a).

Heterarchical interactions between a central neural-cognitive knowledge storage of phonological forms and embodied peripheral structures that perceive and produce these forms continue in importance in this phase of acquisition. As we have noted, there is continued growth in the child's ability to perceive and produce the requirements of phonemic-, phonotactic-, and prosodic-level contrasts in her ambient language. Heterarchical interactions are illustrated as these behavioral patterns facilitate long-term cognitive storage. Repetitions of the child's goal-directed speech actions within linguistic contexts feed into her cognitive knowledge base for more precise tuning of phonological knowledge. In turn, the growing cognitive knowledge base facilitates sharpening of behavioral speech patterns as they are deployed in words and utterances. Mutual facilitations of cognition by action, and action by cognition, illustrate the heterarchy that is foundational to an emergence conceptualization.

Usage-based accounts of the development of phonology and language (Bybee, 2010) and proposals invoking statistical learning and phonology (Pierrehumbert, 2003) are very much in line with the conceptualization of heterarchical interactions across phonological acquisition. Both of these accounts suggest that a key level of representation in speech and language production is the word level. For language learners, words are highly functional units because they convey meaning (as compared to individual sounds or morphemes that carry no meaning on their own). Bybee (2010) argues that words function as the basis for exemplar-based learning. Evidence that words serve as exemplars of phonetic-level units includes the tendency to produce higher-frequency words with greater articulatory reduction. For example, in English, words that are produced more often are more likely to be produced with unstressed vowels or schwas and there is greater weakening of intervocalic stops. In Pierrehumbert's (2003) proposal, phonetic representations can have their origins in word-level exemplars such as these. By learning word pairs like *peas* and *peace*, or *bee* and *pea*, where specific phonetic contrasts are associated with meaning, learners start to attend to and reproduce phonetic contrasts. Once learners are aware of these contrasts they use them to leverage their way to learning more vocabulary. Thus there is interplay between speech and vocabulary learning whereby production of more words is foundational to phonological progress in this period.

PRODUCTION IS THE FOUNDATION

Across the refining patterns period, children's production skills for producing speech sounds and phonotactic patterns change dramatically. They begin to participate fully in using diverse words within conversations that become more spontaneous and cover topics that reflect past and future events. In this regard, changes in oral motor structures and their functioning continue to support the observable emergence of sound types and phonotactic patterns in linguistic output during this later period of phonological learning. On one hand, the same rhythmic open–close "frames" that children use in canonical babbling and in early phonetically consistent forms continue into patterns observed in the early lexicon. Indeed, these preferences are retained in languages (MacNeilage *et al.*, 2000a). This continuity highlights the importance of such frames based on rhythmic jaw oscillations, as a basic building block for complex speech production patterning. During the *refining patterns* period, however, children's oral motor structure and function changes in ways that enables reproduction of more complex ambient language patterns within rhythmic syllabic frames.

Greater space between the tongue and palate allows children more room to articulate a greater variety of sounds (e.g. Kent and Vorperian, 1995a; Ménard *et al.*, 2009). Later acquired sounds such as the /l/ or /r/ take advantage of this space to move, as well as the increasing maturity of tongue-positioning capacities. The ability to finely coordinate movements within the oral cavity is critical. One- and two-year-olds produce integrated articulatory movements which are only gradually refined as the children develop abilities to separately control diverse aspects of vocal tract movement (Green *et al.*, 2000). In this progression, jaw movements become adult-like earlier than their lower- and upper-lip movements (Hodge, 1989; Nittrouer, 1993; Steeve, 2010; Steeve and Moore, 2009).

The process of motor development within the speech production output system continues into late adolescence. Paradigms used to explore this dimension of phonological acquisition employ diverse approaches to understanding the status of movement control underlying linguistic encoding. These include kinematic, acoustic, neural, and transcriptional measurements (see Smith, 2010, for comprehensive overviews of this body of work on the longer term course of physiological development and coordination of speech structures). Kent and Vorperian (1995a, 1995b) have described the physiological and anatomical changes that accompany the slower and larger movements characteristic of young children as being based on "anatomical restructuring." Using MRI methods, Vorperian and colleagues have described changes in both soft and bony tissue from infancy through adulthood (Vorperian *et al.*, 2005). They have confirmed both the rapid changes in early development before 18 months (the period covered in Chapter 4) and the longer term course of maturation of these structures into young adulthood.

From another perspective, work by MacNeilage and Davis based on transcriptional methodologies (e.g. MacNeilage *et al.*, 2000a; Davis *et al.*, 2002) suggests strongly that serial properties of speech movements within and across syllables involve rhythmic jaw movements available for production of rhythmic speech properties earlier than mastery of tongue control. Their transcriptional methodology is confirmed by studies of jaw versus tongue movements, indicating that jaw movements have less complex requirements in speech (Ostry *et al.*, 1997) than tongue goals (Honda, 1996).

Research in production system development using kinematic paradigms employs short samples of speech output targeting limited articulators within the production system complex underlying linguistic articulation. Articulator measurements include the jaw and the upper and lower lips, but not tongue or velar movements. For example, based on lip and jaw kinematic analyses, Riely and Smith (2003) found that 5-year-olds show larger amplitude movements and slower velocity of movement in comparison with adult speakers. They suggested that these outcomes indicate young children's speech movements take longer to plan and may rely more heavily on sensory feedback. These effects have been shown to extend at least until speakers are 16 years of age (Walsh and Smith, 2002).

Goffman and colleagues have considered relationships between motor action via kinematic measurements and the coding of linguistic variables, including speech segments (Goffman and Smith, 1999) and prosodic structures (Goffman *et al.*, 2006). Goffman measured kinematic properties of weak and strong syllables in content and function words in typically developing and language-impaired 4- to 7-year-olds compared with adult speakers (Goffman, 2004). Her findings indicated that adults show differentiation of articulatory movement in content and function words but children do not. Children with language impairment produced less well-organized and stable patterns overall than did their typically developing peers.

Goffman and colleagues have recently studied co-articulation in 5-year-olds and adults. These more recent results indicate that the individual's linguistic goal and the underlying motor processes are interleaved in producing output (Goffman *et al.*, in press). In production of a sentence containing *goose* or *geese*, adults and children showed anticipatory and regressive co-articulation in the *goose* context, with the children showing more variability in rounding movements than adults. Thus, both 5-year-olds and adults shaped motor output related to sentence-level requirements for linguistic output, with variability being the major distinguishing factor across ages studied.

Another supporting element for emergence of intelligible speech is the ability to sustain speech production within longer utterances. As children grow, they are better able to use breath support to sustain utterances, and ultimately, conversation (Boliek *et al.*, 2009). They also produce speech more rapidly (Kent *et al.*, 1987). Williams and Stackhouse (1998) compared the speed and accuracy of children's repeated movements. Three- to 5-year-olds were faster and more accurate in producing tongue than lip (/p/, /b/) movements. Children begin to achieve adult-like rates by age 6. This increase in rate is one key to successful accomplishment of intelligibility within the conversational unit.

Cross-language comparisons reveal many similarities in the acquisition of consonant and vowel output patterns during the refining patterns period. A comparison of four languages with diverse consonant inventories (English, Spanish, Arabic, and Putonghua or Modern Standard Chinese) revealed that sounds such as stops (/p/, /t/, /k/, or /b/ in the case of Arabic) and nasals (/m/, /n/) tend to emerge and stabilize at the age of 3 years or earlier for most learners of these languages (McLeod and Goldstein, 2012). The requirements for articulatory adjustments in production of speech sounds can lead to differences in age of acquisition of those sounds. The phoneme /r/ provides a relevant example. In English (Smit *et al.*, 1990), Arabic (Dyson and Amayreh, 2000), Spanish (flap and trill /r/, Acevedo, 1993), and Putonghua, /r/ emerges around 4 years six months of age. In Spanish and Putonghua, where the sound is a flap production, /r/ stabilizes relatively quickly. In English and Arabic, where the /r/ sound requires more precise tongue adjustment, it stabilizes around age 6 or later. These similarities suggest that an important component of speech development is found in the patterns of maturation of the oral motor mechanism that guide the sound production patterns children must master for speech accuracy and ultimate intelligibility. Children tend to make earlier gains in accuracy for phonemes that can be perfected by the open and close movements of the oral mechanism (including /b/,

/d/, /w/, /m/, for example). Tongue-tip sounds requiring only complete contact with the alveolar ridge (i.e. /t/ or /d/) also tend to emerge earlier. Phonemes that require finer coordination of the articulators based on tongue position or movement (such as an /s/, /r/, or /l/) tend to be acquired later in child inventories across languages studied to date.

In contrast, a subset of phonemes emerges and stabilizes with distinctly different timing across languages studied to date. The existence of these acquisition timing differences suggests that perceptual salience due to frequency in the language or phonological structure might influence children's production acquisition beyond influences of the oral motor mechanism. A comparison of the /tʃ/ in English and Spanish is a good example. The phoneme /tʃ/ is a late acquisition in English but an early acquisition in Spanish (Smit *et al.*, 1990; Acevedo, 1993). While it is a lower-frequency sound in Spanish-learning children, it is frequently produced in the context of "baby talk," at least in Mexican Spanish (Blount and Padgug, 1977). In Chinese, the articulatorily similar sound /ts/ is also an early acquired phoneme (Hua and Dodd, 2000; McLeod and Goldstein, 2012). Another example is the phoneme /h/. The /h/ emerges earlier in Arabic than in English children's speech output (Amayreh and Dyson, 1998), and it is associated with greater frequency of occurrence in Arabic. Glottal stops are more frequent in Arabic languages (Maddieson, 1984). Higher frequency in input to children may contribute to earlier acquisition relative to frequency of occurrence in input to English-language learners. Findings of cross-language similarities highlight the role of oral motor development or skill in the development of speech sounds (see Kern and Davis for a review of cross-language patterns in canonical babbling, in review, 2012). However, the observation of markedly different timing of acquisition in some cases suggests interaction between frequency of occurrence in input and ease of production based on motoric skill with speech articulators.

Age-appropriate intelligibility in a wide variety of settings with a wide variety of communication partners is an outcome of the refining patterns period we are considering. Many well-attested common patterns have been described in young children's output across languages, including use of simple CV syllable shapes and early emerging consonant and vowel properties. However, children also exhibit differences, or variability in output patterning. Indeed, variability in phoneme- and phonotactic-level properties is a hallmark of early speech development in typically developing children as the child's language expands concurrently toward longer and more complex utterances (Stoel-Gammon, 2007).

Variability occurs between children as well (i.e. inter-individual differences in output patterns in a group of children at the same age). In this dimension of variability, children show differing sizes of consonant and vowel inventories, differing levels of accuracy with the sounds they can produce, different types of errors in word forms, and thus, differing levels of intelligibility. Stoel-Gammon and Sosa (2012) studied typically developing children between 12 and 24 months. They found considerable variability in the group (17–59 percent), with a peak in variability at the onset of word combinations. An earlier study (Stoel-Gammon, 2004) found mean variability rates of 60 percent at 21 months, decreasing to 19 percent at 33 months in a cohort of five young children's productions of multiple examples of familiar CVC word forms. Thus variability seems apparent and decreases with age, but persists even at 3 years of age.

Variability is also found across children (i.e. intra-individual variations at the same age). Here, individual children may produce sounds differently in different word positions (i.e. /s/ in initial- or final-word position), in different lexical targets (i.e. /b/ in *table* versus *about*), in different utterance-level targets (i.e. two-word versus four-word utterances), or even in the same word at different times (i.e. *ball* as *ba* at one time and *ball* another time).

Overall, phonetic- and utterance-level context effects may drive both inter- and intra-individual patterns of variability, or simply general variability in an emerging language system. No consensus is available about the likely source of this variability. Neuromotor-based explanations suggest that motor control and accuracy is a developmental process occurring over a long period of time that results in increasing accuracy and decreasing variability in output patterns (e.g. Goffman and Smith, 1999; Kent and Vorperian, 1995b). This theoretical perspective is congruent with the emergence proposal voiced here and gives embodiment a critical role, suggesting that central and peripheral developmental processes are interactive in acquiring phonological complexity. Variability is seen as a product of progressive emergence of mastery over components of speech production output in the presence of a changing landscape of general linguistic and social complexity for the young child. Alternatively, psycholinguistic explanations propose underspecified representations or unstable rules (e.g. Forrest *et al.*, 2000) relative to children's emerging cognitive knowledge base and can account for variability in typically developing and/or children with speech delays. This account is consistent with triggering of maturational processes within the child and does not incorporate social function into the theoretical account of phonological acquisition.

DEVELOPMENTAL TRENDS IN PRODUCTION: EMERGENCE OF WORD PRODUCTION

In addition to ongoing motor development, the emergence of words is a transformational achievement occurring at the end of the moving and sensing period we reviewed in Chapter 4. However, words at the juncture of moving and sensing and the refining period are more often produced based on phonetically consistent forms (a memorized whole or chunk, in the terminology of constructivist language learning theories). Intelligibility at this phase is initially supported by the inclusion of highly practiced sounds and syllables (Vihman and Keren-Portnoy, 2011). The more frequently occurring CV co-occurrences that tend to predominate in babbling and are retained in adult word forms provide another foundation for early speech output patterns (Davis *et al.*, 2002). Early phonetically consistent forms or "templates" proposed by Vihman and colleagues that focus on CC patterns may also contain the same CV elements, emphasizing a convergence across types of analysis. Both approaches suggest that an interleaving of cognitive saliency and production system capacities undergirds earliest word patterns.

As children gain control over individual sound production requirements, these capacities can influence the new words that children learn to produce. Schwartz and colleagues (Schwartz and Leonard, 1982; Schwartz *et al.*, 1987) found that toddlers were more likely to learn new words (e.g. novel words) when they contained sounds from within their repertoire than sounds that they did not yet produce. Thus a child who has /f/ in her repertoire is more likely to learn the novel word /fim/ than /sim/. Storkel (2001) showed that 3- to 6-year-old children learned more novel nouns when they contained common sound sequences than when they contained rare sound sequences. Storkel and colleagues have systematically extended this early finding, showing that across development children are more likely to learn words which contain high-probability sound sequences (e.g. Storkel and Hoover, 2011; Hoover *et al.*, 2010) relative to the likelihood of occurrence of phonemes in a language (i.e. /d/ is higher probability than /w/ in English).

The relationship between input probability and efficiency of learning is stable over time (Storkel, 2009). For verbs, children show an advantage for common sound sequences, particularly in production and in early comprehension trials. As development proceeds, low-frequency sound combinations gain in performance in word comprehension. This finding suggests a disconnection between comprehension and production relative to input frequency. The cognitive advantage of phonetic distance, or discriminability, ultimately takes on a greater role in new vocabulary learning than does ability to produce the target sounds and sequences within the words as the child's language capacities grow. This process affords another relevant example in this period of the ongoing dynamic nature of interactions between components of the complex system underlying emergence of full linguistic knowledge and behavioral expression.

An important consideration is that phonotactic probability is based on characteristics of the language input. Presumably speakers of the same ambient language are similar in this regard. However, individual children's speech patterning is individually unique because their speech sound repertoire is individually determined. As children mature we expect them to have an increasingly larger set of "in" sounds so they can converge on the adult model successfully even in the face of the need to express more general language complexity in word types and utterances. Evaluating older children with phonological delays can offer insight into the role of speech production skill in the interplay between children's production abilities and their general language characteristics. These chronologically older children have the benefit of the same frequency of input as their typically developing peers yet still lack the ability to produce speech sounds and sequences with equivalent accuracy based on that input. This area of developmental delay provides a potentially fruitful site for evaluating claims of emergence but has not been explored from this perspective to date.

DEVELOPMENTAL TRENDS IN PRODUCTION: EMERGENCE OF MULTIWORD UTTERANCES

A key test of a child's level of intelligibility is her ability to maintain accuracy for sounds and sequences within words that occur in utterances of increasing length and complexity. Children's intelligibility in connected speech increases from around 26–50 percent intelligible at age 2 to 100 percent by age 4, even to those who are unfamiliar to the child (Gordon-Brannan and Hodson, 2000; Coplan and Gleason, 1988). Thus by the end of the refining period, children are likely to be fully intelligible in producing the speech sounds and sound sequences of their ambient language. Increasing intelligibility is founded on growth in the complexity of all three of the domains of the complex system underlying phonological acquisition: cognitive, perceptual, and production system abilities. As we have noted, in this later period growth in complexity is based on the mechanism of learning, illustrating operation of a dynamically changing, heterarchically operating system with feedback across domains underlying observable production and perception abilities.

Production skills are enhanced by practice producing speech. The experience of being understood provides input regarding the speaker's success at producing ambient language speech sound and sequence motor targets. Sound production capacities interact with word- and utterance-level complexity in the linguistic context. Children, like adult speakers, are most likely to produce sounds accurately in stressed syllables and in initial word position (Hua and Dodd, 2006). Continuity in learning can be observed at this level as well. Practiced sounds and syllables dominate in production of early word forms in the transition from babbling to word use. Practiced word forms may also play a key role in production of multiword utterances. Intelligibility can emerge around practiced word forms and filter into new word forms as they become more familiar in the child's lexicon.

As children's speech and language skills become more complex they also become more interdependent. Speech production skills play a continuing role in the acquisition of words and structures. Early skill in discriminating speech sounds is associated with larger vocabulary size in early childhood (Kuhl, 2008). By middle childhood, children's knowledge of words allows them to refine their representation of sounds and sequences (Edwards *et al.*, 2011). At the same time, children who have a larger vocabulary and more mature levels of phonological representation develop metaphonological skills needed to develop higher level linguistic knowledge (Walley and Metsala, 1990). Word growth leads the way to this interdependent relationship.

COGNITIVE PROCESSING: THE ROLE OF MEMORY AND ATTENTION

Studies of speech production in child learners highlight the foundational role that production capacities play in the acquisition of intelligibility and the use of speech for increasingly complex and functional linguistic communication. Child-internal changes related to the child's ability to perceptually process and store information about phonological components and their patterns of combinations in the ambient language also shape the growth trajectory of this period. Children's ability to overtly attend to and process speech, dependent on perceptual and attentional processes, also increases significantly over the *refining patterns* period.

As we noted in Chapter 4, work with infants has indicated that they are sensitive to the patterns of their own ambient language by the second six months of life. They recognize strings of sounds as wholes. In experimental paradigms, infants recognize words and speech sounds that correspond to the ambient language they are being exposed to in daily interactions with adults. In the *refining patterns* period, the child's functional need to impose meaning on the salient ambient language speech patterns she hears changes dramatically. Attention demands shift when children begin to process speech as it helps them determine linguistic meanings for specific forms in input. Several changes in children's attention patterns and memory capacities support this qualitative shift in perceptual processing of their daily auditory input in social contexts with others. Children's attention window grows over time as they gain the ability to coordinate attention to multiple events simultaneously and to remember what they have learned over a longer time frame (Sarid and Breznitz, 1997; López *et al.*, 2005).

Phonological working memory, the ability to recall sequences of speech sounds, also increases across the refining patterns period. Experimental work with 3-year-olds shows that children can reproduce one-syllable nonsense words and recall up to three words (Adams and Gathercole, 1995). Across acquisition, the number of words that can be remembered along with the length and complexity of those words increases. Children can soon repeat words of up to four syllables (Dollaghan and Campbell, 1998).

Children's capacities for retaining information interact with the language that they are learning. Thus, the non-word repetition performance of children learning English seems to top out at around three- and four-syllable nonsense words by age 5 (Dollaghan and Campbell, 1998). The role of socially embedded input in learning of ambient language regularities is indicated by cross-linguistic studies. Children who are learning languages such as Portuguese or Greek that contain more multisyllabic words can repeat non-words of up to five and six syllables by age 5 (Masoura and Gathercole, 2005; Santos and Bueno, 2003). Phonological working memory provides a key skill in learning new words. Children must hold strings of information in their memory while they compare these elements to stored representations to determine if the new input matches stored words, or if it might refer to a new meaning about their environment they must encode and store.

At the same time as memory for phonological detail emerges, children's ability to remember longer strings of information generally increases as well. Digit span, referring to the ability to remember strings of objects and words, increases over time. Phonological working memory is a better predictor of memory growth than digit span (Gathercole, 1995). Digit recall interacts with world and language knowledge. When children are asked to recall related objects, they remember more words than when they are asked to recall unrelated words (Tam *et al.*, 2010). The role of language knowledge is highlighted when children are asked to repeat sentences of greater length or complexity. Children remember many more elements when they are put into the context of sentences than if they are asked to recall independent strings of words (Hulme *et al.*, 1991).

Another important change in cognitive processing in this period of development is change in speed of processing. Work by Marchman and colleagues (Marchman *et al.*, 2010; Hurtado *et al.*, 2008) has shown that children's speed of processing starts to increase about the time that children begin the process of learning language. Children who hear more language, and are exposed to more and faster speech, show faster processing times later in acquisition. This pattern of results suggests that the practice of hearing fast speech input has a training effect on the learner. Speed of processing also seems to be influenced by children's knowledge of language. In a "gating" task, children hear parts of words. They can respond based on a shorter gate or less information as they get older and have more language knowledge. Changes in speech of processing for word recognition has been associated with vocabulary size at age 8 (Marchman and Fernald, 2008).

DEVELOPMENTAL PHONOLOGY DIFFERENCES

So far we have argued that the same child-internal and external factors at play in earliest development during the *moving and sensing* period continue to play a role as children are *refining patterns* to achieve use of more diverse and more intelligible speech. Consideration of children who acquire ambient language phonological knowledge and behavioral patterns under different circumstances allows another avenue to consider the extent to which the process of phonological acquisition is impacted by differences in capacities available to children developing typically. In this section, we will consider how acquisition in the face of differences in input patterns resulting from a bilingual language experience as well as differences in child-internal factors due to communication disorders highlights the interactions proposed in an emergence model.

PHONOLOGICAL ACQUISITION IN BILINGUAL LEARNERS

Children who acquire two (or more) languages need to separate their representations of sounds and the rules for combining them (i.e. phonotactics) in their language(s) to achieve intelligibility within each of their speech communities. Although multilingual acquisition is the norm rather than the exception worldwide, more studies have documented monolingual acquisition. The differences between monolingual and bilingual acquisition in childhood can be seen in the accuracy of production of sounds and phonotactics, and in the rate of acquisition of phonological knowledge and behavioral patterns.

Simultaneous bilinguals are children who acquire both of their languages at the same time in early childhood. In this period, the production of the two languages is often thought to be merged into a single system up until about 18–24 months of age because children are observed to use words from both systems to communicate. While this is accurate in some cases, it is not universally the case. Use of words from both languages tends to occur when the child is surrounded by speakers who understand both languages (Deuchar and Quay, 1999; Paradis and Nicoladis, 2007; Paradis et al., 2000). Children are attentive to environmental cues and make few errors addressing speakers in a language that they do not speak beyond 2 years of age. This ability to manage the right language for the environment suggests a meta-awareness of language based on general cues. However, in the early stages of sound and word production, simultaneous-bilingual children are likely to be in the low-average range relative to their peers, producing fewer of the sounds of their target sounds and producing them with greater variability (Gildersleeve-Neumann et al., 2008).

What about sequential bilinguals who start to acquire a second language at preschool age? Some work focusing on Spanish-English bilingual children suggests that second language acquisition is accelerated relative to first language acquisition. After only 9 to 12 months of exposure, children are producing sounds and sequences with over 90 percent accuracy in single word production while they appear to maintain high levels of accuracy in their first languages (Fabiano-Smith and Barlow, 2010). At the same time single-word production tasks may overestimate children's phonological development. A hallmark of phonological skill is the production of highly intelligible speech by about 5 years of age. Recall that monolingual children are estimated to be fully intelligible by this age. There are no comparable estimates for bilingual children. Ongoing work indicates that both parents and teachers rate bilingual children to be only moderately intelligible by kindergarten age (Ruiz-Felter, Bedore, and Peña, in preparation) even though their production accuracy is over 90 percent on average (Gildersleeve-Neumann et al., 2008, 2009). The strongest predictor of speech sound acquisition of these children is current use of the language. The precise source of this rating is not clear, but children with low single-word production scores in both languages have lower-than-expected scores in grammatical and morpho-syntactic production (Cooperson, Bedore, and Peña, in review).

These patterns of production support the emergence perspective suggesting that maturation of the speech mechanism plays a critical role in the acquisition of children's phonological systems. Data on other aspects of these same children's language show that phonology differs in the rate of normalization from reports for monolingual learners. Here it would appear that the child's more mature production abilities allow her to quickly take advantage of the input she receives. The combination of what is observed for young simultaneous and sequential bilinguals highlights the fundamental role of child-internal production abilities and how these abilities provide a base to connect to input more rapidly in older children.

Knowledge of one language may influence how children process their other languages. On one hand, children learning Spanish, with few monosyllabic and many multisyllabic word forms, and English, in which monosyllabic and bisyllabic words predominate, show differences in their ability to repeat nonsense words. Spanish-learning children can repeat more syllables in Spanish than in English, and this presumably experience-based advantage carries over to English where bilingual children are more competent with multisyllabic words (Summers *et al.*, 2010). In contrast, however, sequential-bilingual children who learn Spanish before English do not appear to be advantaged for the production of monosyllabic words.

This relationship seems to break down for bilingual children with speech disorders. Holm *et al.* (1997) evaluated cross-language transfer as result of speech intervention with bilingual children. Where bilingual children lack the ability to produce speech sounds, they are unable to transfer their knowledge of production of sounds and sequences in one language to the sounds and sequences in the other. This observation suggests that the ability to produce a sound (indicating embodied knowledge of the sound) facilitates transfer. Without this level of knowledge bilingual learners may not be able to take full advantage of the input.

PHONOLOGICAL ACQUISITION IN CHILDREN WITH DELAY/DISORDER

Children are most likely to be referred for assessment by speech language pathologists for lack of development of age-appropriate intelligibility (Edwards *et al.*, 1989; Zhang and Tomblin, 2000). The common occurrence of developmental phonological disorder and delay reflects the fundamental importance of speech production intelligibility to the development of effective communication skills in young children. In this section, we will consider how types of communication impairment can impact the acquisition of speech intelligibility. This will help to illustrate how breakdowns in child-internal capacities of production, perception, and cognition compromise emergence of speech intelligibility. We will focus on the co-occurrence of speech and language impairments and hearing impairment as illustrative examples.

Children with Speech Impairment

Children with speech delays have cognitive skills within the typical range but demonstrate deficits in the intelligibility of speech. This deficit, in turn, has consequences for other aspects of language acquisition in many children with developmental speech impairments. Speech and language impairments co-occur in about 11–15 percent of children who are clinically diagnosed with persistent speech delays. About 8 percent of children with language impairment have a history of speech delay (Shriberg et al., 1999). Language impairment (LI) refers to a delay in vocabulary development and/or delays in grammatical development. These deficits further illustrate the interrelated nature of cognition, perception, and production. A look at the developmental patterns of children with speech delays illustrates some of these interconnections.

Typically developing children use phonological cues as they learn to recognize and use new words. There is very little information about the language learning outcomes for children with speech impairment. Children with phonological impairment cannot readily process phonological cues and associate the forms of new words with meanings of new words (Hoover et al., 2010). Gray and Brinkley (2011) explored the extent to which children with language impairment can benefit from phonological cues in word learning using a fast mapping paradigm. Fast mapping focuses on children's initial associations between sound and meaning rather than long-term retention of words. Children with LI were like their typically developing peers in attending more readily to low-frequency sequences. This pattern can be attributed to these being more salient relative to high-frequency sequences. When Gray (2005) compared the ability of children with LI to use meaning based on phonological cues, children could use only one kind of cue at a time to support word learning. In contrast, typically developing children were able to combine cues to support word comprehension at all ages. This limited set of data suggests that a poor foundation of speech representation interferes with the ability to form the connections between form and meaning. Further study should focus on the nature and duration of these difficulties.

Children with Significant Hearing Impairment

The case of hearing impairment allows the observation of effects of differences in degree and kind of perceptual input on phonological outcomes. Communication performance in children with varying degrees of sensori-neural hearing loss (SNHL) has been extensively studied in a number of important domains including language, speech production, speech perception in quiet and noise, and academic achievement (Miyamoto *et al.*, 1999; Serry and Blamey, 1999; Tye-Murray *et al.*, 1995; Davis *et al.*, 2005; Eilers and Oller, 1994; Eisenberg *et al.*, 2004; Geers and Moog, 1992; Moeller *et al.*, 2007a; Paatsch *et al.*, 2004).

Studies of speech output in children whose profound SNHL is identified at older chronological ages indicates a protracted course of development that plateaus without normalization to age-appropriate intelligibility (Blamey *et al.*, 2001; Chin, 2003; Dillon *et al.*, 2004; Peng *et al.*, 2004; Tobey *et al.*, 2003). Tobey and colleagues report reduced speech intelligibility in elementary school-age children using cochlear implants (CIs), characterized by inaccurately produced consonant and vowels (Tobey *et al.*, 2008, 2003, 2004). In Tobey *et al.* (2008), overall speech intelligibility continued to improve, with 79 percent of the children reporting that other people understood their speech as older teenagers. Poor speech intelligibility has also been associated with reduced utterance lengths, poor adjacent word intelligibility, reduced phonological complexity, and simpler syllable structures in older identified CI children who achieve more complex language output (e.g. Chin, 2002, 2006, 2003; Tobey *et al.*, 2008). Optimal outcomes appear sensitive to type and length of device use, as well (Svirsky *et al.*, 2004). Thus speech production outcomes in this population can be seen as diversely determined by both speech and language variables with outcomes that likely do not match those of children with typical hearing profiles.

These performance measures appear to be correlated with several general child-intrinsic variables including gender, nonverbal performance intelligence quotients (IQs), etiology, age of identification of hearing loss, age of first intervention, and experience with intervention (Geers and Brenner, 2003; Geers *et al.*, 2003; Geers, 2004; Tobey *et al.*, 2000, 2003). Several issues related to family environment also have an impact on speech and language outcomes, including parental education, socio-economic status, and size of the family (Davis *et al.*, 2005; Eilers and

Oller, 1994; Eisenberg *et al.*, 2004; Fink *et al.*, 2007; Geers and Moog, 1992; Moeller *et al.*, 2007a; Paatsch *et al.*, 2004; Sarant *et al.*, 2001; Schauwers *et al.*, 2008; Tye-Murray *et al.*, 1995; Warner-Czyz and Davis, 2008). Previous studies examining the effects of such variables on speech production, speech perception, language, and reading in elementary school-age children with SNHL who use CIs report positive outcomes when there is early identification of deafness and an early age of first hearing aid intervention (Eisenberg, 2007; Jerger, 2007; Moeller *et al.*, 2007b; Tomblin and Hebbeler, 2007). This body of research emphasizes the multiple environmental determinants that support emergence of speech and language skills of children with significant hearing impairment.

Environmental effects are not only confined to family variables in older children with hearing impairment. Several studies indicate educational placement settings are related to levels of speech intelligibility and sound accuracy in children using CIs (Tobey *et al.*, 2003, 2004, 2008). These studies report higher levels of speech intelligibility and sound accuracy for CI children who participate in programs emphasizing speaking and listening in their educational settings. Emphasis on listening and speaking appears more important to overall levels of speech intelligibility than setting (private versus public), hours of therapy, or type of classroom (Tobey *et al.*, 2003). Classroom communication mode and amount of mainstreaming also contribute significantly to outcomes in children using CIs (Geers and Brenner, 2003). Children enrolled in programs with an auditory-oral emphasis scored higher on tests of speech perception (Geers *et al.*, 2003), speech production (Tobey, *et al.*, 2003), and language (Geers and Brenner, 2003) than children whose programs included sign. Children who spent more time in mainstream classrooms had higher speech intelligibility (Tobey *et al.*, 2003, 2004) and higher reading scores (Geers and Brenner, 2003; Geers, 2004) than children in special education classrooms.

These data on longer term outcomes in the areas of speech production and both spoken and written language in the presence of compromised auditory perception capacities support the conceptualization of phonological emergence as being based on a heterogeneously determined complex system. Child-intrinsic variables as well as extrinsic environmental input co-create children's individual outcomes for speech and language in children with auditory compromise. Long-term speech and language abilities are not consistently optimal in these children based on the combination of variables that they experience, both in terms of their intrinsic capacities and in available types of extrinsic input over time both inside and outside their family. This long-term picture, which reflects both educational experiences as well as early family issues, supports the proposal that input values expand with age and continue to determine output in children with developmental differences.

A SUMMARY OF REFINING

What have we been able to discern about the period of *refining* as it relates to evaluating evidence for an emergence proposal? Continuity is a key word describing this phase. Although diversity explodes in all directions in the use of the phonological system for myriad functions, the same components that underlie emergence in this period were present at the beginning. Clearly, learning is the dominant mechanism in this period, aided by growth in memory for neural storage of phonological knowledge. Components of the production system continue to mature physically over a protracted period. This maturing system is concurrently and critically tuned by input from communication partners providing raw material on phonological forms and cultural norms for deploying them in linguistic interchanges. Perception capacities provide an ongoing conduit for the child to access the patterned regularities of her ambient language(s) available from social input. And the child is concurrently processing input about phonology as well as other aspects of language that are intimately tied to the use of language form for linguistic purposes. Neural-cognitive functions are refined in service of storage, retrieval, and planning in speaking and listening as the child becomes increasingly efficient using her phonological capacities. Interaction abilities for joint-attention, turn-taking, and intention-reading continue enabling the child to sustain necessary connections for optimal function in her social environment. This social interactional "glue" allows the child to refine her phonology through learning and storage. Thus, the same themes we raised in Chapter 4 in the earliest period of phonological development are abundantly apparent as the young child continues to refine patterns of knowledge and behavior. These capacities also enable the young child to expand use of her phonological system for diverse and new types of linguistic, social, and academic pursuits in this period.

6 Contemporary Theories and Paradigms

The predictions and paradigms of contemporary acquisition theories illuminate diverse issues relevant to evaluating an emergence perspective for phonology. Contemporary theoretical proposals for phonological acquisition are dominated by conceptualizations from linguistics (phonetics and phonology), and cognitive science, in particular, the domain of psycholinguistics.

These scholarly traditions emphasize distinct aspects of acquisition. What the child can *do* with peripheral physical capacities of the production and perceptual system generally falls within the domain of phonetics. What the child knows about language structures and how output may be constrained by mental rules is the domain of phonology. The process by which the young child *acquires, stores,* and *retrieves* knowledge is within the domain of cognitive science. Within cognitive science, the subdomain of psycholinguistics focuses directly on both the process and the products of phonological acquisition, synthesizing questions posed both by linguists and cognitive scientists about the nature of phonological acquisition. Of course, the boundaries of these research cultures traditions are fluid in some respects. Our review is designed to highlight their unique perspectives as well as their overlapping contributions.

Within linguistically oriented conceptualizations, phonetic sciences consider peripheral actions of the production and perception systems in producing prelinguistic vocal output and emergence of language-based speech forms. Phonetic science approaches focus strongly on biological capacities of the child as they are revealed in observable behaviors. In contrast, in phonological perspectives, acquisition is considered a product of an extant system of language knowledge based on mental representation and/or computations based on language input. Behavioral output is viewed as revealing the status of phonological knowledge.

Within cognitive science and psycholinguistic perspectives, considerations of phonological acquisition largely emphasize the process of acquisition rather than considering the structure of observable output forms or of putative underlying structures and rules. Acquisition is conceptualized in terms of general mechanisms underlying cognitive development (e.g. the role of input frequency in perceptual processing or rule-based learning, long- and short-term memory processes). The ways in which learning mechanisms enable young children to acquire, store, and implement phonological knowledge is the primary focus.

WHAT ARE SOME ISSUES TO BE EVALUATED WITH CONTEMPORARY ACQUISITION APPROACHES?

In Chapter 1, we proposed a system-based metaphor. Issues we have outlined as necessary to a system-based emergence approach are not consistently present in contemporary theories. The variety of contemporary research paradigms implemented within diverse research traditions also demonstrates the quantity and quality of information considered as providing support within differing scholarly perspectives.

Within an emergence view, acquisition rests on the emergence of complexity in stored knowledge and in goal-directed speech behaviors. Emergence of these dual dimensions of phonology is founded on diverse general capacities available to the young child for acquiring the complex knowledge and behavioral patterns that support linguistic communication. System components and their interactions responsible for emergence of complexity in the phonological dimension of language are heterogeneous. The system includes peripheral physical systems, neural-cognitive, and social capacities.

Critical facets also include input from more mature users of the ambient language that guide the child in use of her intrinsic capacities for acquiring phonological knowledge and behavioral patterns. Input occurs within social interactions in the child's daily environment connected to salient functional experiences. These experiences guide her in understanding what and how to communicate using her language system. In this chapter, the strengths and challenges to contemporary phonological acquisition theories will be considered in light of the multifaceted components that comprise a complex system-based emergence view.

WHAT DOES THE HISTORY OF PHILOSOPHICAL FOUNDATIONS OF CONTEMPORARY THEORY CONTRIBUTE TO AN EMERGENCE PERSPECTIVE?

The historical context of inquiry into understanding how human infants gain knowledge of their world is long and varied. Considering this history enables a broader context for thinking about the diverse ways in which scholars have viewed phonological acquisition.

Historically, the "nature versus nurture" debate has been a core aspect of continuing controversy related to the origins of complex capacities in humans (Descartes, 1637; Kant, 1924). Debate on this topic has been a fundamental area of difference in the epistemological study of the origins of children's acquisition of knowledge across multiple areas of description. This debate is pertinent to diverse domains, not limited to phonology or even to language (see Woolhouse, 1988). Areas of inquiry have included motor, social, perceptual, and cognitive domains. A brief overview of nature–nurture in phonological acquisition provides a conceptual background on alternative hypotheses to illuminate our consideration of an embodied-emergence proposal.

Plato was the first to propose innateness as a solution to the question of the origins of knowledge. Platonic philosophy counted essences as necessary building blocks to the construction of knowledge. In contemporary terms, this is "essentialism" (e.g. Gelman, 2003). In this view, categories crystallize as "natural kinds" found in nature. Natural kinds capture many of the regularities of their component elements. In the context of phonological theory, for example, the English nasal consonants (i.e. /m/, /n/, and /ŋ/) are said to constitute a natural class, or kind, based on the congruence of their production characteristics (Vihman, 1996) and perceptual access (Narayan *et al.*, 2010; Seidl *et al.*, 2009).

These proposed natural kinds enable children to discover types of environmental categories, such as living things, more readily. From the essentialist perspective, such categories are highly stable in the environment. Critically, however, the class, not the components of the class, is "natural." As an example, in Spanish, the same natural class is composed of a different set of nasal consonants (e.g. /m/, /n/, and /ñ/). This difference necessitates a more finely grained definition requiring that the membership of a "natural class" is not the same across languages. Thus, information about phonetic categories must be available in the ambient language speech input the child hears. The presence of this finely grained information in the input implicates a role for experience in supporting emergence of patterns of sound production and resulting knowledge about their use in linguistic utterances.

Locke, an early 17th-century associationist, presented an early counterpoint to essentialism. He argued that the child is a "tabula rasa" or blank slate on which knowledge is written. He emphasized the role of experience in the acquisition of this knowledge. His contemporary, the philosopher Descartes (1637), following Platonic philosophy, asserted that humans are the only living creatures who possess innate ideas.

Descartes saw the source of innate human ideas as divine, albeit the God of Christian divinity rather than the Platonic Greek gods. These early competing hypotheses about the origin of knowledge formed the basis for later focus on language knowledge.

The philosopher De Saussure (1916) conceived of language as a cultural phenomenon with a distinction between underlying "langue" (language) and surface "parole" (speech) components. The arbitrary nature of language was the result of input from cultural inventions unrelated to biology. De Saussure's view was compatible with empiricism. Empiricists owe their philosophical descent to Locke (Woolhouse, 1988) and other 17th-century British associationists. In these perspectives, the origin of complex behaviors resided outside of the individual. There was no proposal of internal, pre-existing competence to guide the acquisition of knowledge. For De Saussure, language diversity came from outside the individual. His position was in contrast to Platonic philosophy that placed the language capacity within the individual.

Roman Jakobson (1941), often credited as being the first phonologist (see a review by Fikkert, 2007), focused attention on children's phonological acquisition. He conceptualized speech acquisition as the process of developing a set of (mental) representations of perceptual contrasts. The first contrasts were nasal versus non-nasal (/m/–/b/), followed by labial versus velar (/b/–/g/) or voiced versus unvoiced (/d/–/t/). Jacobson's viewpoint was deterministic, in that he saw the order of acquisition as invariant across languages and individuals, and as based on universal feature or contrast hierarchies unrelated to biological constraints (following de Saussure, 1916). Children were proposed to learn sound contrasts that are common across languages early on, while contrasts that are relatively infrequent across languages occur later in development. The young child's vocal production provides evidence for these perceptually driven contrasts.

Chomsky and Halle's (1968) early work on linear generative phonology expressed in *The Sound Pattern of English* (*SPE*) formed a first driving force for knowledge-based phonological essences in the philosophical tradition of Plato and Descartes. Proposing the phonological component as an interface between performance and mental function, Chomsky's original generative grammar (termed universal grammar, or UG) contained two aspects. *Syntax* was considered responsible for grammatical categories and the rules for forming lawful rule-governed sentences. *Phonology* contained phonemes employed in word forms. Within UG, these two aspects of language competence were genetically available to human speakers. Competence was "housed" in a modular, linguistically bound, psychologically real mental system (Fodor and Katz, 1964) not present in non-human communication systems. The phonological system within UG contained abstract feature-based representations that followed ordered rules to produce syllables, prosodic regularities, and phonemic combinations observable in surface output structures in human languages.

In a recent review of language evolution perspectives (Scott-Phillips, 2010), this conceptualization has been termed a "code" model that falls within the information theory of Shannon and Weaver (1949). In this regard, Chomsky's perspective implies a symbol manipulation system based on computational properties shared by speakers and listeners. Both speaker and listener are viewed as computational devices utilizing a modular system to communicate with formal linguistic symbols.

Within phonology, markedness has been an intrinsic component of historical treatments of phonological competence. Originally the concept of markedness emerged from the Prague linguistics circle (see Hymes, 1962, for an English introduction), influenced heavily by original work of Jakobson (1941) and Trubetzkoy (1939). In the original proposals on markedness, an "unmarked" form was a basic, default form at the underlying representation level. Unmarked forms were characterized as occurring more frequently in languages. They also occurred more frequently in early output inventories of young children in this perspective. In contrast, a "marked" form was a non-basic or less natural form. As an example, voiceless unaspirated stops have been designated as unmarked. The phoneme /r/ is, in contrast, a marked form. Markedness has often been defined by how frequently phones occur in output. Marked forms are said to emerge later in acquisition and are less common in phonemic inventories of languages.

In the same period as Chomsky was proposing his sweeping theoretical perspective in *SPE*, Lenneberg (1967) worked out a biologically oriented treatment of language consistent with Chomsky's linear generative phonology. While he reviewed the developmental performance or behavioral output data available at that time, Lenneberg's biologically oriented treatment still emphasized the passive nature of ontogeny as an uncovering of pre-existing language complexity available to the infant at birth in the innate UG. Performance in observable speech output was merely a reflection of competence or knowledge.

These diverse traditions have formed the historical background for contemporary inquiries into understanding of the nature of phonological acquisition. What is acquired and how it is acquired has been answered from a number of philosophical traditions that are largely captured within the nature/nurture debate. In the following section, we will consider the state of contemporary theory relative to phonological acquisition. Theoretical perspectives include a proliferation of approaches dedicated to the biological and social capacities of the young child, as well as to the general cognitive underpinnings of acquisition as they apply to phonology. We will start with phonological acquisition, as consideration of this tradition is directly in line with the history of scholarly inquiry in this area.

WHAT ARE THE PARAMETERS OF PHONOLOGICAL APPROACHES TO ACQUISITION?

Phonological approaches have changed in critical aspects from those of early perceptually based theorists (Jakobson, 1941) and classic *SPE* linear generative phonology (Chomsky and Halle, 1968). Although quite diverse, contemporary phonological approaches are linked conceptually. Current constructions of phonological theory center largely on optimality theory (OT) approaches (Prince and Smolensky, 2004). Non-linear phonology (e.g. Bernhardt and Stemberger, 1998) and other phonological approaches have assumed a relatively minor role in contemporary phonological conceptualizations relative to these OT-based accounts.

An initial question arises about the status of emergence in contemporary phonology. Emergence as an underlying conceptualization for acquisition is outside of the theoretical boundaries of classic *SPE*-based phonological theory. The *SPE* pre-formationist approach continues to be apparent in controversy surrounding formalist versus functionalist views in more recent treatments of phonological (Boersma and Hayes, 2001) and syntactic acquisition (Jackendoff, 2002; Newmeyer, 1998; O'Grady, 2008). Some contemporary OT perspectives (e.g. Boersma and Hayes, 2001) incorporate emergent constraints. However, proposal of a complex system, based on multiple heterogeneous inputs founded within socially relevant function of phonological capacities for the young child in communication, is not a critical element of contemporary phonological theories. In particular, support provided by social interpersonal interactions via joint-attention and turn-taking capacities (e.g. Oller, 2000), which serve a critical communication function for the infant and adult, are not considered as an aspect of constraint reranking in phonological theory.

The role of input has been integrated into some contemporary views of the acquisition process (e.g. Stemberger and Bernhardt, 1999; Rose, 2009). In these perspectives, ambient language regularities observable in young children's output are triggered passively via frequency of input. These input processes support parameterization of precise ambient language knowledge. However, emphasis is on frequency of phonological structures in input rather than the biologically embodied nature of attention processes or the function of social communication for the child. The cultural context in which phonological input occurs falls explicitly outside of phonological theory. Culturally proscribed rules for deployment of phonological forms must of necessity incorporate social-cognitive input from the environment.

Research paradigms within phonological theory focused on child data have historically centered on relatively small corpora to illustrate putative underlying representations, rules, or constraints in the child system. The earliest acquisition studies were based on parent diaries (Leopold, 1970; Menn, 1979; Weir, 1962) wherein parent linguists phonetically transcribed phonological structures present in their own child's output. Data were largely not audio-recorded. This data collection and transcription approach had the potential to distort characterization of the child's output system toward exemplars that fitted the diarist's theoretical model. In addition, the transcription of the child's output could not be evaluated for reliability by other transcribers, as there was no permanent record for verification.

Some more recent analyses have included relatively small corpora using audio and video recordings (e.g. Goad and Rose, 2003; Pater *et al.*, 2004; Stemberger and Bernhardt, 1999). However, with the advent of open access databases (e.g. CHILDES; PHON), some researchers are beginning to analyze larger corpora for patterns (e.g. see Kager *et al.*, 2007). Ability to generate rules or determine the status of faithfulness and markedness constraints for linguistically relevant surface units in child data is the focus of analysis. Markedness constraints are said to impose requirements on the structural well-formedness of the output in acquisition. Faithfulness constraints prevent each instance of input from being realized as some unmarked form. Research is largely based on perceptually based phonetic transcription using adult phonemic distinctions.

The goal of more recent psycholinguistic experimental paradigms is to consider experimental evidence for underlying representations in very young children who are beginning the process of phonological acquisition. Investigations of segmentation cues using head turn (Johnson, 2008) or visual tracking paradigms (Swingley, 2009b; Quam and Swingley, 2010) have considered the varied ways in which young infants may begin to segment the incoming speech signal and develop phonological knowledge

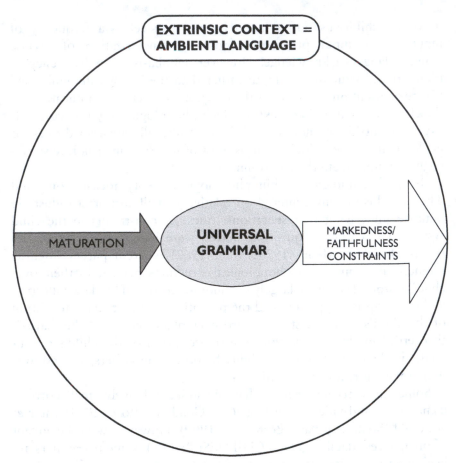

FIGURE 6.1   Components of Acquisition in Phonological Theory

representations. These newer paradigms illustrate the overlapping nature of questions addressed by phonologists traditionally and how they are being implemented within a psycholinguistic experimental tradition (see Goudbeek *et al.*, 2005, for a review of these issues).

The proposed underlying knowledge base includes *units*, potentially of differing sizes in contemporary multi-linear and non-linear phonological theories (e.g. Archangeli and Pulleyblank, 1994; Goudbeek *et al.*, 2005; Prince and Smolensky, 2004). Prosodic effects and proposals of units larger than the phoneme are seen as counteracting inadequacies in the comprehensiveness of description in Chomsky's linear generative phonology (Chomsky and Halle, 1968). Blevins (see Blevins, 2004, for a review) has suggested a set of "phonological primitives" to include distinctive features, segments, length, and prosodic categories (mora, syllable, foot, etc.). The reality and status of these diverse kinds of underlying knowledge units is a topic of scholarly controversy relative to contemporary phonological accounts. The critical status of knowledge/ representation as the driving force behind acquisition is far less debated in these phonologically based conceptualizations.

OPTIMALITY THEORY

Optimality theory (OT) (Prince and Smolensky, 2004) is a prominent example of current phonological theory applied to consideration of acquisition. OT is the dominant paradigm from a structuralist linguistic perspective for the phonological component of language (see deLacy, 2007, for a review of contemporary phonological theory). Within OT, the child learner is seen as moving toward adult language competence by reranking a set of mentally available constraints. Observed "surface" forms in child output and in languages arise from the resolution of conflicts between these ranked grammatical constraints. When initiating an utterance, a "generator" provides a set of potential output forms for a given word. An "evaluator" then uses language-specific constraints to select the most optimal output from the set of potential outputs supplied by the generator. In some OT perspectives, constraints are considered innate and universal (e.g. Dekkers, 2000). Other OT approaches do not assume innate or universal status (e.g. Boersma, 1998).

The notion of constraints introduces a new texture to the universal grammar (UG) proposed in *The Sound Pattern of English* (Chomsky and Halle, 1968). Emphasis on computation relative to when and how putative underlying constraints are reranked based on input to the learner supplants the earlier focus on UG-based underlying representations (see Scheer, 2010, for a helpful critique on this contrast). The origin or source of the constraints reranked by input is not specified. However, their presence still implies some type of a priori capacities in advance of acquisition. Additionally, the state of UG is unresolved in alternative theoretical conceptualizations.

In contemporary OT accounts, surface forms in child output and in languages arise from the resolution of conflicts between the ranked grammatical constraints. As indicated above, they are designated as markedness (M) and faithfulness (F) constraints. In acquisition, M > F occurs in initial stages. The young child thus begins with structural or unmarked constraints above faithfulness constraints, and demotes structural constraints as needed to admit into her inventory marked structures evidenced in her ambient language. The reranking process supplants early markedness constraints with faithfulness constraints, closer to the unique patterns of the ambient language. Systematic cross-linguistic variation is seen as the result of reranking of universal constraints. Inputs to the grammars of all languages are the same. Universal input is implicit in OT analyses in the way that universal UG was implicit in *SPE*.

A second OT construct includes "richness of the base" (Smolensky, 1996). The concept of richness of the base is proposed as a means to accommodate cross-language variation. Richness of the base indicates that the set of inputs (i.e. the richness of the base) to the underlying grammars of all languages is the same. The source of systematic cross-linguistic variation is found in constraint reranking. The resulting diverse grammatical inventories of languages are conceptualized as the outputs that emerge from the grammar when it is fed this universal set of all possible inputs.

Boersma (1998) proposes an emergent approach to markedness within an OT framework. In his treatment, differences in markedness are based on frequency differences in the learner's input (i.e. richness of the base, see Boersma and Levelt, 2000), not on innately available markedness or faithfulness constraints. He asserts the concept of "licensing by cue" (Boersma and Hamann, 2009). Licensing by cue refers to differences in auditory cue reliability in the learner's input. This cue reliability enables marked sound patterns to emerge. Overall, while markedness is a central feature of various classical and contemporary phonological theories, no consensual criteria are available to determine markedness status precisely for phonemes.

Alternative OT proposals suggest that constraints are phonetically grounded (e.g. Bernhardt and Stemberger, 1998). A series of constraints on phonology and morphosyntax are seen as interacting to guide production of possible well-formed output. Conceptual focus falls on how constraint ranking and reranking results in observable output. As an example, phonological constraints such as "complex onset" and "no coda" lead speakers to avoid complexity. An example would be *blue* with a cluster onset and no final consonant. Constraints can be violated and rankings can vary across languages and over time within speakers, leading to the variation observed across languages and in acquisition (Stemberger and Bernhardt, 1999).

Overall, acquisition from a phonological perspective focuses largely on the child's expression of knowledge and on constraint ranking in contemporary accounts. This cognitive emphasis is in contrast to emergence conceptualizations of behavioral complexity based on interactions of peripheral or central biologically based systems that are tuned by functional uses within socially based environmental contexts. Again, the underlying conceptualization is that of acquisition of an abstract code, revealed through maturation and triggered by input.

WHAT ARE THE PARAMETERS OF PHONETIC APPROACHES TO ACQUISITION?

The general stance of phonetic conceptualizations for understanding complex speech patterns, including the acquisition phase, is quite different than phonological approaches. Phonetic approaches consider the nature of speech knowledge via understanding of the development and function of peripheral speech structures and observable speech behaviors. Peripheral subsystems are not seen as passive vessels for channeling knowledge. In contrast, they are centrally involved in exerting pressure on the forms of knowledge perceived, stored, and produced in infants and in languages.

Phonetic science emphasizes the amalgamation of biologically based peripheral production (e.g. Davis *et al.*, 2002) and perceptual system operations (Kluender and Alexander, 2008) as basic to shaping the system toward implementation for producing and perceiving contrasts to communicate linguistically based meanings. As an example, consonant place of articulation (i.e. lip /b/, tongue tip /d/, tongue back /k/, or glottal stops /ʔ/) might be considered in descriptions of behavior patterns, as well as to characterize underlying units of knowledge. Extrinsic input is seen in some approaches as supporting the child in tuning output patterns as well as in enhancing contrast (Kluender *et al.*, 2003).

Neural/cognitively instantiated knowledge is thus rooted in production and perception system manipulations across multiple function-driven interactions in the external world. However, phonetic science generally has been far less invested as a discipline in specifying the properties of underlying representation than has phonology, for which the question of representation is a central focus.

Phonetic approaches are consistent with the heterogeneity of underlying factors characterizing emergence (see Figure 6.2). They do not generally require a priori form as a basic tenet. The child's knowledge about his ambient language phonology emerges from heterarchical interactions between central (i.e. neural and cognitive) and peripheral (i.e. anatomy and physiology of the production and perception system) capacities. These philosophical implications bring phonetic approaches closer to conceptualizations of complexity science and embodiment approaches as we have described them in Chapter 1.

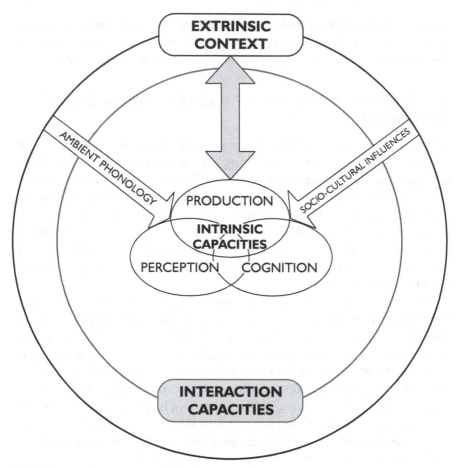

FIGURE 6.2   Components of Acquisition in Phonetic Science

Phonetic perspectives do not consistently address the potential role of social interaction capacities in scaffolding the very early stages of the acquisition process. Research paradigms are not designed to test the role of these issues in acquisition of phonetic capacities. Some research programs focused on acquisition of speech physiology do not consider interaction components of the acquisition process (e.g. Goffman *et al.*, in press). In other perspectives, interactions are a critical piece of the puzzle to be assembled in understanding phonological acquisition (Oller and Griebel, 2008b). These perspectives incorporate interaction capacities at the level of description, but do not test assertions directly in experimental or observational paradigms.

As an example, gestural phonology (Brownman and Goldstein, 1992) proposes imitative visual/auditory attunement between child and adult as a critical mechanism underlying early emergence of language-like sound properties (Studdert-Kennedy and Goodell, 1995). The Frame-Content theory (MacNeilage and Davis, 1990) proposes learning from the environment as critical to emergence of precise ambient language regularities (Kern *et al.*, 2010; Kern and Davis, 2009). Computer modeling paradigms focused on phonetic properties concentrate on the process of learning of sound properties via frequency of input and production system properties, but not on the social interactions in which those systems are embedded (Ménard *et al.*, 2004).

Two current perspectives within phonetic science explicitly incorporate social interactional capacities into modeling the process of acquisition. Oller (2000) has proposed an infra-phonological system whereby the phonetic characteristics of human infant sound systems are viewed in the context of their communicative value. He emphasizes the importance of understanding infant sound systems by comparison with other primates (see Oller and Griebel, 2008b; Snowdon, 2004), as well as the evolutionary history of sound systems in ancestral speakers. As such, Oller's approach to understanding speech acquisition is embedded within the social context in which these systems are deployed on both contemporary (modern human infants) and historical (evolution of the language capacity) time scales.

Based on a long-term program of research related to understanding the basis of acquisition in phonetic factors (Locke, 1983), John Locke has proposed that infant vocal behaviors are adaptive. In his view, they compel adult responsiveness and caregiving for the helpless young human (Locke and Bogin, 2006; Locke, 2008). His "parental selection" hypothesis places social factors at the center of an emergence proposal for earliest stages of phonological acquisition. In short, Locke argues that interactions motivate the use of the vocal system and the initial forms used for communication. Locke's program centers on the evolutionary question of the deep history of use of the vocal system for communication. He restricts his arguments largely to initial parent–child interactions in early infancy rather than the longer term process of ambient language-focused phonological acquisition.

Phonetically oriented views place far less emphasis than phonological theory on genetic mechanisms as being a prominent underlying cause for complex developmental outcomes. The unique anatomy and physiology of the input–output system in young humans is endowed genetically. This endowment supports basic functions of breathing (respiratory system), airway protection (phonatory system), and eating (articulatory system). However, these systems, as they function in typically developing infants and mature across development, account for only one aspect of the starting raw materials available for acquiring a complex knowledge and output system. Thus, maturation is a necessary, but not sufficient, boundary condition on acquisition of perception, storage and retrieval, and production capacities (see Chapter 4 for a review of data on maturation of peripheral capacities).

In addition to physical maturation, general-purpose mechanisms including self-organization and learning also are proposed in a variety of phonetic perspectives as being available to the human infant for assembling a complex knowledge and behavioral repertoire in support of the emergence of a fully expressed mature phonological system. In Chapter 3, we defined self-organization as order emerging without hierarchical preplanning, based on the structural and functional capacities of the system – termed order for free (Kauffman, 1995). Applying the construct of self-organization to phonological acquisition implies that in the earliest speech-like behaviors (e.g. open CV syllables containing a restricted range of sound types, mostly stop consonants such as /b/ or /d/ and front and central vowels such as /i/ or /a/), the young child is assembling adaptive behavioral patterns. These behavioral resources are marshaled to exploit intrinsic peripheral system dynamics to respond to local communication contexts later at the onset of language acquisition.

A strong hypothesis for the role of self-organization would suggest that early phonetic capacities and patterning in languages are based on self-organizing principles. Ubiquitous patterns common across languages (see Ladefoged and Maddieson, 1986, for a review) could be viewed as based on self-organization related to the necessity of economy of implementation of the human production system in the face of perceptual pressure from listeners to use the system to differentiate messages and transmit them quickly.

While not a consistent facet of research within phonetic science, self-organization has been applied to considerations of evidence within varied research programs. Several proposals have suggested self-organization as a supporting mechanism in emergence of output complexity. MacNeilage and colleagues (MacNeilage et al., 2000a) proposed emergence of initial place differentiation within early words (i.e. lip and tongue tip consonant /b-d/ sequences such as bad) as an example of self-organization operating to support initial steps into place variegation for consonant sequences in early words. They argued that initiation of action is a separable functional role of motor systems (Gazzaniga and Heatherton, 2003), and initiation is more difficult when it occurs in the context of more complex output targets. When children are simulating an adult word with inter-cyclical variegation, they are most likely to begin with a lip closure and then add a tongue movement. Lip closure only requires jaw movement. Tongue tip engagement requires a non-neutral tongue placement. Thus, the output system self-organizes, based on motor system principles, into an ease of operation initiating movement (labial), followed by an active tongue tip movement (alveolar) for the second closure.

Lindblom (2000, 2008) has also emphasized self-organization mechanisms. Lindblom's perspective incorporates perception and production system capacities as dual influences on emergent cognitive organization underlying emergence of phonological knowledge. He has proposed a "reuse" hypothesis. Reuse refers to consistent matching between the child's production output and the requirements for generating perceptual distinctiveness. These requirements for successful communication dictate reuse by the child of available movement patterns. Characterizing the child as managing universal physiological constraints on early movements and reusing these available motor patterns for coding meanings with needed perceptual distinctiveness is seen as being favored, based on metabolic constraints on memory formation, according to Lindblom.

The gestural phonology perspective (Brownman and Goldstein, 1992) includes the proposal that earliest steps in vocal acquisition are based on self-organization. In this view on self-organization, oral constrictions shared by adults and children are produced based on a process of mutual auditory and visual attunement (Studdert-Kennedy, 1998). Attunement illustrates self-organization in the implicit assumption of optimization of the system without blueprints.

The status of learning as a general supporting mechanism is related to recent emphasis on the role of input in instantiation of knowledge. Phonetic paradigms investigating early learning in phonological acquisition center on cross-linguistic comparisons (Kern *et al.*, 2009; Lee *et al.*, 2010; Vihman *et al.*, 1986) of spontaneously occurring vocalizations occurring in natural communication settings. This body of research considers the young child's replication of precise ambient language regularities through comparison of spontaneously occurring output with ambient language patterns.

In some recent investigations (Kern and Davis, in review, 2012), phonological characteristics of languages based on computerized dictionaries have been employed in comparisons with child patterns of output. These comparisons of child speech patterns have been considered a means to understand which patterns observable in child output may be related to physical maturation constraints and which may reveal basic properties of the speech production system retained in adult speakers of languages (MacNeilage *et al.*, 2000a).

These observational paradigms focus on perceptually based learning observable in children's spontaneous output as illustrated by appearance of ambient language regularities. Use of spontaneous naturalistic data enables a view of child output systems in the earliest stages when young children are not consistently capable of complying with experimental paradigms requiring behavioral output responses.

Research paradigms implemented under the umbrella of phonetic science have been largely motivated by the status of biological capacities of the developing child. The general philosophy, however, is that peripheral structures and their function have an impact on the nature of long-term mental knowledge structures (e.g. MacNeilage, 2008). Thus, knowledge is not only an abstract system of representation or constraints, but is embodied in actual production and perception processes of the peripheral speech mechanisms.

Development of articulatory system physiology (Kent and Vorperian, 2006) has been outlined from birth through puberty. Generally, phonetic paradigms are centered on the prelinguistic and early-word periods of the acquisition process. As such, predictions of these theories are not well specified relative to modeling the full spectrum of emergence for ambient language knowledge across acquisition. Instead, they are oriented largely to characterizing emergence of physiological capacities supporting early goal-directed action (e.g. Buder *et al.*, 2008; Green *et al.*, 2002; Kent, 1999; Ménard *et al.*, 2009; Steeve *et al.*, 2008) or emergence of phonetic properties available at the onset of speech-like behaviors (Davis and MacNeilage, 1995; Davis *et al.*, 2002; Studdert-Kennedy, 2005).

Studies from diverse production-oriented perspectives present a mosaic of paradigms focused on distinct aspects of acquisition related to the peripheral anatomy and physiology of the production system. Several production system-oriented research programs (e.g. Koopmans-van Beinum and van der Stelt, 1986; Kent and Vorperian, 2006) have detailed emergence of coordination across respiratory, phonatory, and articulatory output subsystems in the first 18 months of life.

Early oral motor development (Green *et al.*, 1997, 2002; Moore and Ruark, 1996) has been described beginning shortly after birth using kinematic measurement techniques. Kinematic measurement techniques are also employed to infer speech-motor control processes across the period of early development of speech production capacities (e.g. Barlow *et al.*, 1997; Smith *et al.*, 1995), or physiological-linguistic system links in later periods of acquisition (Goffman and Smith, 1999; Goffman, *et al.*, 2008).

Growth and coordination of respiratory capacity underlying speech production has been studied (e.g. Boliek *et al.*, 1996; Moore *et al.*, 2001) to outline respiratory function across formative periods during the first six years of life (Parham *et al.*, 2011). In this research, physiological measurement of the chest wall is recorded during varied speech tasks as well as during at-rest breathing in infants and young children. The goal is to understand the emergence of speech-related dynamics from the respiratory capacities available to the young child.

This type of paradigm is consistent with perspectives proposing emergence of speech production capacities from domain-general capacities dedicated to basic life functions. In this case, speech-based respiration emerges from a system employed for supporting the respiratory needs of the body for oxygen–carbon dioxide exchange (Kent and Vorperian, 2006).

Consistent with dominant paradigms in phonological research, perceptually based phonetic transcription and/or acoustic analyses are broadly employed to describe behavioral output patterns. In addition, due to the emphasis on the integral importance of peripheral systems, peripheral physiological measurement techniques, including kinematic measures of muscle function and measures of respiratory function, have been essential to some approaches.

Vocal tract models have also been employed in phonetically based programmatic research to simulate the process of acquisition of complexity in sound systems. Proposed critical characteristics of the vocal tract, including tongue, lips, jaw, and velum, are built into articulatory models and resulting sound properties are observed (Boë and Maeda, 1997; Ménard *et al.*, 2004; Vorperian *et al.*, 2005). As an example, Boë and Maeda's model (1997) includes seven articulatory factors (lip protrusion, lip height, jaw height, tongue body, tongue dorsum, tongue tip, and larynx height) and two scaling factors (oral and pharyngeal cavity length, and fundamental frequency) to explore differences in output between infants and adults across time.

Ménard *et al.* (2004) modeled vocal tract changes from birth to 21 years of age and employed a panel of listeners to infer vowels produced by the model. These vocal tract models consider the interface between articulatory settings reflecting characteristics of the articulatory mechanism and patterns of observable output, as well as perceptual responses from listeners to that output (Ménard *et al.*, 2007).

Vocal tract models are often designed to address the tension between production ease and perceptual distance in understanding maximization of potential for message transmission, a seminal question in phonetic science (see Lindblom, 1992, for a discussion). Tension between production ease and perceptual distinctiveness is a basic question relative to successful linguistic communication between speakers and listeners. Vocal tract models enable a precise specification and adjustments of vocal tract settings and observation of resulting output patterns in a way that is not possible with human speakers.

These modeling paradigms reflect on underlying units of knowledge differently than phonological theorists. They employ learning simulations in artificial computer systems that emphasize the process of acquiring sound systems from peripheral mechanism structures and their functioning. They are congruent in that units of emergent knowledge are characterized by being based on peripheral production output characteristics (de Boer, 2005). Putative units are specified in computer models used to derive data (i.e. tongue or lips, or vowel space configurations, Boë and Maeda, 1997).

Consideration of neural/cognitively instantiated units underlying human speech encoding and decoding has been one of the seminal questions of phonetic science across more than 50 years of scientific inquiry. Underlying invariance in knowledge structures that enables reliable linguistic communication in the face of peripheral variance in articulatory and acoustic raw materials occurring in real-time interactions remains an unsolved scientific problem. Apparent lack of compatibility between central knowledge and peripheral performance components illustrate the conceptual difficulties involved in determining the nature of knowledge units underlying linguistic communication.

Early research considering the status of underlying units from a phonetic perspective (e.g. Stevens and House, 1963) sought a single phonetic goal in the face of a motor system constrained by biomechanics in the time domain. Theories relied on the concept of underlying targets (Lindblom, 1963) or internal spatial targets (MacNeilage, 1970) masked by articulation system dynamics. In this context, "target" refers to the positioning of articulators in the vocal tract relative to movement trajectories required to achieve them. In contrast, in biology the visual and auditory systems have long been known to be more attracted to change in the time dimension (i.e. auditory or visual "movement") than to static properties (Kandel and Schwartz, 1981). This attribute is observable in early language acquisition in studies of edge detection in infancy (Smith et al., 2003; von Hofsten et al., 1998). In early detection of object boundaries, infants employ motion as means to develop early categories for objects in conceptualizing distinct properties within their social environment (Baird and Baldwin, 2001).

Some more recent phonetic and phonological characterizations of underlying units of speech production have moved to dynamically specify units of knowledge (see Lindblom, 2008, for a review) rather than assuming static knowledge structures or reranking of mentally available constraints. Theoretical treatments such as the task-dynamic modeling of Saltzman and Kelso (Kelso, 2008; Saltzman and Kelso, 1987) propose underlying units based on specification of a general movement goal, postulating a region of underlying specification related to task dynamics, rather than a static target.

At a more general level in the area of speech motor control, optimal control accounts within the non-speech literature propose that the movement task is specified initially and movement details are then filled in to optimize performance of the movement goal (i.e. movement optimization, see Berthier *et al.*, 2005; Bernstein, 1967; Lindblom, 2008). This perspective requires a specification of a movement goal (i.e. lip closure for /b/), but not a precise a priori phonemic plan in advance of use.

The issue of the mentally specified units underlying speech production is at the core of conceptual differences between phonological and phonetic theoretical perspectives. Phonological theory centralizes universal knowledge units, albeit with no consensus about what those units are. Indeed, constraints-based OT theories (McCarthy and Prince, 1993) implicate a non-falsifiable hypothesis for the nature of underlying units in emphasizing the tension between faithfulness and markedness, constraints which require continual changes across acquisition and across languages. Importantly, however, developmental changes are related to access and implementation of knowledge, not to the underlying knowledge units themselves within OT.

Alternatively, phonetic perspectives focus on biomechanics of the production and the operation of the peripheral psychoacoustic levels of the perception system as enabling construction of knowledge across acquisition. However, phonetic perspectives show a corresponding lack of consensus on the precise nature of underlying knowledge units. In general, however, the implication of production system approaches is that underlying knowledge units should be characterized with reference to parameters of the production and perception systems, most prominently articulatory and phonatory characteristics (Pierrehumbert, 2000), rather than a priori mental units.

What are examples of phonetic research programs? Some phonetically based approaches have explored acquisition via comprehensive programmatic research. Consideration of these programmatically supported theories enables a look at the ways in which components of an emergence perspective are expressed within this scholarly tradition.

GESTURAL PHONOLOGY

Gestural phonology (Brownman and Goldstein, 1992) provides an example. One prominent goal of gestural phonology is to neutralize the competence–performance dichotomy: "Speech and phonology are low and high dimensional descriptions of a *single* (emphasis ours) complex system" (Brownman and Goldstein, 1992: 180). No translation is deemed necessary between aspects of the system. Cognitive and motor aspects of the system are integral to one another, in contrast to phonological perspectives requiring translation rules (Keating, 1990). The context-free base units of cognition, termed *gestures*, are characterized as being behaviorally coded and temporally embedded in actual action sequences.

Cognitively instantiated gestural units are proposed to be context independent while physical properties of gestures vary according to linguistic context. These two levels of the overall system are intertwined in "mutual constraint" (Browman and Goldstein, 1990). Mutual constraint dictates that properties of cognitive phonological gestures are limited by the need for articulatory contrast. Contrast, or distinctiveness, at the cognitive level is driven by ambient language phonemic choices. Behavioral articulatory or acoustic properties are limited in turn by the cognitive contrast necessary for linguistic communication.

Gestural phonology is based on action theory (Kelso *et al.*, 1986). Contrast at the action system level is driven by the systematic consequences of the coordinated system of speech articulators operating in real time toward speech-related goals. Each physical structure is constrained by membership in the overall production system. Emergent behaviors are seen as products of self-organization (Kugler and Turvey, 1987; Kauffman, 1995) based on local interactions among system components leading to patterns of global order (Browman and Goldstein, 1990).

The gestural scores are proposed as basic within gestural phonology. These scores are employed to support the proposal that output gestures (e.g. velum open/closed, lips closed/open) are the "notes," and phase relationships between the gestures are representative of the time domain in speech output. The closest analogy to a gestural score is a music staff with varied notes occurring simultaneously as well as sequentially. The notes indicate varied articulators and their relative positions (i.e. velum open/closed). The process of acquisition is characterized initially by undifferentiated syllables, followed by differentiation into individual articulatory gestures (i.e. the "particulate principle," Abler, 1989; Studdert-Kennedy, 1998; Studdert-Kennedy and Goodell, 1995). Via self-organization, the child's behavior converges on oral, velar, and laryngeal constrictions. These constrictions, crucially, are shared by child and communication partner as human speakers. Imitative visual/auditory attunement is said to drive the acquisition process. Children recover their communication partner's degree of articulator constriction from acoustics and visual input within functional communicative interactions.

FRAME–CONTENT THEORY

A contrasting phonetic perspective, the Frame/Content (F/C) theory (Davis and MacNeilage, 1995; Davis et al., 2002; MacNeilage and Davis, 1990), has generated a comprehensive set of theoretical predictions about within- and across-syllable patterns in speech acquisition. In this view, the task facing the infant is to gain independent control of coordinated articulators in the time domain, thus addressing for speech the general problem of serial order in action systems posed by Lashley (1951).

Rhythmic mandibular oscillation (i.e. the "frame") accompanied by phonation is proposed to be the aspect of the infant movement system available for the initial approximation of the serial organization of adult speech at the onset of canonical babbling (MacNeilage and Davis, 1993). The "unit" in babbling is considered the rhythmic mandibular cycle. Rhythmic mandibular movement cycles yield perceptually apparent simulations of consonants in the closure phase, vowels in the open phase, and syllables as the consequence of these rhythmic alternations between consonants and vowels. No sub-cycle independence of component articulators such as tongue, lips, or soft palate is required for the infant to produce speech-like sequences that are apparent to listeners.

Rhythmic close-and-open phases of the jaw (Dolata et al., 2008) result in listener perception of consonants and vowels. These consonant-like and vowel-like perceptual qualities are not based on independent articulatory movements of active articulators within the rhythmic jaw cycle. Based on lack of independent movements of articulators in rhythmic cycles, labial consonants with central vowels (/ba/), coronal consonants with front vowels (/di/), and dorsal consonants with back vowels (/ku/) are predicted to be more frequent in infant output inventories beginning in prelinguistic babbling. Based on the conceptualization of rhythmic mandibular oscillations without the necessity of active movements of other articulators within the vocal sequence (Davis et al., 2002), across syllables, manner variegation is predicted to occur more often than place variegation (i.e. /bawa/ over /bada/). Vowel height variegation is predicted over front–back changes (e.g. /daedi/ over /daedu/). In the case of this variegation, change is related to relative degree of closure of the jaw in successive mandibular cycles.

What does this theory add to understanding of an emergence perspective on acquisition? MacNeilage and Davis have suggested that F/C provides a movement-based principle for characterizing the predominant types of syllable-based movements observed in young children during babbling and early speech (Davis and MacNeilage, 1995; Davis et al., 2002). At a more general level, predominant, although not universal, confirmation of these predictions in English and across widely diverse languages studied (Gildersleeve-Neumann et al., 2011; Lee et al., 2010; Kern et al., 2010) suggests the importance of considering the movement system in understanding the precise characteristics of early syllable types in acquisition (Teixeira and Davis, 2002). In addition, in analysis of language patterns, predominance of the two lingual syllable types (i.e. coronal front and dorsal back) were found at higher than chance levels (MacNeilage et al., 2000b; Rousset, 2004) in a survey of 26 diverse languages. These results for languages indicate that the within-CV co-occurrences predicted by the F/C theory may be retained in languages as an aspect of production ease in the tension between production ease and perceptual distinctiveness.

Progressive refinements in speech production capacities relative to ambient language properties are based on differentiation (i.e. Fentress, 1984) of "content" or capacities for executing individual movement patterns for phonemes from the gestalt pattern produced by rhythmic jaw oscillations. Fentress's original work described differentiation of precision in mouse grooming movements across development as an example of differentiation. Early movements in young mice showed more global and imprecise movements but contained all the components of later refined movements for grooming.

Differentiation in speech acquisition refers to the assumption that the components supporting skilled movements are present but must be refined across development via maturation with corresponding gain in control of motor system function for goal-directed speech actions. Perceptual input demonstrating the sound types employed for linguistic communication is also required. Differentiation as a perspective on acquisition is quite different from auditory or movement based integration of smaller units into larger wholes, as is proposed in the particulate principle of gestural phonology (Studdert-Kennedy, 2005).

In the F/C theory, segmental "content" elements (consonants or vowels) are gradually differentiated from the rhythmic "frame" of mandibular open–close movements to become independently programmable entities underlying speech-motor control processes. Differentiation of these independent segmental-related movements (i.e. /r/ or /θ/) occurs as the infant acquires increasing control over the coordination of articulators within the rhythmic jaw cycle. For example, as the tongue becomes relatively more independent of the jaw and capable of finer adjustments of the articulators, the infant is predicted to produce place variegation (i.e. /bada/) in consonant sequences rather than only manner variegation (i.e. /bawa/) that is based on relative closure of the jaw in rhythmic cycles. Production of sounds such as /ʃ/, /r/, or /l/ requires finely grained articulator placements to be superimposed on the rhythmic jaw cycle during the closure phase. Control over soft palate closure predicts growth in alternation of nasals and orals rather than pervasive nasal or oral quality throughout sequences. Most importantly, action in the time domain is a basic tenet in contrast to descriptions of the status of underlying rules or phonological representations.

WHAT ARE PARAMETERS OF COGNITIVE/PSYCHOLINGUISTIC APPROACHES?

Cognitively oriented perspectives within psycholinguistics form a third category of theoretical proposals on phonological acquisition. Cognition generally relates to the mental functions underlying knowing and using information for interactions with the environment. Contemporary cognitively oriented approaches to phonological acquisition are addressed as they co-occur with the child's attainment of more general knowledge of the world. The tenet that knowledge is available in advance of use, characteristic of structuralist phonological approaches, is not a necessary starting assumption for cognitive paradigms.

Theoretical proposals within cognitive science and psycholinguistic domains have typically centered on issues related to how the process of acquisition proceeds. Process-oriented approaches ask how acquisition proceeds and what mechanisms underlie the process as they can be observed in experimental paradigms. Some proposals address self-organization and learning, as well.

Subdomains of cognitive science include neural and social cognition, as well as perceptually oriented computer models and laboratory-based perceptual experimental paradigms. The coexistence of these subdomains emphasizes the diverse factors needed to consider children's acquisition of the cognitive complexity characteristic of adult humans. These diverse factors are investigated relative to a number of important axes of growth in knowledge complexity in the young child, including language properties, as well as social and emotional learning.

Developmental psycholinguistic studies within cognitive science consider how young children learn language. Psycholinguistic proposals, in particular, extend the general focus of developmental cognitive science on characterizing the acquisition of complex behavior by infants and young children into the specific realm of language acquisition. Psycholinguistics is a synthetic discipline, including linguistics, biology, information theory, and neuroscience under the larger umbrella of the discipline of psychology.

Psycholinguistic models for language acquisition attempt to portray key aspects of the cognitive subsystems involved in acquiring language knowledge. The goal of experimental paradigms is to consider how these key aspects are related in the process whereby young children learn to decode and encode language. Input processing, as well as storing, planning, and retrieving mentally stored phonological forms for implementation, are the central focus. Diverse experimental traditions emphasize potential interfaces between phonological knowledge and other aspects of the language system.

In contrast to phonological theories based on the psychological reality of underlying representations or constraints, psycholinguistic research is concerned with how cognitive properties instantiated in neural tissue operate to enable young children to produce and comprehend language(s). Psycholinguistic traditions focus on ways in which input is converted to stored language knowledge for retrieval in output. Physical factors related to the structures and functions of the peripheral perception and production systems are not central. The role of input, important in learning theories within psycholinguistics related to neural-cognitive growth, is conceptualized relative to frequency of linguistic input, rather than to the operations of the peripheral auditory system, in the biology of the young human.

However, compared with both phonological and phonetic characterizations, psycholinguistic/cognitive researchers are more likely to assume the necessity of a cross-domain understanding of acquisition where phonology is not seen as being acquired in isolation from other aspects of language knowledge (e.g. Dell, 1988; Edwards *et al.*, 2004; Luce *et al.*, 2000). Semantic (Coady and Aslin, 2004; Yu *et al.*, 2005) and syntactic (Tomasello, 2003) domains of language knowledge are implicated as interactive aspects associated integrally within cognitive processing domain in some proposals.

Early cognitive-linguistically-oriented theories centered on phono-logical acquisition arose in response to the Jakobsonian (Jakobson, 1941) assertion of a universal linguistic timetable for expression of phonological knowledge. Jakobson proposed that initial vocal patterns were reflective of a universal series of perceptually based distinctions (e.g. sonorant-obstruent, /a/ and /b/; oral-nasal, /b/ and /m/). Data on early acquisition did not confirm Jakobson's universal sequence (e.g. Menn, 1983; Ferguson and Farwell, 1975; Macken and Ferguson, 1983). In early data-based work, observed differences in behavioral patterns within and across children were seen as reflective of individual cognitive strategies. Conceptual emphasis was placed on how the child's mind stores and processes knowledge for language acquisition. Commitment to a priori form that is basic to phonological theory was less central to these early cognitively oriented proposals.

Contemporary cognitively oriented paradigms have also centered on later developmental periods. They include "neighborhood density" approaches (Luce and Pisoni, 1998; Storkel, 2006; Charles-Luce and Luce, 1995). The construct of neighborhood density focuses on linguistic processing and retrieval issues above the level of peripheral perceptual and production system operation. Phonological and semantic properties are seen as interactive rather than isolated. Crucially, this approach gives a great role to perception and input as the relationships between these aspects must be accessed from word forms the child hears.

Recognition accuracy is related to the number of "neighbors" a word has (Storkel, 2006). Preschool children have been found to learn novel words with common sound sequences more rapidly than novel words with rare sound sequences in a number of studies (Beckman and Edwards, 2000; Storkel and Morrisette, 2002). Common phonotactic sound sequences are correlated with word forms in dense "phonological neighborhoods" (Vitevitch et al., 1999). This relationship connotes an important link between phonological and lexical aspects of storage and retrieval.

In addition to the more general view of phonology as interactive with other aspects of language, contemporary psycholinguistic accounts are characterized by integration of constructs across disciplinary boundaries more than is typical of traditional phonological or phonetically oriented theories. Connectionist neural net models (e.g. Elman, 2005) explicitly model neural and cognitive aspects of acquisition. Their paradigms include computer simulations of change in neural structures in response to frequency of input of phonological forms. These neural nets reflect machine-based modeling of brain learning in responses to input consistent with information theory accounts of knowledge acquisition (Shannon and Weaver, 1949).

More comprehensive theoretical proposals on phonological acquisition also reach across disciplinary boundaries to incorporate linguistic structure as well as processing accounts in considering acquisition. For example, Vihman, DePaolis, and Keren-Portnoy's (Vihman, in press) "articulatory filter" hypothesis includes perception and production. Vihman and colleagues incorporate laboratory perceptual experiments with consideration of the path of emergence for sound patterns in early words occurring in spontaneous production output. Guenther's DIVA model (Guenther, 1995) focuses on auditory perceptual input processing and neural instantiation of cognitive knowledge as tightly interactive subcomponents supporting emergence of a complex phonological system.

Cognitively/psycholinguistically oriented proposals are consistent with the construct of emergence. Both cognitive and production/perception aspects of the complex system typified by the young child in acquisition are incorporated into contemporary cognitively oriented models (i.e. Vihman and Croft, 2007; Werker and Curtin, 2005). Diverse mechanisms underlying acquisition of knowledge are primary components. These components are integral to understanding the nature of information processing and how it is implemented to support increases in system complexity, in this case, phonological knowledge.

Figure 6.3 depicts the core variables of our complex system emergence proposal as they are demonstrated in contemporary cognitively oriented psycholinguistic proposals. Child-intrinsic capacities are emphasized at different levels than in phonetic perspectives. In particular, the role of perceptual capacities and neural-cognitive instantiation are central (Molfese and Pratt, 2007; Sanders *et al.*, 2008). The critical status of input for instantiation of a complex knowledge system forms a basic component of cognitively oriented accounts of acquisition, including phonological acquisition (e.g. Fikkert, 2007; Zamuner *et al.*, 2005). Perceptual (e.g. Jusczyk, 1997; Werker and Curtin, 2005) or perceptual-neural proposals (e.g. Guenther, 1995; Werker and Curtin, 2005) have been employed to characterize the capacities of the auditory-perceptual system as the seminal influence in support of the acquisition of phonological knowledge.

Production system capacities are not frequently a central aspect of cognitive science/psycholinguistically oriented theoretical proposals (although, see Fikkert, 2005, for a synthesizing view). However, memory and learning are frequently a focus within developmental psycholinguistics. These mechanisms are incorporated as general-

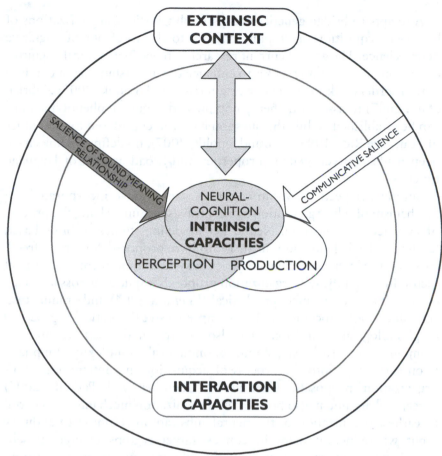

FIGURE 6.3 Components of Acquisition in Cognitively Oriented Approaches

purpose capacities supporting acquisition of knowledge. Each of these components is implicitly tied with input from the extrinsic context to stimulate and refine the child's knowledge of phonological knowledge.

The recent emphasis in the perception literature on the role of input is viewed as interacting with the child's growing capacities to employ learning as a tool for acquiring precise knowledge. This laboratory-based experimental literature (e.g. Coady and Aslin, 2004; Newport and Aslin, 2004) centers on attention capacities for detecting sequence regularities. This approach de-emphasizes social-cognitive linkages within functional communication dyads, as is the emphasis in work by Tomasello on syntax acquisition (Tomasello, 2003). There, the social component is viewed as supporting emergence of cognition (although, see Kuhl, 2007, for work integrating these two perspectives).

Attempts to bridge genetics and psycholinguistic characterizations of language acquisition are rapidly coming to the forefront of cognitive neuroscience. The goal of current research is to evaluate typical cognitive development. A second focus is to enhance the understanding of children with disorders of known genetic origin (Rice and Smolik, 2007; Zubrick *et al.*, 2007) to assess whether genotypic and cognitive phenotypic links can be established. While the question has been considered for a number of years (see Rice, 1996; Rice and Smolik, 2007), no definitive links have been made between genetic properties and broad aspects of language function.

Several perspectives within cognitive science have incorporated the mechanism of self-organization as a central aspect underlying the process of knowledge acquisition. Neural net modeling studies of brain-based learning (McClelland and Elman, 1986) have proposed "order for free," based on the interactive characteristics of system components as a critical factor. Importantly, self-organization proposals implicate across language domain interactions, including lexical (Li *et al.*, 2004) and grammatical (Li *et al.*, 2004) associations. More comprehensive theoretical approaches to phonological acquisition have also incorporated a self-organization component for early steps into phonological complexity. Emphasis is on early steps into the process of acquisition in contemporary self-organization proposals. Guenther's (Guenther and Perkell, 2004) perceptual argument also posits a self-organization mechanism as central to earliest organization of the neural substrate in response to auditory input where neural maps in convex target regions emerge in self-organizing ways to support instantiation of phonemes across acquisition.

Learning mechanisms are central to all contemporary cognitive science research. Neural net models have more generally been implemented to test general learning theories (e.g. Bates and MacWhinney, 1988). Connectionist modeling represents a well-studied proposal within this genre relative to speech acquisition. In these models, learners are assumed to weigh specific, differing elements, such as phonemes or words, according to their frequency of occurrence in the input, and generate grammatical utterances based on a critical mass of information (Plunkett and Marchman, 1991).

A variety of experimental methods are encompassed within current cognitively oriented approaches. Phonologically oriented experimental paradigms spring from a homogeneous approach to considering the basis of knowledge. In contrast, cognitive paradigms spring from a variety of research cultures, including computer science (Elman, 2005), perception-oriented laboratory experimental paradigms (e.g. Vitevitch and Luce, 2005) and psycholinguistic paradigms exploring memory storage, retrieval and planning for output (e.g. Beckman and Edwards, 2000; Munson, 2001).

Within perceptual approaches to understanding the nature and course of acquisition, experimental laboratory paradigms are most common (see Jusczyk, 1997, for a review of classic studies on this topic). Studies of perceptual processing early in the first year employ physiological response paradigms. These paradigms do not require intentional response by the infant. They analyze biological responses including heart-rate deceleration and non-nutritive sucking. Laboratory experimental paradigms have considered the capacities of the infant auditory system at birth as well as refinements toward the ambient environment available by the second half of the first year (Kuhl *et al.*, 2006; Kuhl, 2007).

Later in the first year and into the second year, perceptual paradigms include contemporary looking-time measurements (e.g. Werker and Fennell, 2008; see Aslin, 2007, for a review of this paradigm). Reaction-time measurements (e.g. Luce, 1986; Vitevitch and Luce, 2005) provide another paradigm within experimental psychology to test questions about cognitive processing and representation in somewhat older children. In these experimental procedures, children's capacities are measured through behavioral responses. As an example, they may include behavioral responses to auditory content varied in dimensions crucial to phonological knowledge (i.e. F2 changes relative to consonant place of articulation distinctions) and response latencies (i.e. length of response time for critical speech cues).

Perceptual mechanisms by which young infants come to recognize language-specific phonemic categories are not agreed upon. Hypotheses include the perceptual magnet effect in which goodness of fit determines categorization (Kuhl *et al.*, 1992), the extremes of vowel space as an organizing mechanism (Polka and Werker, 1994), and discovery of recurring gestural coordination patterns and phonemes (Best, 1994).

Auditory perceptual approaches carry the implicit assumption that underlying units should be characterized in auditory-acoustic terms to match proposed mechanisms for instantiating long-term knowledge structures (e.g. Guenther, 1995). Guenther's perceptual approach is reliant on convex region targets (adapted from Keating, 1990). Contemporary perceptually driven conceptualizations (e.g. Gebhart *et al.*, 2009) emphasize the infant's capacities for rapid learning of sequence regularities from perceptually available auditory input. These experimental paradigms imply one underlying representation built from input regularities.

PERCEPTUAL–NEURAL MODELING

Guenther's auditory perceptual account (Guenther, 1995; Guenther and Perkell, 2004), the Directions Into Velocities of Articulators (DIVA) model, illustrates an input-oriented view. DIVA focuses on linkages between the child's perceptual capacities for finding patterns with neural instantiation of those patterns. The result, in Guenther's view, is a progressive emergence of neural-acoustic maps supporting underlying knowledge instantiation.

The primary focus of the DIVA models is in auditory planning of speech movements. Goals of speech movements founded in auditory temporal space are characterized as one site of emergent phonological knowledge. Movement planning represents a mapping between articulation movements and their neurally coded auditory consequences. Importantly, Guenther's auditory neural mapping account lies squarely within an emergence perspective on the process of knowledge acquisition. It does not require a priori form in advance of use.

One aspect of Guenther's model is his conceptualization of convex region targets (adapted from Keating, 1990), wherein phoneme targets are seen as occurring in multidimensional regions rather than as points. He proposes that consideration of phoneme targets as regions rather than discrete points enables accommodation of important speech phenomena, including co-articulation, and contextual variability characteristic of infant vocalizations, as well as adult-connected speech patterns. His perspective suggests that the locus of speech acquisition lies in neurally coded auditory representations.

Guenther employs computational modeling. A set of neurons illustrating putative neural representations are model parameters. Parameters are tuned during a babbling phase. Random articulator movements provide auditory feedback used to train neural mappings. Neural phoneme representations emerge across "generations."

NEIGHBORHOOD DENSITY

Cognitively oriented proposals centered on later developmental periods for speech accuracy include "neighborhood density" approaches (Edwards *et al.*, 2004; Munson and Soloman, 2004). This approach is based on work by Luce and colleagues who proposed a "neighborhood activation" model of spoken word recognition (Luce, 1986; Luce and Pisoni, 1998), whereby words are organized in memory into "similarity neighborhoods" based on their frequency of occurrence in the language and the density of words in their lexical neighborhood. In adults, words occurring often in the language from sparse lexical neighborhoods (i.e. few phonemically similar words, or lexical neighbors with which to compete for lexical selection) are recognized faster and more accurately than words occurring infrequently from dense lexical neighborhoods (i.e. many similar-sounding words with which to compete for lexical selection). The construct of neighborhood density emphasizes linguistic processing and retrieval issues above the level of peripheral perceptual and production system operations, focusing on psycholinguistic processes rather than neural variables supporting cognition.

Considered as an integral aspect of the process of speech acquisition, incorporation of linguistic processing variables emphasizes the functional load of cognitive processing as foundational to emergence of intelligible speech. This inclusion implies that speech acquisition is not modular in the sense portrayed in phonological theories, but based on a complex system necessarily including cognitive processing in somewhat older children. In these characterizations, the size of the child's lexicon is integral to accuracy of retrieval for phonological forms. Like many other models related to the process of speech acquisition presented in this chapter, this particular model is not inclusive of the whole process of acquisition, only of the phase of the process related to full emergence of word intelligibility. It strongly emphasizes the interface of the lexicon with phonological processing.

WHERE ARE WE NOW?

The present universe of theoretical perspectives on the acquisition of phonological knowledge and behavior is varied and philosophically diverse. Both conceptualizations and paradigms for testing those conceptualizations reflect largely autonomous scholarly research cultures. Several unique and overlapping scholarly traditions contribute to consideration of what, how, and why acquisition of phonology should be understood.

Phonological traditions emphasize the structure of phonological forms as a modular and non-function-driven process. A priori knowledge is revealed by maturation and parameterized toward ambient language regularities by input. Emphasis is on the state of phonological knowledge accessed by frequency counts of observable behavioral forms.

Phonetic perspectives, in dramatic contrast, emphasize the importance of the peripheral action system in instantiation of phonetic behavioral patterns and growth in complexity of those patterns. Behavioral action system patterns are the focus, as they can reveal organization of phonological systems for producing and perceiving output optimally in human speakers and listeners. This central question is accessed by a variety of measurement paradigms devoted to understanding the action system, as well as accessing action system properties through analysis of behavioral patterns.

Cognitive science emphasizes the process of acquiring knowledge as an input-driven process that is required for instantiation of neurally and cognitively described knowledge. Output is not considered strongly in cognitive conceptualizations of phonological acquisition. Interrelationships with other aspects of language knowledge and performance are central, particularly lexical development in some contemporary conceptualizations.

What about parameters of emergence in these current proposals? Phonological proposals are less congruent with an emergence perspective as they focus on phonological structure without incorporating other aspects of language or child capacities or the social functions of language. Language is modular and unique to humans. This "language is special" view negates consideration of a strong form of emergence hypothesis that views language as another example of complexity in the natural world.

In contrast, phonetic and psycholinguistic proposals operate on a conceptual foundation closer to emergence. A priori form is not a requirement for understanding the action, perceptual, or neural-cognitive subsystems that are a frequent area of emphasis within these traditions. Neither phonetic nor cognitive science proposals are comprehensive relative to issues we have proposed as being relevant to emergence of complexity in phonological knowledge or behavior. Both have elements of reductionism in that they do not encompass the wide variety of domain-general properties we have proposed as necessary for emergence. In particular, they do not consistently incorporate interactional capacities and extrinsic social function into their paradigms.

The challenge to understanding phonological acquisition and testing emergence proposals is synthesis and comprehensiveness. Synthesis of the most fruitful methods and paradigms and experimental methods across these scholarly disciplines is needed. Comprehensiveness in considering multiple factors impinging on acquisition of this complex system is also a necessary goal. Many powerful paradigms and theoretical questions are present in contemporary science to address an emergence proposal comprehensively.

Each of the philosophical traditions addressing the nature of phonological acquisition in contemporary scholarly inquiry carries with it a set of conceptual "baggage" and a way of addressing the issues involved in evaluating emergence. Our goal here has been to consider what each of these traditions offers to consideration of the tenets of emergence as we have conceptualized it.

7   The Present State and a Future For Emergence

WHAT IS EMERGENCE?

We have addressed the requirements for an emergence claim as it might motivate understanding children's acquisition of phonology. At the simplest level, phonology can be viewed as the "carrier" for ideas the child receives and uses as she learns about her environment and begins consistently communicating across the first years of her life. Her task is to acquire this carrier system and employ it for linguistic communication with others who understand it. *Ball* with a /b/ /a/ /l/ sequence of sounds is perceived with the child's ears and eyes as she begins to understand the word within social experiences. To say "ball," she needs to retrieve and organize phonological components she has stored in her growing knowledge base. Her respiratory, phonatory, and articulatory systems have to coordinate so that she can talk about "ball" with others. Over time she learns to attach "ball" to all sorts of objects that fit within that semantic category and to use it in a variety of communication contexts.

Social interactions and words like "ball" that are used within them occur consistently in a child's daily life. These interactions supply multiple examples for the child to construct her phonological knowledge base and refine her behavioral repertoire to begin to produce and perceive "ball" accurately. The phonological system the child is refining is exhibited in her ability to understand and say "ball" as well as in the growing number of lexical items she is adding daily to her repertoire. From an emergence perspective, her lexicon is embodied in a neural-cognitive system and evidenced by ambient language perception–action abilities. None of the dimensions we have proposed as being responsible for knowing and using phonology is sufficient alone to support emergence; all are necessary to enable a fully functional system. Thus knowing and doing are both required to characterize the complex system.

Emergence presents one option for considering how children acquire this socially functional system of knowledge observable in understanding what others say and in generating goal-directed speech behaviors. Emergence conceptualizations for acquiring phonology have been characterized in our narrative as being founded on dynamic interactions within a complex system. This complex system is embodied and dynamically changing across acquisition. From an emergence perspective, bodily actions linking with the child's social environment provide a critical stream of experience for her in gaining knowledge about the world and ways to express that knowledge. "Knowing" and "doing" capacities provide support to the child in connecting socially with people around her to grow and learn in her world.

We have situated emergence of phonology within three global dimensions. The young child's *intrinsic* biological and cognitive abilities and her social *interaction* capacities enable gathering and organizing knowledge about the components of her ambient language phonology for understanding language forms. These capacities support her as she refines her output repertoire toward ambient language requirements for using speech forms accurately to speak to others across the first five years or so of her life.

Extrinsic input from communication partners accounts for a third dimension supporting emergence of this complex system. Communication partners scaffold and tune both the child's abilities for knowing about phonological patterns in her language and for doing them as she produces words that others begin to understand. Tuning based on input from other people occurs through repetitions within the daily events that are important to the young child. These daily routines and play experiences enable her to maintain functional connections with other people in recurring activities. Reliable connections with people around her allow them to "show the way" toward phonological precision for the ambient language, while rewarding her with the caregiving and stimulation she needs to grow and thrive. Functional pressure to connect and to communicate underlies growth in interconnections between her *intrinsic* and *interaction* capacities and the critical *extrinsic* guidance she receives from her communication partners.

These three dimensions of the complex system are not language dedicated in an emergence view. All three have other purposes in the young child's world. They serve functions as diverse as eating, breathing, and learning about objects and actions of all kinds. Information about the world supports the child in basic survival, and in achieving consistent attachments for receiving care and eventually giving care to other people. Viewed as members of a neural-cognitively instantiated biological and social system, these three dimensions have served to enhance the survival of humans on an evolutionary time scale. They have been progressively co-opted and organized to support emergence of complex language in human speakers and listeners. What we see in the short time scale of young children's acquisition of phonology is a partial picture of what that evolutionary process for human language might have been like.

We have raised some philosophical themes that are inherent in considering an emergence proposal. As we have noted, these themes are congruent with biological and social science foundations. In some cases, they have not been a part of contemporary theories of phonological acquisition. One major theme we have explored extensively in this narrative is heterogeneity of the components that support emergence of phonology. Early constructions of language (e.g. Fodor and Katz, 1964; Chomsky and Halle, 1968) considered language to be a modular capacity, non-interactive with other human capacities supporting complex action and other types of knowledge. In particular, Chomsky's conceptualization proposed that language is fully described as an abstract system of symbol manipulations. This conceptualization is still basic to some contemporary arguments about the language faculty in humans (e.g. Pinker, 1994, 2009).

Emergence proposals strongly suggest an alternative conceptualization to "language is special and humans are special." In an emergence proposal, general-purpose mechanisms interact in a heterarchy to support emergence of complexity. Relative to phonological acquisition, a heterarchy implies feedback across dimensions of the system. Feedback occurs from peripheral to central, as well as from central to peripheral system components. Thus the central nervous system communicates with the peripheral production and perception organs. But these organs also communicate with central control centers in the tuning process supporting emergence of phonological knowledge and organized behavioral patterns. Production system capacities may influence perception of relevant phonological input. Additionally, there is the clear tie of the child's perception of ambient language regularities to refining production output patterns. In Chapters 4 and 5, we reviewed available acquisition data that evaluate the strength of this generalization about an emergence view. While available data are not comprehensive in enabling evaluation of tenets of emergence, they point the way toward considering what we know about acquisition of phonology as supportive of a functional heterogeneously determined process.

Relative to social interactions, the child and her communication partners must be able to connect with one another. Within these social connections, the child refines her output and her partner refines input so that the child can master ambient language requirements. Thus, the child and her communication partners reciprocally influence and are influenced by one another. Each of the mutually influencing dimensions of the system reflects operation of the feedback-based heterarchy conceptualization central to emergence. The concept of a heterarchy is not compatible with the view of a hierarchically based and abstract modular system developed in isolation from diverse interactions or from functional pressures toward intelligibility for linguistic communication.

General-purpose *mechanisms* are also involved in maintaining the interconnections among these system dimensions. These mechanisms are the metaphorical mortar that enables the dynamic system to support endpoint capacities of a fully developed long-term knowledge store and mature ambient language listening and speaking capacities. We have termed these two outcomes of the system as knowing and doing. Self-organization and learning are two primary mechanisms for facilitating change in the system toward these two ends.

Self-organization, as we have defined it, refers to emergence of patterns of knowledge and behavior at a global level based on interactions among lower-level components of the complex system. In an emergence view, self-organization does not require a blueprint or cookbook. As one mechanism underlying phonological acquisition, self-organization reflects optimization of interactions among organization of system components (see Chapter 3), based on children's physical attributes and their optimal interaction for functional purposes. Functional purposes are accomplished by growth in the child's repertoire of abilities for perceiving and storing knowledge, and producing recognizable phonological properties in output. These goal-directed behaviors are based on connections of the child's intrinsic and interaction capacities interacting with extrinsic input from other speakers.

Perceptual capacities enable a first site for evaluating the validity of a self-organization proposal. We have noted that perceptual abilities are present from at least three months before the infant's birth to aid her in acquiring relevant input for constructing a phonological system. Sensation and psychoacoustic processing by the human auditory system funnels the raw materials available for building a linguistic sound system to higher neural-cognitive centers by six months after birth. The optimal sensory frequencies to which this system responds and the ways sounds are sorted at the psychoacoustic level as they are forwarded to higher cognitive centers constitutes a basic level of self-organization toward the end of generating long-term phonological knowledge. As we have noted, no blueprint or external director is required to guide the process. The child's outward focus and the organized knowledge that results is supported by self-organization at the peripheral processing level based on auditory system characteristics of human listeners. These peripheral processes are organized to provide optimal response systems that operate within the frequent and intimate interactions of the newborn and her caregivers. Intrinsic capacities also undergird progressive attunement as the child grows and social interactions continue to feed her with relevant auditory raw materials for constructing a detailed ambient language phonological system concurrent with increase in connections with higher cognitive neural centers in the second half of the first year of life.

Neural organization illustrates another site for operation of self-organization mechanisms. Local interactions, based on neural interconnections constructed by listening and using sound patterns, self-organize neural tissue interconnections optimally. Neurons in the brain form a vast network of synaptic interconnections. All these interconnections support a system of great complexity that is the foundation for general cognition as well as for storing language knowledge. A limited amount of genetic material guides this neural complexity. The genetic material available could not logically generate all the patterns of interconnections in the brain for all the diverse operations of humans in their world. The general-purpose mechanism of self-organization is one means to support growth in the network of neural connections that is the embodied home to cognitive processes. This mechanism can be viewed as instrumental in building stable neural connections related to exposure to ambient language phonological regularities as well as embodied "practice" via production output experiences. Thus the emergence of an organized neural network is based on phonological raw material from intrinsic output that the child produces herself as well as extrinsic input that she perceives from persons around her. These rich sources of raw material provide the input into the neural substrate. Input results in organization of neural networks supporting eventual emergence of a fully realized neural-cognitive system of phonological knowledge for the child's ambient language or languages.

The production system is a third site for implementation of self-organization mechanisms in phonological acquisition. This system is founded in interactions of the respiratory, phonatory, and articulatory subsystems as they operate in goal-directed ways in young humans. In daily life, these subsystems support eating, breathing, and other non-language-dedicated functions. They achieve these organized behaviors for supporting general functions through increasingly efficient interconnections across subsystems.

In the domain of phonological acquisition, predominance of common behavioral patterns in canonical babbling across languages by 8–10 months (Kern and Davis, submitted) which occur despite diversity of language input to children suggests that the output system is self-organizing based on the characteristics of children's intrinsic capacities for producing rhythmic, speech-like vocalizations. Thus, optimal organization of the respiratory, phonatory, and articulatory subsystems results in rhythmically organized, syllable-like behaviors. These perceptually syllable-like behaviors are confined to a small and largely common set of sound and sequence patterns. These language-like patterns exist in a milieu of diverse sound variations produced by young children (Oller *et al.*, 2010), reflecting the range of available sound-making options. However, speech-like output interfaces with perception and neural-cognitive processing from the beginning. And relevant sound patterns have already been selectively attended to by infants and reinforced by listeners in social contexts (Kuhl, 2009) since birth.

Phonological input from adult speakers is also similar in many ways to the predominant patterns observable in children from the onset of speech-like behaviors in canonical babbling. There are many opportunities in modern languages to observe the maintenance of patterns that are observable in young children in output of adult speakers (Ladefoged and Maddieson, 1986). Phonological theories have assigned these sounds and patterns to unmarked status based on frequency of occurrence of patterns in children and in languages. We would assert that the biological status of young humans, as well as the reliable presence of social connectivity in early development, provides an alternative explanatory, rather than descriptive, source for these complementary patterns in adult and child speakers. They can be viewed as basic to the optimal operation of the biologically based input-storage-output system of human speakers. Languages retain core properties of phonological knowledge and organized behavioral patterns observable in young children. But adult speakers explore diversification in perceptual distinctiveness for maximal diversity in message transmission. These diversifications in service of distinctiveness for sending and receiving more messages are observable in the unique properties of phonological systems in modern languages.

Like self-organization, learning provides an undedicated and powerful mechanism available to the young child in service of mastery over ambient language-specific phonological forms. Young humans are, simply put, "learning sponges" during seminal early periods of phonological acquisition. As with self-organization, learning provides a foundational mechanism for achieving age-appropriate function in a broad set of areas of the child's daily life. Phonology is only one case of the application of learning mechanisms for enhancement of interactivity with the world. Interactivity includes connections with people, objects, and events to learn what they do and how they do it. Within this broader learning milieu, the child must learn how to initiate and respond in myriad social contexts to accomplish the functional phonologically focused goals of knowing and doing.

Diverse types of learning mechanisms are concurrently applied by children to the problem of acquiring phonological knowledge and an organized behavioral repertoire of goal-directed sound patterns. Interactive with the basic design of the system provided through self-organization, learning is a crucial means toward accomplishing refinement of each child's ambient phonological system. The child produces vocalizations within communicative interactions and receives input from communication partners. The socially embedded input refines the base vocal and/or verbal qualities the child is capable of within the heterarchical system we have described. The child and the adult both change and are changed by consistent interactions with one another through learning.

WHAT UNIQUE INSIGHTS DOES EMERGENCE OFFER?

Review of the parameters of emergence becomes an academic exercise if there is no rationale for emergence that matters. Thus, an overarching question becomes, "What is the value of an emergence perspective for enhancing our understanding of phonological acquisition?" We have emphasized across our narrative that embracing emergence reflects a philosophical chasm relative to other available claims about the nature of the acquisition process for phonology. In Chapter 6, we broadly characterized available options as phonological, phonetic, and psycholinguistic. Research programs in all of these academic cultures carry implications for what phonological acquisition is actually about. These implications and the subsequent theoretical claims were noted as being unique and overlapping in some respects. However, they form a critical context for asking the "Why emergence?" question.

Phonological perspectives suggest that some version of a priori mental representations (Chomsky and Halle, 1968), rules, or constraints (see Blevins, 2004, and deLacy, 2007, for reviews) supply the critical focus for understanding acquisition of phonology. These conceptualizations hold in common a singular emphasis on the status of a child's knowledge base driving observable output patterning. Mental constructs underlying the child's behavioral output patterns are parameterized by perceptual access and/or maturation, and described by perceptual processing responses in experimental paradigms or frequency counts of behavioral output in observational paradigms.

Phonetically oriented perspectives emphasize the anatomy and physiological function of peripheral output systems. The nature of the constraints that these physical implementation systems place on phonological output patterns in developing children and in mature adult speakers of languages is a predominant focus of phonetic science. In contrast to phonological theory, phonetic perspectives call attention to phonological systems as they reflect structure and functioning of peripheral body systems for speech production and perception in children and in languages. The philosophical underpinnings of this research culture lie in exploring the potential of a non-arbitrary relationship between structure and function of the human body and what children know and do with that knowledge.

In children, diverse means of characterizing maturing physical mechanisms and observable behavior patterns are evaluated to consider lawful relationships between bodily capacities and observable sound patterns. In adults, the relationship between perception-production processes and phonological patterns is viewed as being retained in the observable phonological patterns in languages (see Lindblom and Maddieson, 1988, for consideration of consonant patterning; de Boer, 2001, regarding vowel systems). The status of underlying long-term phonological knowledge is relatively de-emphasized in consideration of the embodied processes underlying phonological patterns.

Experimental investigations related to the processes by which phonological knowledge is acquired are the dominant topic of psycholinguistic/cognitively oriented proposals. Modelers employ computational approaches to perceptual processing and instantiation of neural knowledge. Infant perception studies test how young infants learn from frequency of input as well as how they evidence development of phonological representation of varied aspects of the phonological system in early periods. Studies of later periods of acquisition explore how dimensions of language (e.g. lexical and phonological) may be interdependent.

Principal emphasis in these approaches is on processing of input, as this input is said to enable the infant and young child to lay down a foundation of phonological knowledge. Relatively less weight is given to considerations of the operations of peripheral production and perceptual systems. In contrast, correspondingly more importance is given to cognitive processing, including memory and attention processes and the mental computations required for acquiring and storing long-term phonological knowledge. Learning from perceptual input is paramount, rather than assumptions of a priori representations or constraints. Production system operations are de-emphasized.

These scholarly traditions give us the contemporary theoretical background for addressing the "Why emergence?" question. They illustrate what types of solutions we may presently have available. A critical review of theory has not directly provided an answer for why we should consider emergence as an alternative for understanding phonological acquisition. The overarching conclusion from consideration of these research traditions and the ways they have considered phonological acquisition is that they are congruent with the "blind man and the elephant" metaphor. In this venerable metaphor, three different blind men perceive uniquely diverse aspects of the elephant as they are in contact with the animal through their sense of touch. Each constructs a partial view. None of these research cultures enables a comprehensive understanding. Scholarly traditions focused on considering the nature of phonological acquisition have considered pieces of the "elephant" in the same way. Research cultures focus on underlying knowledge and rules (phonology), the physiological function of speech-related structures and functions (phonetics), or input processing, storage, and retrieval of output (psycholinguistics). Each gives a varied and partial picture of acquisition. A comprehensive view would be well served by a synthesis across these research traditions. That needed synthesis is at the heart of why a comprehensive focus founded in multiple neural-cognitive, biological, and socially based capacities may offer a new avenue to comprehensive understanding of acquisition of phonology. To better understand the potential contributions of an emergence approach to phonology we need to study speech acquisition more broadly and in different contexts.

GENERAL-PURPOSE CAPACITIES

As we have evaluated the "Why emergence?" question, a complementary issue accompanies the "blind man and the elephant" reductionism that is inherent in present theoretical proposals. Emergence includes the overarching philosophical orientation that general-purpose capacities and mechanisms available to the young human can be marshaled for phonological acquisition. As we reviewed in Chapters 4 and 5, these general purpose capacities are subsumed within the biological, social, and neural-cognitive dimensions of human abilities. As well, interaction capacities and the extrinsic input available to the child serve acquisition of general knowledge and behavioral pattern complexity, in addition to scaffolding language acquisition. While contemporary approaches and the corresponding research agendas pursued incorporate these issues to varying degrees, they do not presently emphasize the general nature of these capacities as they are implemented in service of phonological acquisition.

Lack of consideration of the potential for broad-spectrum capacities to be used for special purposes in language acquisition cedes proposals on the nature of the acquisition to being a special-purpose ability that is pre-specified genetically. While the end product, human language, is undoubtedly specialized and unique to humans, the foundations and the processes by which it develops do not have to be based on a language-dedicated system. Indeed, that type of solution lacks parsimony as well as congruence with the overlaid nature of the biological, social, and cognitive foundations of complex behavioral patterns and knowledge in humans.

Philosophical constructs underlying emergence suggest evaluation of a proposal that domain-specific phonological knowledge and complex phonological behavioral patterns may be acquired using available general-purpose capacities. Thus, general capacities are marshaled for precise ends. While this view of emergence is more consistent with phonetic and psycholinguistic approaches than current phonological theory, both of the former focus on single dimensions of the complex system we have proposed. Phonetic theory is centered on peripheral system operations, and psycholinguistic theory largely considers perceptual processing leading to neural-cognitive instantiation of phonological knowledge.

THE ROLE OF FUNCTION

A corollary to the lack of strong emphasis on a general-purpose foundation for phonological acquisition is acknowledgment of the functional pressures to acquire phonology. Emergence conceptualizations are embedded in a foundational principal that language (in this case, phonology) is directed toward supporting optimal function of the human organism within the environment. In Chapter 4 we reviewed data supporting the primacy of biological and social capacities enabling the young infant to function optimally across the first year to year and a half of her life. A critical look at this data indicates that the infant's development of perceptual, neural, and vocal systems facilitates consistent connections related to survival as a neotenous organism in this early period. Far from "poverty of the stimulus," the infant experiences a rich set of environmental inputs available to guide her own powerful biological and interaction capacities in growth toward independent function within her environment.

Diverse research paradigms have provided data to converge on the generalization that both the infant's capacities and the social scaffolding present from birth are functional for survival and for learning critical pieces of information to maintain viability in the world. Using these dimensions of a complex system that operates in a variety of domains, the child can also acquire knowledge and behaviors relevant to starting her own unique process of mastering ambient-language phonological patterns.

As we found in Chapter 5, data on later periods of phonological acquisition suggest interactive functioning of language systems with a shifting emphasis to implementation of learning mechanisms and the primacy of cognitive processing and storage of phonological information. In this later period of acquisition, the child masters perceptual and production system operations for producing intelligible phonological forms of her ambient language. The neural-cognitive substrate for storing and retrieving the phonological component of linguistically oriented communication grows exponentially to respond to the functional goal of ambient language mastery across this period. At the same time, these capacities are undergirding growth in comprehension and behavioral expressions across a variety of domains of function in the child's life.

Lack of emphasis on the function of phonological knowledge and behavioral patterns is embedded in differing ways in linguistic, phonetic, and psycholinguistic research cultures. None of these traditions emphasize the potential importance to the child of the functioning of the phonological system in characterizing its acquisition. As an example, considerations of the role of input, which are of increasing importance in many characterizations, are related to the frequency of input of ambient-language phonological structures, not more generally to the function of parent–child interactions in facilitating and tuning the child's function in her environment by means of a growing phonological output repertoire and understanding of input that is coded using those phonological patterns (Kuhl *et al.*, 2003; Brooks and Meltzoff, 2008; Goldstein *et al.*, 2003; Kinzler *et al.*, 2007).

NATURE–NURTURE

A comprehensive emergence proposal also has the conceptual scaffolding to integrate both nature and nurture more fully within a system-based theory. Emergence proposals imply a neutralization of the sharp divide between potentially innate capacities and the role of the environment. Neutralization of boundaries between nature and nurture is a legitimate outgrowth of a heterarchical and dynamic system enabled by social feedback. Biologically motivated child-intrinsic capacities (nature) are central to phonological acquisition. However, these capacities – while absolutely necessary – are not sufficient to drive the emergence of phonology. Aspects of acquisition associated with nurture, including ambient-language input and general aspects of cultural implementation for phonological forms in listening and speaking from extrinsic models, are also necessary.

DEVELOPMENTAL STAGES AND INDIVIDUAL VARIATIONS

One issue that has created theoretical tension in characterizing the process of phonological acquisition is the importance of group trends versus individual and unique paths. An emergence perspective can encompass the issue of developmental stages common to most children acquiring phonology, as well as child-individual differences in acquisition trajectories. In particular, the mechanism of self-organization connotes a set of largely common intrinsic physiological and social properties in the first year of life. Additionally, stage descriptions of production output behaviors and development of sound system-related perceptual capacities have also emphasized commonalities. We have reviewed these well-described milestones in Chapter 4. However, these common properties (e.g. growth of the respiratory system toward a more mature configuration; "cooing" and "gooing," and "raspberry" vocalizations at 4–6 months, followed by the onset of rhythmic syllables) are observable in infants within a widely varied set of behaviors on a day-to-day basis. At 7–8 months, rhythmic, speech-like syllables emerge reliably in typically developing infants based on a more mature neural substrate enabling vocal rhythmicity. But these syllable-like vocalizations also occur within a diverse milieu of less mature sound types within individual children on a day-to-day basis, implicating a concurrent substrate of individual variation.

We have noted in Chapter 5 that in subsequent periods of acquisition after the first 12 months, the seminal influence of learning begins to dominate in understanding the emergence of phonological knowledge and behaviors. Learning is evident from the child's perceptual and cognitive readiness for acquiring and beginning the process of storing sound system properties. It is also evident from the types of perceptual, cognitive, and production behaviors that can be observed with increasingly sophisticated research paradigms requiring active child participation (e.g. looking while listening).

This "learning heavy" phase of phonological acquisition can be considered a stage as well as a potential site for flowering of individual differences in child profiles. At the behavioral level, milestones for acquisition of consonant aspects of the sound system are widely available, at least for English-learning children. These behavioral milestone approaches emphasize stages or common timetables for acquisition. However, normative milestones for consonants exist in a relative vacuum of corresponding information about vowels, or phonotactic or prosodic properties of the phonological system. Phonotactic structure refers to the ways that sounds can be combined in syllables, and syllables into words (Ladefoged and Johnston, 2011). A sound structure that is phonotactically legal in English (e.g. /st/ in the syllable-initial position or /rd/ in syllable-final position) is not permissible in the Nahuatl language (Maddieson, 1984). Nahuatl, on the other hand, permits sound combinations that are not legal in English (e.g. /tl/ in the word *tlascal*, tortilla). Languages also vary in their phonotactic word structure preferences. English and Chinese represent languages with a predominance of one- or two-syllable words. In contrast, multisyllabic words are more common in Spanish, Russian, and Greek.

Normative information about the acquisition milestones for sounds and phonotactic structures is not available for most languages other than English. So at present, it is not known whether stage-related milestones can characterize consonant acquisition in most other languages or, indeed, whether stages are characteristic of other aspects of phonological patterning. As with earlier periods of acquisition, emergence conceptualizations can encompass both common and stable trends and individual departures as valid aspects of this period of acquisition of the sound system.

Within the emergence conceptualization we have been considering, both common trends and individual differences may be seen as characterizing emergence of complexity. The general notion of "both," not "either–or," is consistent with the complex system conceptualization of emergence. In considering this proposition, it should be noted that stage theories have provided information as to the sequence, but not the process, by which development unfolds. Often, the process is not linear. If development evolves as a nonlinear process with periods of acceleration and deceleration, then linear statistical methods such as linear regression analysis might not accurately capture the estimation of growth. Rather, nonlinear statistical methods such as growth curve modeling (Bryk and Raudenbush, 1992; Hox, 1995; Singer, 1998) and the general estimating equation (Horton and Lipsitz, 1999; Zeger *et al.*, 1988; Liang and Zeger, 1986) may better match the nonlinear aspects of developmental growth. Also, significant individual differences may require the addition of multilevel modeling (Bryk and Raudenbush, 1992) that allows the examination of both general trends and individual differences over time. These contemporary quantitative methods enable a means to encompass both common trends and individual trajectories into characterizing the nature of emergence of phonological properties.

DEVELOPMENTAL DIFFERENCES IN ACQUISITION

The case of developmental differences in acquisition of phonology has provided another potential site for considering a "Why emergence?" proposal. The heterogeneous components that we propose as enabling emergence suggest an avenue to understand how within-child differences in the presence and operation of intrinsic and extrinsic system factors can account for unique acquisition trajectories in children with communication disorders of different origins.

Studies of children within communication disorders have often focused on developmental differences in single domains. Within the language domain, studies of speech development, vocabulary development, and grammatical development are largely conceptualized and analyzed independently of one another in children with clinically relevant differences in acquisition profiles. Studies reviewed in Chapter 5 indicate a different insight; semantic and phonological development may more likely be interdependent in development. In the physical implementation dimension, phonological acquisition profiles of children with cleft palate (structural production system deficit), and others with hearing loss (perceptual deficit), provide relatively clear-cut examples of multifactorial influences on developmental outcomes. Both speech and language may be delayed in children with either cleft palate or hearing impairment. But given differences in perception and production system capacities, do speech production output patterns provide the same support for vocabulary acquisition observed when children have a compromised speech and language repertoire due to structural oral-motor constraints in cleft palate, than when children have a compromised repertoire due to perceptual constraints with a differing auditory history? What happens when there are cognitive constraints in addition to perceptual or production constraints, as in the case of children born with Down syndrome who are hearing impaired, or have large tongues and thus structural differences, as well? By systematically identifying broad areas of deficit to characterize speech and language profiles in children with differences in speech production, perception, neural-cognition, and social components of development, we can gain insight into how factors in the dynamic system interact when some part or parts of the system are impaired or non-functional. In particular, these more comprehensive questions about the bases of speech and language deficits are consistent with considering acquisition of phonology as an example of emergent complexity when there are unique and differing profiles of child-intrinsic biological, social, and cognitive-neural foundations.

To move out of the domain of child-intrinsic biological capacities, from an emergence perspective one might ask about the impact of differences in interactional capacities on acquiring phonology. In particular, how are joint-attention, turn-taking, and perspective-taking influenced in children who are significantly impaired in acquiring phonology based on known etiologies of difference? For example, what differences in phonological acquisition profiles are associated with the social interaction differences observable in children with autism spectrum disorder (ASD) (Shriberg *et al.*, 2011)? And how do their unique perceptual processing and neural-cognitive profiles complicate this question? Persistent speech disorders have recently been identified as a growing concern in children identified with ASD, suggesting that differences in one or several factors unique to ASD may also contribute to a higher than expected incidence in complications related to the phonological component of their language abilities as well.

Considering the extrinsic dimension of this complex system relative to emergence, what is the quality and quantity of extrinsically available phonological input to these children? How is this input similar to and/or potentially quite different from that received by typically developing children? Studies of varying types of children with developmental language differences have indicated significant effects on parent input style inherent in parent–child interactions. These input differences could be viewed from an emergence perspective as interfering with feedback between extrinsic and intrinsic aspects of the complex system.

CROSS-LANGUAGE CULTURAL DIFFERENCES

The case of cross-language differences in phonological acquisition is also a potential site for considering a positive impact of complex system conceptualizations on understanding of acquisition trajectories and outcomes. Across cultures, young children acquire their ambient language phonologies based on intact intrinsic and similar biological and social capacities, but different interactional styles. Spanish-learning children in Mexico do not initiate topics, but respond to adult initiations. Inuit-learning children in Alaska are not rewarded for verbal interactions. Quichua-learning children are not responded to in the early-word-learning period until they have "something to say" (Gildersleeve-Neumann, 2001). Children who spend time strapped to their mothers, versus children who grow up in daycare settings, do not have the same opportunities to integrate visual and auditory information. These cultural interaction styles are robust for supporting emergence of phonology in differing cultural circumstances across these diverse phonological systems. Integrating these cultural styles into a view of the nature of acquisition requires an incorporation of function into conceptualizing the scope of what young children must learn as they master the ability to deploy the phonology of their language. Phonology is a tool founded in child-internal capacities and external use as well as a computational system. Emergence views imply a broader view of what must be acquired to successfully master functional use of phonological knowledge and behaviors.

Exposure to More Than One Language

Another area where an emergence conceptualization may contribute to a more comprehensive view of the phonological acquisition process is acquisition in bilingual children. These children present a unique opportunity to explore emergence. They need to integrate different cultural interaction styles for successful use of their ambient language(s). In addition, the nature of more than one set of ambient-language inputs is a central site of diversity. Bilingual children receive extrinsic input from two or more languages in varying degrees related to the array of languages spoken to them consistently by communication partners. Relative to these circumstances of their daily input, children who acquire two (or more) languages simultaneously are challenged because they must learn more than one phonological system concurrently. These phonological systems contain both shared and unshared features (e.g. consonant place characteristics, number of vowels, and phonotactic rules for each input language). The child must map the unique features onto two (or more) different languages to understand and use them.

Simultaneous bilinguals are children exposed to two or more languages from the onset of language learning. Studies of relationships between speech- and language-acquisition trajectories in these young bilingual children can provide information about the role of information demands on the pace and unique quality of phonological emergence. Such studies would be logical complements to studies of cross-linguistic acquisition where the complexity of the phonological repertoire and the complexity of the language vary in children learning one language.

Within the scope of bilingual studies, the sequential bilingual offers another avenue to consideration of the value of an emergence perspective to a comprehensive view of the phonological acquisition process. Many sequential bilinguals start to learn a second language in the early school years or later. These individuals have relatively more mature speech production and perceptual systems when they begin the process of acquiring a second language. They have already experienced the growth of a neural-cognitive phonological system for acquiring, storing, and retrieving phonological knowledge. Consideration of how children who already have knowledge of a phonological system and the ability to produce relatively complex speech sounds learn to master a new phonology can enable insights into the interaction between the limitations in speech production abilities characteristic of infancy and acquisition of a phonological system in more cognitively and socially mature individuals. The relative contribution of a more mature cognitive knowledge base of how phonological patterns occur in a language may give a different picture of the course of acquisition than in the case of the young simultaneous bilingual who does not yet have a knowledge base to start the acquisition process for two languages.

WHAT ARE SOME APPLICATIONS OF AN EMERGENCE PROPOSAL?

A complex system proposal for the phonological component of language can impact some non-acquisition-related questions as well. These are the larger questions concerning the origins of complex knowledge that have been posed both historically and in contemporary scientific inquiry. These questions illuminate the bigger picture into which human language acquisition and, more precisely, phonological acquisition may properly be contextualized. The heterogeneous and functional basis for emergence conceptualizations enables a broad-based metric for considering these questions, and may suggest some options for addressing them fruitfully.

THE LONGER TIME SCALE OF HUMAN LANGUAGE CAPACITIES

The ethnographer Nikko Tinbergen (Tinbergen, 1963) has suggested four questions that should be addressed comprehensively in characterizing the evolution of the human language capacity. One of those questions concerns ontogeny in modern organisms, including human infants. In Tinbergen's terms, the ethnographer needs to ask how the young organism's behavior changes with age, what early experiences are necessary for the behavior to be manifest, and which developmental steps and environmental factors play a role in ontogenesis. Modern children's acquisition of phonology potentially enables a short time-scale view across ontogeny of the phylogeny of human language capacities in Tinbergen's conceptualization.

Human infants' intrinsic capacities and general-purpose enabling mechanisms mature on an extended developmental timetable when compared with other species. This extended timetable for development of adult complexity is characterized as neoteny. Since the process of development is extended in human infants relative to other modern species, the human ontogenetic process affords an opportunity for examining emergence of a complex system when it is in its simplest early phases. This examination is consistent with Tinbergen's conceptualization that ontogeny can motivate understanding of the phylogenetic origins of language. Emergence conceptualizations of the process of phonological acquisition are consistent with consideration of ontogeny in questions related to the phylogeny of language and may prove to be a fruitful framework.

GENETIC BASES OF PHONOLOGY

Contemporary researchers have addressed the potential for a genetic basis for language faculties in modern humans (see Tomblin, 2003, for a review). To date, this ongoing question about the bases of speech and language capacities has not been resolved. Present research methods have largely encompassed family-based epidemiological studies of disordered populations, including children and families with specific language impairment (O'Brien et al., 2003), autism (Tomblin et al., 2003), and childhood apraxia of speech (Shriberg et al., 2008). Regions of chromosomes shown as being associated with reading and language disorders have also been linked to speech sound disorders (e.g. Sices et al., 2007). Data and implications have been limited to consideration of the adequacy of speech and language expression (or phenotype) within families considered to show transmission of speech and language differences (e.g. Tomblin et al., 2009). Conclusions have been based on identification of clinical patterns of behavioral output in comparison with molecular genetic data analyses.

In the context of the emergence proposal we have explored here, one question that must be addressed within contemporary research into genetic bases of speech and language is the heterogeneity of determination of speech and language capacities proposed. At present, genetic studies are limited to characterizing goal-directed speech behaviors of individuals expressing clinical phenotypes within families. This conceptualization is strongly related to defining speech and language as a computational system rather than more broadly as a functional tool. Consideration of underlying physical, neural-cognitive, and social capacities proposed as co-determinates of phonological acquisition have not been addressed. Inquiries into genetic relationships with phenotypes for cognitive processing capacities, including memory, storage, and retrieval for phonological forms, are not available for these children. And considerations of how children may process input from the extrinsic environment, considered to be central to understanding the process of speech and language acquisition, have not been addressed. Presumably, these features of the process of acquiring phonology would also be of interest for their genetic bases as well. Also unresolved is the role of issues other than genetic factors, implying that genetics may be a sole determinate of speech and language capacities. A more comprehensive view of determinates of speech and language acquisition could lead potentially to a more solid foundation for suggestions of a genetic basis for language in the future. But the definitional boundaries on language constitute a strong barrier at present to moving genetics of language research programs toward emergence conceptualizations.

BOUNDARY VALUES FOR PHONOLOGY AND HUMAN LANGUAGE

Cross-species considerations relative to boundaries for language or, more generally, boundary values between humans and other species at a general level, constitute another relevant topic that could be well-served by the conceptual structure of an emergence proposal. One of the ongoing dialogues in understanding language is the kinds of characteristics that can be used to define what is uniquely human. An emergence proposal enables consideration of questions related to intrinsic–extrinsic differences in body systems, capacities for interaction, and consideration of social and cultural dimensions of input, as well as sound pattern frequencies. In this regard, Savage-Rumbaugh's extensive studies of bonobos (Savage-Rumbaugh *et al.*, 2001) have emphasized the effects of the extrinsic environment as well as the function of culturally embedded communication in learning, components that are often missing in studies of phonological acquisition. Views of animal learning relative to human language acquisition are, like questions about genetic bases of language, unresolved. The larger issues of boundary values for language, especially whether it emerges from domain-general properties of the organism, or is a specialized human modular capacity evidenced by genetically determined, maturational processes, remains a seminal issue for science. Considerations of this dimension could be well-served by the complex systems framework of an emergence proposal.

WHERE DO WE GO FROM HERE?

We have proposed some topics where a complex system-emergence perspective can enhance our conceptualization of issues that have been the subject of long-term interest to scholars from a variety of scientific disciplines. Our review of contemporary theories and their associated research cultures and data indicates strongly that scientific research cultures have tested only some aspects of an emergence perspective. Within their own conceptualizations of the nature of phonological acquisition, scholars have not evaluated tenets of emergence comprehensively. The real challenge for testing emergence as a potential solution to understanding how phonology is acquired is to marshal both new and existing paradigms to ask more comprehensive questions than are presently characteristic of research cultures in this area.

Computer and statistical analysis of comprehensive child databases as they may compare with ambient-language data across diverse languages can be used to consider a variety of the dimensions of emergence. The new PhonBank database generated by Brian MacWhinney and Yvan Rose as a part of CHILDES is based on donations of data from scholars working in a variety of languages. PhonBank makes large databases on these languages available to scholars to test hypotheses. This open database can enable evaluation of questions about child-intrinsic and extrinsic environmental influences that have not been easily accessible to scholars from a broad base of disciplines due to the overheads of gathering and processing child data. Most of the corpora available on PhonBank have been gathered in naturalistic settings in a variety of language environments, so that parent-caregiver interactions within their functional-cultural context are also accessible.

To achieve these goals, modeling that accounts for speech production in the context of language will help. We need to consider speech acquisition in the context of larger speech units (i.e. greater focus on words, sentences, and connected speech production). Questions related to the emergence of phonological properties in the context of other aspects of language including the lexical, semantic, syntactic, and morphological, must be tested as well. At the same time, we need to work on understanding the acquisition of speech in the context of communication. A step forward in that direction will include considering how speech is acquired and used in the context of change in language knowledge (content form and use all are potential influences) and cognitive change.

In addition to corpora analyses, new methods of accessing perceptual and neural-cognitive capacities have centered on children's behavioral and neuro-physical responses in experimental settings. These methods can enable consideration of how phonological knowledge is acquired, stored, and deployed in varied circumstances of phonological acquisition. As we have noted, typical development, as well as diverse circumstances of cultural and language learning difference and clinical differences in children's profiles as they acquire phonology, can teach us a lot. In these diverse circumstances, the ways in which components of a complex system might operate as the system is intact in typically developing children, and as it is altered in different ways in children with diverse types of developmental differences, can be illuminated.

New paradigms that can be used to gain insight into the ways that speech interacts with other aspects of language and cognition include speed of processing tasks. As an example, one promising paradigm for evaluating the automaticity of phonological representation in young humans is the "looking while listening" paradigm. In this type of experiment, children hear speech and see visual stimuli on a split computer screen. Researchers track how long it takes them to orient toward the corresponding scene. Shorter orienting time suggests that the speech signal has been processed more efficiently. A variant of looking while listening uses "gated" speech. By providing only part of the phonological input, it is possible to test the strength of representation of other parts of the input. This experimental approach can help tease apart the roles of frequency in the input versus the role of practice, for example.

Eye-tracking paradigms use computer software and hardware to track eye movements over a visual field in response to stimuli. In contrast to work with speed of processing that focuses on how fast a response is made, eye tracking can be used to gain insight into the ways that variation in the speech input impacts processing time and accuracy. Eye tracking is a tool that could enable researchers to evaluate how data about frequency and input impact children's comprehension.

Studies using event related potentials (ERP) can be used to explore the nature and extent of neural representation of speech or auditory input. Event related potentials are measurements of brain responses to perceptually based stimuli. Their use is particularly appealing for use with young children because of their non-invasive nature, in that the child can actually talk while being tested. ERP studies can give us insights into the time course and map of brain activation related to variations in speech stimuli as they are related to language input over time.

These corpora and experimental methods provide examples of contemporary options for considering the nature of phonological acquisition from the diverse perspectives required to evaluate emergence. They illustrate only a sample of the rich new array of paradigms available to ask needed questions for evaluating an emergence proposal. This is a key step to evaluating emergence given that evidence for the two-way interactions that characterize this approach can only be tested if we consider multiple dimensions of production and processing

A FINAL WORD

The larger scope question we have considered in this narrative was proposed very early in the history of philosophy: Where does knowledge come from? As we saw at the beginning of our narrative, this question has been addressed in a variety of ways across a long span of scholarly inquiry. Our answer, centered on the problem of phonological acquisition, has been to propose a multifaceted approach wherein individual internal factors and external environmental factors are necessary for acquiring complex phonological knowledge and action. Knowledge is embodied, as the neural-cognitive system that stores phonological knowledge and the capacities of the body for perception and action to deploy it are interdependent. These essential components of a complex system emergence proposal present an alternative to earlier philosophical renderings on the nature of phonological acquisition that have largely investigated single factors either inside or outside individuals to explicate the origins of complex capacities.

We have, moreover, suggested that the phonological component of language illustrates the human child's repertoire of tools that enable optimal function in the world around her. This assertion is at the heart of emergence proposals. It also challenges a view of phonology as primarily an abstract computational system without a demonstrable tie to supporting function of the young child in her environment. Function-based proposals require that the complex system encompasses the ways that the child grows in using available resources to gain independence in her surroundings through the vehicle of phonological capacities.

An emergence view asserts that phonological acquisition is a dynamic and active process. It is a process founded within operation of a complex physical, neural-cognitive, and social system. The system operates based on shared domain-general resources that support diverse areas of function for humans. It serves as an embodied tool for achieving optional function by human speakers and listeners rather than an abstract computational system. Such a conceptual stance on understanding the nature of phonological acquisition has profound consequences for what we study and how we study it. Put another way, what you see is what you look for. We are embracing a broader view as the eventual avenue to valid and comprehensive understanding of phonological acquisition as emerging from interactive human capacities operating as a complex system.

References

Abitz, M., Damgaard-Nielsen, R., Jones, E. G., Laursen, H., Graem, N., and Pakkenberg, B. (2007). Excess of neurons in the human newborn mediodorsal thalamus compared with that of the adult. *Cerebral Cortex*, 17(11), 2573–8.

Abler, W. L. (1989). On the particulate principle of self-diversifying systems. *Journal of Social and Biological Structures*, 12(1), 1–13.

Acevedo, M. A. (1993). Development of Spanish consonants in preschool children. *Journal of Childhood Communication Disorders*, 15(2), 9–15.

Adams, A.-M., and Gathercole, S. E. (1995). Phonological working memory and speech production in preschool children. *Journal of Speech and Hearing Research*, 38(2), 403–14.

Alcock, K. J., Passingham, R. E., Watkins, K. E., and Vargha-Khadem, F. (2000). Oral dyspraxia in inherited speech and language impairment and acquired dysphasia. *Brain and Language*, 75, 17–33.

Amayreh, M. M., and Dyson, A. T. (1998). The acquisition of Arabic consonants. *Journal of Speech Language and Hearing Research*, 41(3), 642–53.

Archangeli, D., and Pulleyblank, D. (1994). *Grounded Phonology*. Cambridge, MA: MIT Press.

Arnold, K., and Zuberbuhler, K. (2006). Language evolution: Semantic combinations in primate calls. *Nature*, 441(7091), 303. doi: 441303a.

Aslin, R. N. (2007). What's in a look? *Developmental Science*, 10, 48–53.

Aslin, R. N., Saffran, J., and Newport, E. L. (1998). Computation of conditional probability statistics by 8-month-old infants. *Psychological Science*, 9(4), 321–4.

Baird, J. A., and Baldwin, D. A. (2001). Making sense of human behavior: Action parsing and intentional inference. In B. F. Malle, L. J. Moses and D. A. Baldwin (eds), *Intentions and Intentionality: Foundations of Social Cognition* (pp. 193–206). Cambridge, MA: MIT Press.

Baldwin, D. A. (1995). Understanding the link between joint attention and language. In C. Moore and P. J. Dunham (eds), *Joint Attention: Its Origin and Role in Development* (pp. 131–58). Hillsdale, NJ: Lawrence Erlbaum.

Baldwin, D. A., and Markman, E. M. (1989). Establishing word–object relations: A first step. *Child Development*, 60, 381–98.

Baldwin, D. A., Andersson, A., Saffran, J., and Meyer, M. (2008). Segmenting dynamic human action via statistical structure. *Cognition*, 106(3), 1382–1407. doi: S0010-0277(07)00183-7.

Bannard, C., Lieven, E., and Tomasello, M. (2009). Modeling children's early grammatical knowledge. *Proceedings of the National Academy of Sciences*, 106(41), 17284–9.

Barlow, S. M. (1998). Real time modulation of speech-orofacial motor performance by means of motion sense. *Journal of Communication Disorders*, 31(6), 511–34.

Barlow, S. M., Finan, D. S., and Andreatta, R. (1997). Neuronal group selection and emergent orofacial motor control: Towards a unifying theory of speech development. In W. Hulstijn, H. F. M. Peters and P. H. H. M. van Lieshout (eds), *Speech Production: Motor Control, Brain Research, and Fluency Disorders* (pp. 529–46). Amsterdam: Elsevier.

Barr, R., Rovee-Collier, C., and Campanella, J. (2005). Retrieval protracts deferred imitation by 6-month-olds. *Infancy*, 7(3), 263–83.

Bates, E., and MacWhinney, B. (1988). What is functionalism? *Papers and Reports on Child Language Development*, 27, 137–52.

Bates, E., Camaioni, L., and Volterra, V. (1975). The acquisition of performatives prior to speech. *Merrill-Palmer Quarterly*, 21(3), 205–26.

Bates, E., Benigni, L., Bretherton, I., Camioni, L., and Volterra, V. (1978). *The Emergence of Symbols: Cognition and Communication in Infancy*. New York: Academic Press.

Bauer, P. J. (2002). Early memory development. In U. Goswami (ed.), *Blackwell Handbook of Childhood Cognitive Development* (pp. 127–46). Malden, MA: Blackwell.

Beckman, M. E., and Edwards, J. (2000). The ontogeny of phonological categories and the primacy of lexical learning in linguistic development. *Child Development*, 71, 240–9.

Bernhardt, B., and Stemberger, J. P. (1998). *Handbook of Phonological Development: From the Perspective of Constraint-Based Nonlinear Phonology*. San Diego, CA: Academic Press.

Bernstein, N. (1967). *The Coordination and Regulation of Movements*. Oxford: Pergammon Press.

Bernstein-Ratner, N. (1984). Phonological rule usage in mother–child speech. *Journal of Phonetics*, 12, 245–54.

Bernstein-Ratner, N. (1986). Durational cues which mark clause boundaries in mother–child speech. *Journal of Phonetics*, 14, 303–9.

Berthier, N. E., Rosenstein, M. T., and Barto, A. G. (2005). Approximant optimal control as a model for motor learning. *Psychological Review*, 112, 329–46.

Best, C. C., and McRoberts, G. W. (2003). Infant perception of non-native consonant contrasts that adults assimilate in different ways. *Language and Speech*, 46(2–3), 183–216. doi: 10.1177/00238309030460020701.

Best, C. T. (1993). Emergence of language-specific constraints in perception of native and non-native speech: A window on early phonological development. In B. Boysson-Bardies, P. W. Jusczyk, F. P. MacNeilage, J. Morton and S. Schonen (eds), *Developmental Neurocognition: Speech and Face Processing in the First Year of Life*. Dordrecht: Kluwer Academic Publishers.

Best, C. T. (1994). The emergence of native-language phonological influences in infants: A perceptual assimilation model. In J. C. Goodman and H. C. Nusbaum (eds), *The Development of Speech Perception*. Cambridge, MA: MIT Press.

Best, C. T., McRoberts, G. W., and Sithole, H. (1988). The phonological basis of perceptual loss for non-native contrasts: Maintenance of discrimination among Zulu clicks by English-speaking adults and infants. *Journal of Experimental Psychology: Human Perception and Performance*, 14, 207–40.

Best, C. T., McRoberts, G. W., LaFleur, R., and Silver-Isenstadt, J. (1995). Divergent developmental patterns for infants' perception of two nonnative consonant contrasts. *Infant Behavior and Development*, 18(3), 339–50.

Bishop, D. V. M., Laws, G., Adams, C., and Norbury, C. F. (2006). High heritability of speech and language impairments in 6-year-old twins demonstrated using parent and teacher report. *Behavior Genetics*, 36(2), 173–84.

Blamey, P. J., Barry, J. G., and Jacq, P. (2001). Phonetic inventory development in young cochlear implant users 6 years postoperation. *Journal of Speech Language and Hearing Research*, 44(1), 73–9.

Blevins, J. (2004). *Evolutionary Phonology: The Emergence of Sound Patterns*. New York: Cambridge University Press.

Bloom, K., D'Odorico, L., and Beaumont, S. (1993). Adult preferences for syllabic vocalizations: Generalizations to parity and native language. *Infant Behavior and Development*, 16(1), 109–20.

Bloom, K., Russell, A., and Wassenberg, K. (1987). Turn taking affects the quality of infant vocalizations. *Journal of Child Language*, 14(2), 211–27.

Bloom, L., and Lahey, M. (1968). *Language Development and Language Disorders*. New York: John Wiley & Sons.

Blount, B. G., and Padgug, E. J. (1977). Prosodic, paralinguistic, and interactional features in parent–child speech: English and Spanish. *Journal of Child Language*, 4(1), 67–86. doi: 10.1017/s0305000900000489.

Bock, K. (1982). Toward a cognitive psychology of syntax: Information processing contributions to sentence formulation. *Psychological Review*, 89(1), 1–47.

Boden, M. (2006). *Mind as Machine*. Oxford: Oxford University Press.

Boë, L.-J., and Maeda, S. (1997). Modélisation de la croissance du conduit vocal: Espace vocalique des nouveaux-nés et des adultes. Conséquences pour l'ontogenèse et la phylogenèse. *Journées d'Études Linguistiques: La voyelle dans tous ces états*, 98–105.

Boersma, P. (1998). *Functional Phonology: Formalizing the Interactions between Articulatory and Perceptual Drives*. The Hague: Holland Academic Graphics.

Boersma, P., and Hamann, S. (2009). Cue constraints and their interactions in phonological perception and production. In P. Boersma and S. Hamann (eds), *Phonology in Perception* (pp. 55–110). Berlin: Mouton de Gruyter.

Boersma, P., and Hayes, B. (2001). Empirical tests of the gradual learning algorithm. *Linguistic Inquiry*, 32(1), 45–86.

Boersma, P., and Levelt, C. (2000). Gradual constraint-ranking learning algorithm predicts acquisition order. Paper presented at the Child Language Research Forum 30, Stanford, CA.

Bolhuis, J., and Gahr, M. (2006). Neural mechanisms of birdsong memory. *Nature Reviews Neuroscience*, 7, 347–57.

Boliek, C. A., Hixon, T. J., Watson, P. J., and Morgan, W. J. (1996). Vocalization and breathing during the first year of life. *Journal of Voice*, 10(1), 1–22. doi: S0892-1997(96)80015-4.

Boliek, C. A., Hixon, T. J., Watson, P. J., and Jones, P. B. (2009). Refinement of speech breathing in healthy 4–6 year old children. *Journal of Speech, Language, and Hearing Research*, 52(4), 990–1007.

Bornstein, M. H., and Tamis-LeMonda, C. S. (1990). Activities and interactions of mothers and their firstborn infants in the first six months of life: Covariation, stability, continuity, correspondence, and prediction. *Child Development*, 61(4), 1206–17.

Bosch, L., and Sebastián-Galles, N. (1997). Native-language recognition abilities in 4-month-old infants from monolingual and bilingual environments. *Cognition*, 65(1), 33–69.

Bosch, L., and Sebastián-Galles, N. (2003). Simultaneous bilingualism and the perception of a language-specific vowel contrast in the first year of life. *Language and Speech*, 46(2), 217–43.

Brooks, R., and Meltzoff, A. N. (2008). Infant gaze following and pointing predict accelerated vocabulary growth through two years of age: A longitudinal, growth curve modeling study. *Journal of Child Language*, 35(1), 207–20.

Browman, K., and Goldstein, L. (1990). Gestural specification using dynamically-defined articulatory structures. *Journal of Phonetics*, 18, 299–320.

Brown, C. M., and Hagoort, P. (eds) (1999). *The Neurocognition of Language*. New York: Oxford University Press.

Brownman, C. P., and Goldstein, L. (1992). Articulatory phonology: An overview. *Phonetica*, 49, 155–80.

Bruner, J. S. (1973). Organization of early skilled action. *Child Development*, 44, 1–11.

Bruner, J. S. (1983). *Child's Talk: Learning to Use Language*. New York: Norton.

Bryk, A. S., and Raudenbush, S. W. (1992). *Hierarchical Linear Models: Applications and Data Analysis Methods*. Newbury Park, CA: Sage Publications.

Buder, E. H., Chorna, L. B., Oller, D. K., and Robinson, R. B. (2008). Vibratory regime classification of infant phonation. *Journal of Voice*, 22(5), 553–64. doi: S0892-1997(07)00002-1.

Budwig, N. (1995). *A Developmental-Functionalist Approach to Child Language*. Mahwah, NJ: Lawrence Erlbaum.

Burns, T. C., Yoshida, K. A., Hill, K., and Werker, J. F. (2007). The development of phonetic representation in bilingual and monolingual infants. *Applied Psycholinguistics*, 28(3), 455–74.

Burt, J. M., O'Loghlen, A. L., Templeton, C. N., Campbell, S. E., and Beecher, M. D. (2007). Assessing the importance of social factors in bird song learning: A test using computer-simulated tutors. *Ethology*, 113(10), 917–25.

Butterworth, G. (1995). Origins of mind in perception and action. In C. Moore and P. J. Dunham (eds), *Joint Attention: Its Origins and Role in Development* (pp. 29–40). Hillsdale, NJ: Lawrence Erlbaum.

Bybee, J. L. (2010). *Language, Usage and Cognition*. Cambridge and New York: Cambridge University Press.

Camazine, S., Deneubourg, J.-L., Franks, N., Sneyd, J., Theraulaz, G., and Bonabeau, E. (2001). *Self-Organization in Biological Systems*. Princeton, NJ: Princeton University Press.

Carey, S., and Bartlett, E. (1978). Acquiring a single new word. *Proceedings of the Stanford Child Language Conference*, 15, 17–29.

Carpenter, M., Nagell, K., and Tomasello, M. (1998). Social cognition, joint attention, and communicative competence from 9 to 15 months of age. *Monographs of the Society for Research in Child Development*, 21, 315–30.

Chapman, K. L., Hardin-Jones, M., and Halter, K. A. (2003). The relationship between early speech and later speech and language performance for children with cleft lip and palate. *Clinical Linguistics and Phonetics*, 17(3), 173–97.

Chapman, K. L., Hardin-Jones, M., Schulte, J., and Halter, K. A. (2001). Vocal development of 9-month-old babies with cleft palate. *Journal of Speech Language and Hearing Research,* 44(6), 1268–83.

Chapman, K. L., Hardin-Jones, M. A., Goldstein, J. A., Halter, K. A., Havlik, R. J., and Schulte, J. (2008). Timing of palatal surgery and speech outcome. *Cleft Palate Craniofacial Journal,* 45(3), 297–308. doi: 06-244.

Charles-Luce, J., and Luce, P. A. (1995). An examination of similarity neighborhoods in young children's receptive vocabularies. *Journal of Child Language,* 22(3), 727–35.

Chin, S. B. (2002). Aspects of stop consonant production by pediatric users of cochlear implants. *Language, Speech, and Hearing Services in Schools,* 33(1), 38–51.

Chin, S. B. (2003). Children's consonant inventories after extended cochlear implant use. *Journal of Speech, Language, and Hearing Research,* 46(4), 849–62.

Chin, S. B. (2006). Realization of complex onsets by pediatric users of cochlear implants. *Clinical Linguistics and Phonetics,* 20(7–8), 501–8.

Chirotan, I., Coupé, C., Marsico, E., and Pellegrino, F. (eds) (2009). *Approaches to Phonological Complexity.* Berlin: Mouton de Gruyter.

Cholin, J., Levelt, W. J. M., and Schiller, N. O. (2006). Effects of syllable frequency in speech production. *Cognition,* 99(2), 205–35.

Chomsky, N., and Halle, M. (1968). *The Sound Patterns of English.* New York: Harper & Row.

Clark, A. (1997). *Being There: Putting Brain, Body, and World Together Again.* Cambridge, MA: MIT Press.

Coady, J. A., and Aslin, R. N. (2004). Young children's sensitivity to probabilistic phonotactics in the developing lexicon. *Journal of Experimental Child Psychology,* 89, 183–213.

Colman, A. M. (2001). *A Dictionary of Psychology.* Retrieved from <http://www.oxfordreference.com/views/ENTRY.html?subview=Main&entry=t87.e1594>

Comrie, B. (1989). *Language Universals and Linguistic Typology: Syntax and Morphology* (2nd edn). Oxford: Basil Blackwell.

Conel, J. L. R. (1963). *The Post-Natal Development of the Human Cerebral Cortex,* vol. 7. *The Cortex of the Four Year Old Child.* Cambridge, MA: Harvard University Press.

Conel, J. L. R. (1967). *The Post-Natal Development of the Human Cerebral Cortex,* vol. 8. *The Cortex of the Six Year Old Child.* Cambridge, MA: Harvard University Press.

Cooperson, S. J., Bedore, L. M., and Peña, E. D. (in review). The relationship of phonological skills to language skills in Spanish–English speaking bilingual children.

Coplan, J., and Gleason, J. R. (1988). Unclear speech: Recognition and significance of unintelligible speech in preschool children. *Pediatrics* 82(3/2), 447–52.

Crago, M. B. (1992). Ethnography and language socialization: A cross-cultural perspective. *Topics in Language Disorders,* 12(3), 28–39.

Croft, W. (2003). *Typology and Universals* (2nd edn). Cambridge: Cambridge University Press.

Cross, T. G. (1977). Mothers' speech adjustment: The contributions of selected child listener variable. In C. E. Snow and C. A. Ferguson (eds), *Talking to Children: Language Input and Acquisition* (pp. 151–88). Cambridge: Cambridge University Press.

Cutler, A., and Clifton, C. (1999). Comprehending spoken language: A blueprint of the listener. In C. M. Brown and P. Hagoort (eds), *The Neurocognition of Language* (pp. 123–66). New York: Oxford University Press.

Damasio, A. R. (1994). *Descartes' Error: Emotion, Reason, and the Human Brain.* New York: G. P. Putnam.

Damasio, A. R. (1996). The somatic marker hypothesis and the possible functions of prefrontal cortex. *Philosophical Transactions of the Royal Society of London Bulletin of Biological Sciences, 351*(1346), 112–42.

Davis, B. L., and Lindblom, B. (2000). Prototype formation in speech development and phonetic variability in baby talk. In F. Lacerda, C. Von Hofsten and M. Heineman (eds), *Emerging Cognitive Abilities in Infancy* (pp. 59–71). Cambridge: Cambridge University Press.

Davis, B. L., and MacNeilage, P. F. (1990). Acquisition of correct vowel production: A quantitative case study. *Journal of Speech and Hearing Research, 33*(1), 16–27.

Davis, B. L., and MacNeilage, P. F. (1995). The articulatory basis of babbling. *Journal of Speech and Hearing Research*, 38(6), 1199–1211.

Davis, B. L., and MacNeilage, P. F. (2000). An embodiment perspective on the acquisition of speech perception. *Phonetica*, 57, 229–41.

Davis, B. L., and MacNeilage, P. F. (2002). The internal structure of the syllable: An ontogenetic perspective on origins. In T. Givon and B. Malle (eds), *The Rise of Language out of Pre-language*. Amsterdam: Benjamin.

Davis, B. L., MacNeilage, P. F., and Matyear, C. L. (2002). Acquisition of serial complexity in speech production: A comparison of phonetic and phonological approaches to first word production. *Phonetica*, 59, 75–107.

Davis, B. L., Tobey, E. A., and Moore, J. M. (2004). The effect of auditory experience on early speech production characteristics. Paper presented at the American Speech, Language, and Hearing Association Convention, Philadelphia, PA.

Davis, B. L., McCaffrey, H., von Hapsburg, D., and Warner-Czyz, A. (2005). Perceptual influences on motor control: Infants with varied hearing levels. *Volta Review*, 105(1), 7–27.

de Boer, B. (2001). *The Origins of Vowel Systems*. Oxford: Oxford University Press.

de Boer, B. (2005). Evolution of speech and its acquisition. *Adaptive Behavior, 13*(4), 281–92.

DeCasper, A. J., and Spence, M. J. (1986). Prenatal maternal speech influences newborns' perception of speech sounds. *Infant Behavior and Development, 9*, 133–50.

DeCasper, A. J., Lecanuet, J.-P., Busnel, M.-C., Granier-Deferre, C., and Maugeais, R. (1994). Fetal reactions to recurrent maternal speech. *Infant Behavior and Development, 17*, 159–64.

Dekkers, J. (2000). *Optimality Theory: Phonology, Syntax, and Acquisition*. Oxford: Oxford University Press.

deLacy, P. (ed.) (2007). *The Cambridge Handbook of Phonology*. Cambridge: Cambridge University Press.

Dell, G. (1988). The retrieval of phonological forms in production: Tests of predictions from a connectionist model. *Journal of Memory and Language*, 27, 124–42.

DePaolis, R., Vihman, M. M., and Kunnari, S. (2008). Prosody in production at the onset of word use: A cross-linguistic study. *Journal of Phonetics*, 36, 406–22.

de Saussure, F. (1916). *Course in General Linguistics,* tr. R. Harris. Peru, IL: Carus Publishing Co.

Descartes, R. (1637). *The Philosophical Works of Descartes,* tr. E. S. Haldane and G. T. R. Ross, vol. 1. New York: Cambridge University Press.

Deuchar, M., and Quay, S. (1999). Language choice in the earliest utterances: A case study with methodological implications. *Journal of Child Language*, 26(2), 461–75. doi: 10.1017/s0305000999003852.

Dietrich, C., Swingley, D., and Werker, J. F. (2007). Native language governs interpretation of salient speech sound differences at 18 months. *Proceedings of the National Academy of Sciences of the U.S.*, 104(41), 16027–31.

Dillon, C., Pisoni, D. B., Cleary, M., and Carter, A. K. (2004). Nonword imitation by children with cochlear implants: Consonant analyses. *Archives of Otolaryngology Head and Neck Surgery*, 130(5), 587–91. doi: 10.1001/archotol.130.5.587.

Dodd, B. J. (1972). Effects of social and vocal stimulation on infant babbling. *Developmental Psychology*, 7(1), 80–3.

Dolata, J. K., Davis, B. L., and MacNeilage, P. F. (2008). Characteristics of the rhythmic organization of vocal babbling: Implications for an amodal linguistic rhythm. *Infant Behavior and Development*, 31(3), 422–31. doi: 10.1016/j.infbeh.2007.12.014.

Dollaghan, C., and Campbell, T. F. (1998). Nonword repetition and child language impairment. *Journal of Speech, Language, and Hearing Research*, 41(5), 1136–46.

Dyson, A. T., and Amayreh, M. M. (2000). Phonological errors and sound changes in Arabic-speaking children. *Clinical Linguistics and Phonetics*, 14(2), 79–109. doi: 10.1080/026992000298850.

Edelman, G. M. (1992). *Bright Air, Brilliant Fire: On the Matter of the Mind*. New York: Basic Books.

Edwards, J., and Beckman, M. E. (2008). Methodological questions in studying consonant acquisition. *Clinical Linguistics and Phonetics*, 22(12), 937–56.

Edwards, J., Beckman, M. E., and Munson, B. (2004). The interaction between vocabulary size and phonotactic probability effects on children's production accuracy and fluency in nonword repetition. *Journal of Speech, Language, and Hearing Research*, 47, 421–36.

Edwards, J., Munson, B., and Beckman, M. E. (2011). Lexicon–phonology relationships and dynamics of early language development: A commentary on Stoel-Gammon's 'Relationships between lexical and phonological development in young children'. *Journal of Child Language*, 38(1), 35–40. doi: 10.1017/S0305000910000450.

Edwards, M., Cape, J., and Brown, D. (1989). Patterns of referral for children with speech disorders. *Child: Care, Health and Development*, 15(6), 417–24. doi: 10.1111/j.1365-2214.1989.tb00632.x.

Eggermont, J. J., Brown, D. K., Ponton, C. W., and Kimberly, B. P. (1996). Comparison of distortion product otoacoustic emission (DPOAE) and auditory brain stem response (ABR) traveling wave delay measurements suggests frequency specific synapse maturation. *Ear and Hearing,* 17: 386–94.

Eilers, R. E., and Oller, D. K. (1994). Infant vocalizations and the early diagnosis of severe hearing impairment. *Journal of Pediatrics,* 124(2), 199–203. doi: S0022-3476(94)70303-5.

Eimas, P. D., Siqueland, E. R., Jusczyk, P. W., and Vigorito, J. (1971). Speech perception in infants. *Science,* 171, 303–6.

Eisenberg, L. S. (2007). Current state of knowledge: Speech recognition and production in children with hearing impairment. *Ear and Hearing,* 28(6), 766–72. doi: 10.1097/AUD.0b013e318157f01f.

Eisenberg, L. S., Kirk, K. I., Martinez, A. S., Ying, E. A., and Miyamoto, R. T. (2004). Communication abilities of children with aided residual hearing: Comparison with cochlear implant users. *Archives of Otolaryngology Head and Neck Surgery,* 130(5), 563–9. doi: 10.1001/archotol.130.5.563.

Eisenberg, L. S., Shannon, R. V., Martinez, A. S., Wygonski, J., and Boothroyd, A. (2000). Speech recognition with reduced spectral cues as a function of age. *Journal of the Acoustic Society of America,* 107, 2704–10.

Elman, J. L. (2005). Connectionist models of cognitive development: Where next? *Trends in Cognitive Science,* 9(3), 111–17. doi: S1364-6613(05)00024-0.

Elman, J. L., Bates, E., Johnson, M., Karmiloff-Smith, A., Parisi, D., and Plunkett, K. (1996). *Rethinking Innateness: A Connectionist Perspective on Development.* Cambridge, MA: MIT Press.

Fabiano-Smith, L., and Barlow, J. A. (2010). Interaction in bilingual phonological acquisition: Evidence from phonetic inventories. *International Journal of Bilingual Education and Bilingualism,* 13(1), 81–97.

Fadiga, L., Craighero, L., Buccino, G., and Rizzolatti, G. (2002). Speech listening specifically modulates the excitability of tongue muscles: A TMS study. *European Journal of Neuroscience,* 15(2), 399–402.

Felsenfeld, S. (2002). Finding susceptibility genes for developmental disorders of speech: The long and winding road. *Journal of Communication Disorders,* 35(4), 329–46.

Fennell, C. T., and Waxman, S. R. (2010). What paradox? Referential cues allow for infant use of phonetic detail in word learning. *Child Development,* 81(5), 1376–83. doi: 10.1111/j.1467-8624.2010.01479.x.

Fennell, C. T., Byers-Heinlein, K., and Werker, J. F. (2007). Using speech sounds to guide word learning: The case of bilingual infants. *Child Development,* 78(5), 1510–25.

Fentress, J. C. (1984). The development of coordination. *Journal of Motor Behavior,* 16(2), 99–134.

Ferguson, C. A., and Farwell, C. B. (1975). Words and sounds in early language acquisition. *Language,* 51, 419–39.

Fernald, A. (1989). Intonation and communicative intent in mothers' speech to infants: Is the melody the message? *Child Development,* 60(6), 1497.

Fernald, A., and Hurtado, N. (2006). Names in frames: Infants interpret words in sentence frames faster than words in isolation. *Developmental Science,* 9(3), F33–FF40.

Fernald, A., and Morikawa, H. (1993). Common themes and cultural variations in Japanese and American mothers' speech to infants. *Child Development,* 64(3), 637.

Fernald, A., Taeschner, T., Dunn, J., and Papoušek, M. (1989). A cross-language study of prosodic modifications in mothers' and fathers' speech to preverbal infants. *Journal of Child Language*, 16(3), 477–501.

Ferrari, P. F., Gallese, V., Rizzolatti, G., and Fogassi, L. (2003). Mirror neurons responding to the observation of ingestive and communicative mouth actions in the monkey ventral premotor cortex. *European Journal of Neuroscience*, 17(8), 1703–14. doi: 2601.

Field, T., Diego, M., and Hernandez-Reif, M. (2009). Depressed mothers' infants are less responsive to faces and voices. *Infant Behavior and Development*, 32(3), 239–44. doi: S0163-6383(09)00041-1.

Field, T., Diego, M., Hernandez-Reif, M., Figueiredo, B., Ezell, S., and Siblalingappa, V. (2010). Depressed mothers and infants are more relaxed during breastfeeding versus bottlefeeding interactions: brief report. *Infant Behavior and Development*, 33(2), 241–4. doi: S0163-6383(09)00114-3.

Fikkert, P. (2005). Getting sound structures in mind: Acquisition bridging linguistics and psychology? In A. E. Cutler (ed.), *Twenty-First Century Psycholinguistics: Four Cornerstones* (pp. 43–56). Mahwah, NJ: Lawrence Erlbaum Associates.

Fikkert, P. (ed.) (2007). *Acquiring Phonology*. Cambridge, MA: Cambridge University Press.

Fikkert, P., and Levelt, C. (2009). How does place fall in place. The lexicon and emergent constraints in children's developing grammars. In E. Dresher and K. Rice (eds), *Contrast in Phonology*. Berlin: Mouton de Gruyter.

Fink, N. E., Wang, N. Y., Visaya, J., Niparko, J. K., Quittner, A., Eisenberg, L. S., and Tobey, E. A. (2007). Childhood development after cochlear implantation (CDaCI) study: Design and baseline characteristics. *Cochlear Implants International*, 8(2), 92–116. doi: 10.1002/cii.333.

Fodor, J. A., and Katz, J. (eds) (1964). *The Structure of Language*. New York: Prentice Hall.

Forrest, K., Elbert, M., and Dinnsen, D. A. (2000). The effect of substitution patterns on phonological treatment outcomes. *Clinical Linguistics and Phonetics*, 14(7), 519–31. doi:10.1080/026992000750020341.

Frank, M. C., Vul, E., and Johnson, S. P. (2009). Development of infants' attention to faces during the first year. *Cognition*, 110(2), 160–70.

Gathercole, S. E. (1995). Nonword repetition: More than just a phonological output task. *Cognitive Neuropsychology*, 12(8), 857–61. doi: 10.1080/02643299508251405.

Gathercole, S. E. (ed.) (2001). *Short-Term and Working Memory*. Hove: Psychology Press.

Gathercole, S. E., and Baddeley, A. D. (1993). *Working Memory and Language*. Mahwah, NJ: Lawrence Erlbaum Associates.

Gazzaniga, M. S., and Heatherton, T. F. (2003). *Psychological Science*. New York: Norton.

Gebhart, A. L., Newport, E. L., and Aslin, R. N. (2009). Statistical learning of adjacent and non-adjacent dependencies among non-linguistic sounds. *Psychonomic Bulletin and Review*, 16, 486–90.

Geers, A. (2004). Speech, language, and reading skills after early cochlear implantation. *Archives of Otolaryngology Head and Neck Surgery*, 130(5), 634–8. doi: 10.1001/archotol.130.5.634.

Geers, A., and Brenner, C. (2003). Background and educational characteristics of prelingually deaf children implanted by five years of age. *Ear and Hearing*, 24(1 suppl), 2S–14S. doi: 10.1097/01.AUD.0000051685.19171.BD.

Geers, A., and Moog, J. S. (1992). Speech perception and production skills of students with impaired hearing from oral and total communication education settings. *Journal of Speech and Hearing Research*, 35(6), 1384–93.

Geers, A., Brenner, C., and Davidson, L. (2003). Factors associated with development of speech perception skills in children implanted by age five. *Ear and Hearing*, 24(1 suppl), 24S–35S. doi: 10.1097/01.AUD.0000051687.99218.0F.

Gelman, S. A. (2003). *The Essential Child: Origins of Essentialism in Everyday Thought*. New York: Oxford University Press.

Gerken, L. (2004). Nine-month-olds extract structural principles required for natural language. *Cognition*, 93, B89–B96.

Gerken, L. (2006). Decisions, decisions: Infant language learning when multiple generalizations are possible. *Cognition*, 98, B67–B74.

Gesell, A. (1946). *The Embryology of Behavior*. New York: Harper.

Gibson, E. J. (1988). Exploratory behavior in the development of perceiving, acting, and the acquiring of knowledge. *Annual Review of Psychology*, 39, 1–41.

Gibson, J. J. (1966). *The Senses Considered as Perceptual Systems*. Boston: Houghton-Mifflin.

Gibson, J. J. (1979). *The Ecological Approach to Visual Perception*. Boston: Houghton Mifflin

Gierut, J., and Storkel, H. L. (2002). Markedness and the grammar in lexical diffusion of fricatives. *Clinical Linguistics and Phonetics*, 16(2), 115–34.

Gildersleeve-Neumann, C. (2001). Constraints on infant speech acquisition: A cross-language perspective. Unpublished doctoral dissertation, University of Texas at Austin, Austin, TX.

Gildersleeve-Neumann, C., Davis, B. L., and MacNeilage, P. F. (2011). Serial trends in acquisition of Quichua. *Applied Psycholinguistics*, 34, 111–34.

Gildersleeve-Neumann, C. E., Kester, E. S., Davis, B. L., and Pena, E. D. (2008). English speech sound development in preschool-aged children from bilingual English–Spanish environments. *Language, Speech, and Hearing Services in Schools*, 39(3), 314–28.

Gildersleeve-Neumann, C. E., Pena, E., Davis, B. L., and Kester, E. S. (2009). Effects on L1 during early acquisition of L2: Speech changes in Spanish at first English contact. *Bilingualism: Language and Cognition*, 12, 259–72.

Givon, T. (2009). *The Genesis of Syntactic Complexity*. Philadelphia, PA: John Benjamins.

Gliga, T., Elsabbagh, M., Andravizou, A., and Johnson, M. H. (2009). Faces attract infants' attention in complex displays. *Infancy*, 14(5), 550–62.

Goad, H., and Rose, Y. (2003). Segmental-prosodic interaction in phonological development: A comparative investigation. *Canadian Journal of Linguistics: Revue Canadienne de Linguistique*, 48(3–4), 139–48.

Goffman, L. (2004). Kinematic differentiation of prosodic categories in normal and disordered language development. *Journal of Speech Language and Hearing Research*, 47(5), 1088–1102.

Goffman, L., and Smith, A. (1999). Development and phonetic differentiation of speech movement patterns. *Journal of Experimental Psychology*, 25(3), 649–60.

Goffman, L., Heisler, L., and Chakraborty, R. (2006). Mapping of prosodic structure onto words and phrases in children's and adults' speech production. *Language and Cognitive Processes,* 21, 25–47.

Goffman, L., Smith, A., Heisler, L., and Ho, M. (2008). Coarticulation as an index of speech production units in children and adults. *Journal of Speech, Language, and Hearing Research,* 51(6), 1424–37.

Goldin-Meadow, S. (2009). Using the hands to study how children learn language. In J. Colombo, P. McCardle and L. Freund (eds), *Infant Pathways to Language: Methods, Models, and Research Directions* (pp. 195–210). New York: Taylor & Francis.

Goldstein, M. H., and Schwade, J. A. (2008). Social feedback to infants' babbling facilitates rapid phonological learning. *Psychological Science,* 19(5), 515–23.

Goldstein, M. H., and Schwade, J. A. (2009). From birds to words: Perception of structure in social interactions guides vocal development and language learning. In M. S. Blumberg, J. H. Freeman and S. R. Robinson (eds), *The Oxford Handbook of Developmental and Comparative Neuroscience.* Oxford: Oxford University Press.

Goldstein, M. H., King, A. P., and West, M. J. (2003). Social interaction shapes babbling: Testing parallels between birdsong and speech. *Proceedings of the National Academy of Science USA,* 100(13), 8030–5. doi: 10.1073/pnas.1332441100.

Goldstein, M. H., Schwade, J., Briesch, J., and Syal, S. (2010). Learning while babbling: Prelinguistic object-directed vocalizations indicate a readiness to learn. *Infancy,* 15(4), 362–91. doi: 10.1111/j.1532-7078.2009.00020.x.

Gordon-Brannan, M., and Hodson, B. W. (2000). Intelligibility/severity measurements of prekindergarten children's speech. *American Journal of Speech Language Pathology,* 9(2), 141–50.

Gottlieb, G. (1998). Normally occurring environmental behavioral influences on gene activity: From central dogma to probabilistic epigenesis. *Psychological Review,* 105(4), 792–802.

Gottlieb, G. (ed.) (2001). *A Developmental Psychobiological Systems View: Early Formulation and Current Status.* Cambridge, MA: MIT Press.

Goudbeek, M., Smits, R., Swingley, D., and Cutler, A. (eds) (2005). *Acquiring Auditory and Phonetic Categories.* Amsterdam: Elsevier.

Gray, S. (2005). Word learning by preschoolers with specific language impairment: Effect of phonological or semantic cues. *Journal of Speech, Language, and Hearing Research,* 48(6), 1452–67. doi: 10.1044/1092-4388(2005/101).

Gray, S., and Brinkley, S. (2011). Fast mapping and word learning by preschoolers with specific language impairment in a supported learning context: Effect of encoding cues, phonotactic probability, and object familiarity. *Journal of Speech Language and Hearing Research,* 54(3), 870–84. doi: 1092-4388_2010_09-0285.

Green, J. R., Moore, C. A., and Reilly, K. J. (2002). The sequential development of jaw and lip control for speech. *Journal of Speech, Language, and Hearing Research,* 45(1), 66–79. doi: 10.1044/1092-4388(2002/005).

Green, J. R., Moore, C. A., Higashikawa, M., and Steeve, R. W. (2000). The physiologic development of speech motor control: Lip and jaw coordination. *Journal of Speech, Language, and Hearing Research,* 43(1), 239–55.

Green, J. R., Moore, C. A., Ruark, J. L., Rodda, P. R., Morvee, W. T., and VanWitzenburg, M. J. (1997). Development of chewing in children from 12 to 43 months: Longitudinal study of EMG patterns. *Journal of Neurophysiology*, 77(5), 2704–16.

Greenough, W. T., and Black, J. E. (1992). Induction of brain structure by experience: Substrates for cognitive development. In M. Gunnar and C. A. Nelson (eds), *Behavioral Developmental Neuroscience* (vol. 24, pp. 155–200). Hillsdale, NJ: Lawrence Erlbaum.

Gros-Louis, J. G., West, M. J., Goldstein, M. H., and King, A. P. (2006). Mothers provide differential feedback to infants' prelinguistic sounds. *International Journal of Behavioral Development*, 30(6), 509–16.

Grossmann, T., and Johnson, M. H. (2007). The development of the social brain in human infancy. *European Journal of Neuroscience*, 25(4), 909–19. doi: 10.1111/j.1460-9568.2007.05379.x.

Guenther, F. H. (1995). Speech sound acquisition, coarticulation, and rate effects in a neural network model of speech production. *Psychological Review*, 102(3), 594–621.

Guenther, F. H., and Gjaja, M. N. (1996). The perceptual magnet effect as an emergent property of neural map formation. *Journal of the Acoustical Society of America*. 100(2), 1111–21.

Guenther, F. H., and Perkell, J. S. (2004). A neural model of speech production and its application or studies of the role of auditory feedback in speech. In R. Maassen, R. Kent, H. Peters, P. van Lieshout and W. Hulstijn (eds), *Speech Motor Control in Normal and Disordered Speech* (pp. 29–49). New York: Oxford University Press.

Gupta, P., and MacWhinney, B. (1997). Vocabulary acquisition and verbal short-term memory: Computational and neural bases. *Brain and Language*, 59(2), 267–333.

Haken, H. (1977). *Synergetics: An Introduction. Nonequilibrium Phase Transitions and Self-Organization in Physics, Chemistry, and Biology*. New York: Springer-Verlag.

Hall, G. (2005). Psychology of learning. In L. Nadel (ed.), *Encyclopedia of Cognitive Science* (vol. 2, pp. 837–45). London: Wiley.

Hanley, R. J., Dell, G. S., and Kay, J. (2004). Evidence for the involvement of a nonlexical route in the repetition of familiar words: A comparison of single and dual route models of auditory repetition. *Cognitive Neuropsychology*, 21(2–4), 147–58.

Hannon, E. E., and Johnson, S. P. (2005). Infants use meter to categorize rhythms and melodies: Implications for musical structure learning. *Cognitive Psychology*, 50(4), 354–77. doi: S0010-0285(04)00074-X.

Harding, A., and Grunwell, P. (1998). Active versus passive cleft-type speech characteristics. *International Journal of Language Communication Disorders*, 33(3), 329–52.

Hardin-Jones, M. A., and Jones, D. L. (2005). Speech production of preschoolers with cleft palate. *Cleft Palate Craniofacial Journal*, 42(1), 7–13. doi: 10.1597/03-134.1.

Hebb, D. O. (1949). *The Organization of Behavior*. New York: Wiley.

Heimann, M., Strid, K., Smith, L., Tjus, T., Ulvund, S. E., and Meltzoff, A. N. (2006). Exploring the relation between memory, gestural communication, and the emergence of language in infancy: a longitudinal study. *Infant Child Development*, 15(3), 233–49. doi: 10.1002/icd.462.

Helekar, S. A., Espino, G. G., Botas, A., and Rosenfield, D. B. (2003). Development and adult phase plasticity of syllable repetitions in the birdsong of captive zebra finches (Taeniopygia guttata). *Behavioral Neuroscience*, 117(5), 939–51.

Hickok, G., and Poeppel, D. (2004). Dorsal and ventral streams: A framework for understanding aspects of the functional anatomy of language. *Cognition*, 92, 67–99.

Hitch, G. J., and Towse, J. N. (1995). Working memory: What develops? In F. E. Weinert and W. Schneider (eds), *Memory Performance and Competencies: Issues in Growth and Development* (pp. 3–21). Hillsdale, NJ: Lawrence Erlbaum.

Hockett, C. (1960). Logical considerations in the study of animal communication. In W. E. Lanyon and W. N. Tavolga (eds), *Animal Sounds and Communication* (pp. 392–430). Washington, DC: American Institute of Biological Sciences.

Hodge, M. M. (1989). A comparison of spectral temporal measures across speaker age: Implications for an acoustical characterization of speech acquisition. Ph.D. dissertation, University of Wisconsin-Madison.

Hodson, B. W., and Paden, E. (1991). *Targeting Intelligible Speech: A Phonological Approach to Remediation*. Austin, TX: ProEd.

Holland, J. H. (1998). *Emergence: From Chaos to Order*. Redwood City, CA: Addison-Wesley..

Holm, A., Ozanne, A., and Dodd, B. (1997). Efficacy of intervention for a bilingual child making articulation and phonological errors. *International Journal of Bilingualism*, 1(1), 55–69.

Holt, L. L. (2005). Temporally nonadjacent nonlinguistic sounds affect speech categorization. *Psychological Science*, 16(4), 305–12. doi: 10.1111/j.0956-7976.2005.01532.x.

Holt, L. L., and Lotto, A. J. (2008). Speech perception within an auditory cognitive science framework. *Current Directions in Psychological Science*, 17(1), 42–6. doi: 10.1111/j.1467-8721.2008.00545.x.

Holveck, M.-J., de Castro, A. C. V., Lachlan, R. F., ten Cate, C., and Riebel, K. (2008). Accuracy of song syntax learning and singing consistency signal early condition in zebra finches. *Behavioral Ecology*, 19(6), 1267–81. doi: 10.1093/beheco/arn078.

Honda, K. (1996). Organization of tongue articulation for vowels. *Journal of Phonetics*, 24(1), 39–52. doi: 10.1006/jpho.1996.0004.

Hoover, J. R., Storkel, H. L., and Hogan, T. P. (2010). A cross-sectional comparison of the effects of phonotactic probability and neighborhood density on word learning by preschool children. *Journal of Memory and Language*, 63(1), 100–16. doi: 10.1016/j.jml.2010.02.003.

Horton, N. J., and Lipsitz, S. R. (1999). Review of software to fit generalized estimating equation (GEE) regression models. *American Statistician*, 53, 160–9.

Hox, J. J. (1995). *Applied Multilevel Analysis* (2nd edn). Amsterdam: TT-Publikaties.

Hua, Z., and Dodd, B. (2000). The phonological acquisition of Putonghua (modern standard Chinese). *Journal of Child Language*, 27(1), 3–42. doi: 10.1017/s030500099900402x.

Hua, Z., and Dodd, B. (2006). *Phonological Development and Disorders in Children: A Multilingual Perspective*. Clevedon, England, and Buffalo, NY: Multilingual Matters.

Hulme, C., Maughan, S., and Brown, G. D. A. (1991). Memory for familiar and unfamiliar words: Evidence for a long-term memory contribution to short-term memory span. *Journal of Memory and Language*, 30(6), 685–701. doi: 10.1016/0749-596x(91)90032-f.

Hurley, S. L., and Chater, N. (eds) (2002). *Perspectives on Imitation: From Neuroscience to Social Science. Imitation, Human Development and Culture* (vol. 2). Cambridge, MA: MIT Press.

Hurtado, N., Marchman, V. A., and Fernald, A. (2008). Does input influence uptake? Links between maternal talk, processing speed and vocabulary size in Spanish-learning children. *Developmental Science*, 11(6), F31–F39. doi: 10.1111/j.1467-7687.2008.00768.x.

Hymes, D. (1962). The ethnography of speaking. In T. Gladwin and W. C. Sturtevant (eds), *Anthropology and Human Behavior* (pp. 13–53). Washington, DC: Anthropology Society of Washington.

Indefrey, P., and Levelt, W. J. M. (2004). The spatial and temporal signatures of word production components. *Cognition*, 92, 101–44.

Iverson, J. M., and Goldin-Meadow, S. A. (2005). Gesture paves the way for language development. *Psychological Science*, 16, 368–71.

Jackendoff, R. (2002). *Foundations of Language: Brain, Meaning, Grammar, Evolutions*. New York: Oxford University Press.

Jakobson, R. (1941). *Child Language, Aphasia and Phonological Universals*. The Hague: Mouton.

Jakobson, R. (1968). *Child Language, Aphasia and Phonological Universals*, tr. A. Keiler. The Hague: Mouton and Co.

Jerger, S. (2007). Current state of knowledge: Perceptual processing by children with hearing impairment. *Ear and Hearing*, 28(6), 754–65. doi: 10.1097/AUD.0b013e318157f049.

Johnson, E. K. (2008). Infants use prosodically conditioned acoustic-phonetic cues to extract words from speech. *Journal of the Acoustical Society of America*, 123(6), EL144–8. doi: 10.1121/1.2908407.

Johnson, M. H. (1987). *The Body in the Mind: The Bodily Basis of Meaning, Imagination, and Reason*. Chicago, IL: University of Chicago Press.

Johnson, M. H. (1997). The neural basis of cognitive development. In W. Damon, D. Kuhn and R. Siegler (eds), *Handbook of Child Psychology* (5th edn), vol. 2. *Cognition, Perception and Language* (pp. 1–49). New York: Wiley.

Johnson, M. H., Munakata, Y., and Gilmore, R. O. (2002). *Brain Development and Cognition: A Reader* (2nd edn). Oxford and Malden, MA: Blackwell Publishers.

Jones, E. A., and Carr, E. G. (2004). Joint attention in children with autism: Theory and intervention. *Focus on Autism and Other Developmental Disabilities*, 19, 13–26.

Jonsson, C.-O., and Clinton, D. (2006). What do mothers attune to during interactions with their infants? *Infant and Child Development*, 15(4), 387–402. doi: 10.1002/icd.466.

Jusczyk, P. W. (1992). Developing phonological categories from the speech signal. In C. A. Ferguson, L. Menn and C. Stoel-Gammon (eds), *Phonological Development: Models, Research, Implications* (pp. 17–64). Timonium, MD: York Press.

Jusczyk, P. W. (1997). *The Discovery of Spoken Language*. Cambridge, MA: MIT Press.

Jusczyk, P. W., and Aslin, R. N. (1995). Infants' detection of the sound patterns of words in fluent speech. *Cognitive Psychology*, 29(1), 1–23.

Jusczyk, P. W., Cutler, A., and Redanz, N. J. (1993). Infants' preference for the predominant stress patterns of English words. *Child Development*, 64, 675–87.

Kagan, J. (1994). *The Nature of the Child*. New York: Basic Books.

Kager, R., Feest, S. van der, Fikkert, P., Kerkhoff, A., and Zamuner, T. S. (2007). Representations of [voice]: Evidence from acquisition. In J. van de Weijer and E. J. van der Torre (eds), *Voicing in Dutch*. Amsterdam: Benjamins.

Kalan, A. K., and Rainey, H. J. (2009). Hand-clapping as a communicative gesture by wild female swamp gorillas. *Primates*, 50(3), 273–5.

Kandel, E. R., and Schwartz, J. H. (1981). *Principles of Neural Science*. Amsterdam: Elsevier Science Publishing Co.

Kant, I. (1924). *Critique of Pure Reason*. New York: Macmillan.

Kao, M. H., and Brainard, M. S. (2006). Lesions of an avian basal ganglia circuit prevent context-dependent changes to song variability. *Journal of Neurophysiology*, 96(3), 1441–55. doi: 10.1152/jn.01138.2005.

Kauffman, S. (1995). *At Home in the Universe: The Search for the Laws of Self-Organization and Complexity*. New York: Oxford University Press.

Keating, P. A. (1990). The window model of coarticulation: Articulatory evidence. In J. Kingston and M. E. Beckman (eds), *Papers in Laboratory Phonology*, vol. 1. *Between the Grammar and Physics of Speech* (pp. 451–70). Cambridge, MA: Cambridge University Press.

Keller, H., and Schoelmerich, A. (1987). Infant vocalizations and parental reactions during the first four months of life. *Developmental Psychology*, 23(1), 62–7.

Kelso, J. A. S. (2008). Coordination dynamics. In R. A. Meyers (ed.), *Encyclopedia of Complexity and System Science*. Heidelberg: Springer.

Kelso, J. A. S., Saltzman, E. L., and Tuller, B. (1986). The dynamical perspective on speech production: Data and theory. *Journal of Phonetics*, 14, 29–59.

Kent, R. D. (1992). *Intelligibility in Communication Disorders: Theory, Measurements, and Management*. Amsterdam: John Benjamins Publisher.

Kent, R. D. (1999). Motor control: Neurophysiology and functional development. In A. J. Caruso and E. A. Strand (eds), *Clinical Management of Motor Speech Disorders in Children* (pp. 29–71). New York: Thieme Publishers.

Kent, R. D. (2004). The uniqueness of speech among motor systems. *Clinical Linguistics and Phonetics*, 18(6), 495–505.

Kent, R. D., and Vorperian, H. K. (1995a). *Anatomic Development of the Cranifocial-Oral-Laryngeal Systems*. San Diego, CA: Singular Publishing Group.

Kent, R. D., and Vorperian, H. K. (1995b). *Development of the Craniofacial-Oral-Laryngeal Anatomy*. San Diego, CA: Singular Publishing.

Kent, R. D., and Vorperian, H. K. (2006). In the mouths of babes: Anatomic, motor, and sensory foundations of speech development in children. In R. Paul (ed.), *Language Disorders from a Developmental Perspective* (pp. 37–49). Mahwah, NJ: Lawrence Erlbaum.

Kent, R. D., Kent, J. F., and Rosenbek, J. C. (1987). Maximum performance tests of speech production. *Journal of Speech and Hearing Disorders*, 52(4), 367–87.

Kern, S., and Davis, B. L. (2009). Emergent complexity in early vocal acqusition: Cross-linguistic comparisons of cannonical babbling. In I. Chitoran, C. Coupe, E. Marsico and F. Pellegrino (eds), (pp. 353–76). Berlin: Mouton de Gruyter.

Kern, S., and Davis, B. L. (in review, 2012). *First Steps into Language Complexity: Cross Language Patterns in Canonical Babbling*. Monographs of the Society for Research in Child Language.

Kern, S., and Davis, B. L. (submitted). *The Canonical Babbling Period: Sound Patterns across Languages*. Monographs of the Society for Research in Child Language.

Kern, S., Davis, B. L., and Zinc, I. (2010). From babbling to first words in four languages: Common trends, cross-language and individual differences. In J. M. Hombert and F. D'errico (eds), *Becoming Eloquent* (pp. 205–32). Cambridge: John Benjamins.

Kern, S., Davis, B. L., MacNeilage, P. F., Kocbas, D., Kuntay, A., and Zink, I. (2009). Crosslinguistic similarities and differences in babbling: Phylogenetic implications. In J. M. Hombert (ed.), *Towards the Origins of Language and Languages*. New York: Academic Press.

Kim, Y.-j. (1997). The acquisition of Korean. In D. I. Slobin (ed.), *Crosslinguistic Study of Language Acquisition* (vol. 4, pp. 335–443). Mahwah, NJ: Lawrence Erlbaum Associates.

Kinzler, K. D., Dupoux, E., and Spelke, E. S. (2007). The native language of social cognition. *Proceedings of the National Academy of Science USA*, 104(30), 12577–80. doi: 10.1073/pnas.0705345104.

Kiparsky, P., and Menn, L. (1977). On the acquisition of phonology. In J. MacNamara (ed.), *Language Learning and Thought* (pp. 47–78). New York: Academic Press.

Klein, P. J., and Meltzoff, A. N. (1999). Long-term memory, forgetting and deferred imitation in 12-month-old infants. *Developmental Science*, 2(1), 102–13.

Kluender, K. R., and Alexander, J. M. (2008). Perception of speech sounds. In Allan I. Basbaum (ed.), *The Senses: A Comprehensive Reference* (pp. 829–60). New York: Academic Press.

Kluender, K. R., and Walsh, M. A. (1992). Amplitude rise time and the perception of the voiceless affricate/fricative distinction. *Perceptions in Psychophysiology*, 51(4), 328–33.

Kluender, K. R., Coady, J. A., and Kiefte, M. (2003). Sensitivity to change in the perception of speech. *Speech Communication*, 41(1), 59–69.

Kluender, K. R., Diehl, R. L., and Killeen, P. R. (1987). Japanese quail can learn phonetic categories. *Science*, 237, 1195–7.

Koopmans-van Beinum, F. J., and van der Stelt, J. M. (1986). Early stages in the development of speech movements. In B. Lindblom and R. Zetterström (eds), *Precursors of Early Speech* (pp. 37–50). New York: Stockton Press.

Kovacs, Å. M., and Mehler, J. (2009). Flexible learning of multiple speech structures in bilingual infants. *Science*, 325(5940), 611–12.

Kugler, P. N., and Turvey, M. T. (1987). *Information, Natural Law, and the Self-Assembly of Rhythmic Movement*. Hillsdale, NJ: Lawrence Erlbaum Associates.

Kuhl, P. (2004). Early language acquisition: Cracking the speech code. *Nature Reviews Neuroscience*, 5(11), 831.

Kuhl, P. (2007). Is speech learning 'gated' by the social brain? *Developmental Science*, 10, 110–20.

Kuhl, P. (2009). Early language acquisition: Neural substrates and theoretical models. In M. S. Gazzaniga (ed.), *The Cognitive Neurosciences* (4th edn). Cambridge, MA: MIT Press.

Kuhl, P. (2011). Social mechanisms in early language acquisition: Understanding integrated brain systems supporting language. In J. Decety and J. Cacioppo (eds), *The Handbook of Social Neuroscience* (pp. 640–67). Oxford: Oxford University Press.

Kuhl, P., and Meltzoff, A. N. (1996). Infant vocalizations in response to speech: Vocal imitation and developmental change. *Journal of the Acoustical Society of America,* 100(4), 2425–38.

Kuhl, P., and Miller, J. D. (1975). Speech perception by the chinchilla: Voiced-voiceless distinction in alveolar plosive consonants. *Science,* 190, 69–72.

Kuhl, P., and Rivera-Gaxiola, M. (2008). Neural substrates of language acquisition. *Annual Review of Neuroscience,* 31, 511–34. doi: 10.1146/annurev. neuro.30.051606.094321.

Kuhl, P., Meltzoff, A. N., and Yonas, A. (1988). Speech as an intermodal object of perception. *Perceptual Development in Infancy* (pp. 235–266). Hillsdale, NJ: Lawrence Erlbaum Associates.

Kuhl, P., Tsao, F. M., and Liu, H. M. (2003). Foreign-language experience in infancy: Effects of short-term exposure and social interaction on phonetic learning. *Proceedings of the National Academy of Science USA,* 100(15), 9096–101. doi: 10.1073/pnas.1532872100.

Kuhl, P., Williams, K. A., Lacerda, F., and Stevens, K. N. (1992). Linguistic experience alters phonetic perception in infants by 6 months of age. *Science,* 255(5044), 606.

Kuhl, P., Stevens, E., Hayashi, A., Deguchi, T., Kiritani, S., and Iverson, P. (2006). Infants show facilitation for native language phonetic perception between 6 and 12 months. *Developmental Science,* 9, 13–21.

Kuhl, P. K. (2008). Linking infant speech perception to language acquisition: Phonetic learning predicts language growth. In P. McCardle, J. Colombo and L. Freund (eds), *Infant Pathways to Language: Methods, Models, and Research Directions* (pp. 213–44). New York: Erlbaum.

Kuhlman, K. A., Burns, K. A., Depp, R., and Sabbagha, R. E. (1998). Ultrasonic imaging of normal fetal response to external vibratory acoustic stimulation. *American Journal of Obstetric Gynecology,* 158, 47–51.

Ladefoged, P., and Johnstone, K. (2011). *A Course in Phonetics* (6th edn). Boston, MA: Wadsworth/Cengage Learning.

Ladefoged, P., and Maddieson, I. (1986). *Some of the Sounds of the World's Languages.* Los Angeles, CA: Phonetics Laboratory, Dept. of Linguistics, UCLA.

Lai, C. S. L., Fisher, S. E., Hurst, J. A., Vargha-Khadem, F., and Monaco, A. P. (2001). A forkhead-domain gene is mutated in a severe speech and language disorder. *Nature,* 413, 519–23.

Lakoff, G., and Johnson, M. (1999). *Philosophy in the Flesh: The Embodied Mind and its Challenge to Western Thought.* New York: Basic Books.

Lamb, M. E., Bornstein, M. H., and Teti, D., M. (2002). *Development in Infancy: An Introduction.* Mahwah, NJ: Lawrence Erlbaum.

Lashley, K. S. (1951). The problem of serial order in behavior. In L. A. Jeffress (ed.), *Cerebral Mechanisms in Behavior* (pp. 112–46). New York: John Wiley & Sons.

Learmonth, A. E., Lamberth, R., and Rovee-Collier, C. (2005). The social context of imitation in infancy. *Journal of Experimental Child Psychology,* 91(4), 297–314.

Lee, S. (2003). Perceptual influences on speech production in Korean learning infant babbling. Ph.D., dessertation, University of Texas at Austin, Austin, TX.

Lee, S., and Davis, B. L. (2010). Segmental distribution pattern of English infant- and adult-directed speech. *Journal of Child Language*, 35, 591–617.

Lee, S., Davis, B. L., and MacNeilage, P. F. (2008). Segmental properties of input to infants: A study of Korean. *Journal of Child Language*, 35(3), 591–617.

Lee, S., Davis, B. L., and MacNeilage, P. F. (2010). Universal production patterns and ambient language influences in babbling: A cross-linguistic study of Korean- and English-learning infants. *Journal of Child Language*, 37(2), 293–318. doi: 10.1017/S0305000909009532.

Legerstee, M., Markova, G., and Fisher, T. (2007). The role of maternal affect attunement in dyadic and triadic communication. *Infant Behavior and Development*, 30(2), 296–306. doi: S0163-6383(06)00068-3.

Lenneburg, E. H. (1967). *The Biological Foundations of Language*. New York: John Wiley & Sons.

Leonard, L. B. (1998). *Children with Specific Language Impairment*. Cambridge, MA: Bradford Books.

Leopold, W. F. (1970). *Speech Development of a Bilingual Child: A Linguist's Record*. New York: AMS Press.

Levelt, W. J. M. (1993). *Speaking: From Intention to Articulation*. Cambridge, MA: MIT Press.

Levelt, W. J. M. (1999). Producing spoken language: A blueprint of the speaker. In C. M. Brown and P. Hagoort (eds), *The Neurocognition of Language*. New York: Oxford University Press.

Levelt, W. J. M., and Meyer, A. (2000). Word for word: Multiple lexical access in speech production. *European Journal of Cognitive Psychology*, 12(4), 433–52.

Lewis, B. A., Freebairn, L. A., and Hansen, A. (2004). Family pedigrees of children with suspected childhood apraxia of speech. *Journal of Communication Disorders*, 37(2), 157–75.

Li, P., Farkas, I., and MacWhinney, B. (2004). Early lexical development in a self-organizing neural network. *Neural Networks*, 17(8–9), 1345–62. doi: S0893-6080(04)00153-4.

Liang, K.-Y., and Zeger, S. L. (1986). Longitudinal data analysis using generalized linear models. *Biometrika*, 73(1), 13–22. doi: 10.1093/biomet/73.1.13.

Lindblom, B. (1963). Spectrographic study of vowel reduction. *Journal of Acoustical Society of America*, 35, 1773–81.

Lindblom, B. (1992). Phonological units as adaptive emergents of lexical development. In C. A. Ferguson, L. Menn and C. Stoel-Gammon (eds), *Phonological Development* (pp. 131–63). Parkton, MD: York Press.

Lindblom, B. (2000). Developmental origins of adult phonology: The interplay between phonetic emergents and the evolutionary adaptations of sound patterns. *Phonetica*, 57(Special Issue: Studies in Speech Communication and Language Development), 297–314.

Lindblom, B. (2004). The organization of speech movements: Specification of units and modes of control. Paper presented at the Sound to Sense workshop, MIT.

Lindblom, B. (2008). The target hypothesis, dynamic specification and segmental independence. In B. L. Davis and K. Zajdo (eds), *Syllable Development: The*

Frame Content Theory and Beyond (pp. 327–54). New York: Routlege/Taylor & Francis.

Lindblom, B., and Maddieson, I. (1988). Phonetic universals in consonant systems. In L. M. Hyman and C. N. Li (eds), *Language, Speech, and Mind* (pp. 62–78). London: Routledge.

Locke, J. L. (1983). *Phonological Acquisition and Change.* New York: Academic Press.

Locke, J. L. (2006). Parental selection of vocal behavior: Crying, cooing, babbling, and the evolution of language. *Human Nature,* 17, 155–68.

Locke, J. L. (2008). Lipsmacking and babbling: Syllables, sociality and survival. In B. L. Davis and K. Zajdo (eds), *The Syllable in Speech Production* (pp. 327–54). New York: Routledge/Taylor & Francis.

Locke, J. L., and Bogin, B. (2006). Language and life history: A new perspective on the evolution and development of linguistic communication. *Behavioral and Brain Sciences,* 29, 259–80.

Locke, J. L., Bekken, K. E., McMinn-Larson, L., and Wein, D. (1995). Emergent control of manual and vocal-motor activity in relation to the development of speech. *Brain and Language,* 51(3), 498–508.

López, F., Menez, M., and Hernández-Guzmán, L. (2005). Sustained attention during learning activities: An observational study with pre-school children. *Early Child Development and Care,* 175(2), 131–8. doi: 10.1080/0300443042000230384.

Lucas, M. M. (1987). Sentence effects on the processing of ambiguous words in sentence contexts. *Language and Speech,* 30, 25–46.

Luce, P. A., Goldinger, S. D., Auer, E. T., and Vitivich, M. S. (2000). Phonetic priming, neighborhood activation, and PARSYN. *Perception and Psychophysics,* 62, 615–25.

Luce, P. A., and Pisoni, D. B. (1998). Recognizing spoken words: The neighborhood activation model. *Ear and Hearing,* 19(1), 1–36.

Luce, R. D. (1986). *Response Times: Their Role in Inferring Elementary Mental Organization.* New York: Oxford University Press.

Lukowski, A. F., Wiebe, S. A., Haight, J. C., DeBoer, T., Nelson, C. A., and Bauer, P. J. (2005). Forming a stable memory representation in the first year of life: Why imitation is more than child's play. *Developmental Science,* 8(3), 279–98. doi: 10.1111/j.1467-7687.2005.00415.x.

MacDougall-Shackleton, S. A. (2009). The importance of development: What songbirds can teach us. *Canadian Journal of Experimental Psychology: Revue canadienne de psychologie experimentale,* 63(1), 74–9.

Macken, M. A., and Ferguson, C. A. (1983). Cognitive aspects of phonological development: Model, evidence, and issues. In K. E. Nelson (ed.), *Children's Language* (vol. 4, pp. 255–82). Hillsdale, NJ: Lawrence Erlbaum.

MacNeilage, P. F. (1970). Motor control of serial ordering of speech. *Psychology Review,* 77(3), 182–96.

MacNeilage, P. F. (2008). *The Origin of Speech.* Oxford: Oxford University Press.

MacNeilage, P. F., and Davis, B. L. (1990). Acquisition of speech production: Frames, then content. In M. Jeannerod (ed.), *Attention and Performance 13: Motor Representation and Control* (pp. 453–76). Hillsdale, NJ: Lawrence Erlbaum Associates.

MacNeilage, P. F., and Davis, B. L. (1993). Motor explanations of babbling and early speech patterns. In B. de Boysson-Bardies and S. de Schonen (eds), *Developmental Neurocognition: Speech and Face Processing in the First Year of Life* (pp. 341–52). Dordrecht: Kluwer Academic Publishers.

MacNeilage, P. F., and Davis, B. L. (2002). On the origins of intersyllabic complexity. In T. Givon and B. Malle (eds), *On the Rise of Language out of Pre-language*. Amsterdam: Benjamins.

MacNeilage, P. F., Davis, B. L., Kinney, A., and Matyear, C. L. (2000). The motor core of speech: A comparison of serial organization patterns in infants and languages. *Child Development*, 71(1), 153–63.

MacNeilage, P. F., Davis, B. L., Matyear, C. L., and Kinney, A. (2000). Origin of speech output complexity in infants and in languages. *Psycological Science*, 10, 459–60.

MacWhinney, B. (2004). A multiple process solution to the logical problem of language acquisition. *Journal of Child Language*, 31, 883–914.

Maddieson, I. (1984). *Patterns of Sounds*. Cambridge and New York: Cambridge University Press.

Majorano, M., and D'Odorico, L. (2011). The transition into ambient language: A longitudinal study of babbling and first word production of Italian children. *First Language*, 31(1), 47–66. doi: 10.1177/0142723709359239.

Malsheen, B. (1980). Two hypotheses for phonetic clarification in the speech of mothers to children. In G. H. Yeni-Komshian, J. F. Kavanaugh, and C. A. Ferguson (eds), *Child Phonology: Perception* (vol. 2, pp. 173–84). New York: Academic Press.

Mampe, B., Friederici, A. D., Christophe, A., and Wermke, K. (2009). Newborns' cry melody is shaped by their native language. *Currents in Biology*, 19(23), 1994–7. doi: S0960-9822(09)01824-7.

Marchman, V. A., and Fernald, A. (2008). Speed of word recognition and vocabulary knowledge in infancy predict cognitive and language outcomes in later childhood. *Developmental Science*, 11(3), F9–F16. doi: 10.1111/j.1467-7687.2008.00671.x.

Marchman, V. A., Fernald, A., and Hurtado, N. (2010). How vocabulary size in two languages relates to efficiency in spoken word recognition by young Spanish–English bilinguals. *Journal of Child Language*, 37(4), 817–40. doi: 10.1017/S0305000909990055.

Mareschal, D., Thomas, M., and Westermann, G. (eds.) (2007). *Neuroconstructivism, Vol. I: How the brain constructs cognition*. Oxford: Oxford University Press.

Markova, G., and Legerstee, M. (2006). Contingency, imitation, and affect sharing: Foundations of infants' social awareness. *Developmental Psychology*, 42(1), 132–41. doi: 10.1037/0012-1649.42.1.132.

Masoura, E. V., and Gathercole, S. E. (2005). Contrasting contributions of phonological short-term memory and long-term knowledge to vocabulary learning in a foreign language. *Memory*, 13(3–4), 422–9.

McCarthy, J. J., and Prince, A. S. (1993). *Prosodic Morphology: Constraint Interaction and Satisfaction*. New Brunswick, NJ: University of Massachesettes, Amherst and Rutgers University.

McClelland, J. L., and Elman, J. L. (1986). The TRACE Model of Speech Perception. *Cognitive Psychology*, 18, 1–86.

McClelland, J. L., Botvinick, M. M., Noelle, D. C., Plaut, D. C., Rogers, T. T., Seidenberg, M. S., and Smith, L. B. (2010). Letting structure emerge: Connectionist and dynamical systems approaches to cognition. *Trends in Cognitive Science*, 14(8), 348–56. doi: S1364-6613(10)00124-5.

McCowan, B., and Reiss, D. (1995). Whistle contour development in captive-born infant bottlenose dolphins (Tursiops truncatus): Role of learning. *Journal of Comparative Psychology*, 109(3), 242–60.

McCune, L., and Vihman, M. M. (2001). Early phonetic and lexical development: A productivity approach. *Journal of Speech Language and Hearing Research*, 44(3), 670–84.

McLeod, S., and Goldstein, B. A. (eds) (2012). *Multilingual Aspects of Speech Sound Disorders in Children*. Bristol: Multilingual Matters.

Mehler, J., Jusczyk, P. W., Lambertz, G., Halsted, N., Bertoncini, J., and Amiel-Tison, C. (1988). A precursor of language acquisition in young infants. *Cognition*, 29, 143–78.

Meltzoff, A. N., and Goswami, U. (2002). Imitation as a mechanism of social cognition: Origins of empathy, theory of mind, and the representation of action. In U. Goswami (ed.), *Blackwell Handbook of Childhood Cognitive Development* (pp. 6–25). Malden, MA: Blackwell Publishing.

Meltzoff, A. N., and Kuhl, P. (1994). Faces and speech: Intermodal processing of biologically relevant signals in infants and adults. In D. J. Lewkowicz and R. Lickliter (eds), *The Development of Intersensory Perception: Comparative Perspectives* (pp. 335–69). Hillsdale, NJ: Lawrence Erlbaum Associates.

Meltzoff, A. N., and Moore, M. K. (1977). Imitation of facial and manual gestures by human neonates. *Science*, 198, 75–8.

Meltzoff, A. N., and Moore, M. K. (1989). Imitation in newborn infants: Exploring the range of gestures imitated and the underlying mechanisms. *Developmental Psychology*, 25, 954–62.

Meltzoff, A. N., and Prinz, W. (2002). *The Imitative Mind: Development, Evolution, and Brain Bases*. Cambridge: Cambridge University Press.

Ménard, L., Davis, B. L., and Boë, L.-J. (2007). Perceptual categorization of synthesized English vowels from birth to adulthood. Paper presented at the International Congress of Phonetic Sciences, Germany, Aug.

Ménard, L., Schwartz, J.-L., and Boë, L.-J. (2004). Role of vocal tract morphology in speech development: Perceptual targets and sensorimotor maps for synthesized French vowels from birth to adulthood. *Journal of Speech, Language, and Hearing Research*, 47(5), 1059–80.

Ménard, L., Davis, B. L., Boë, L. J., and Roy, J. P. (2009). Producing American English vowels during vocal tract growth: A perceptual categorization study of synthesized vowels. *Journal of Speech Language and Hearing Research*, 52(5), 1268–85. doi: 10.1044/1092-4388(2009/08-0008).

Menn, L. (1979). *Pattern, Control, and Contrast in Beginning Speech: A Case Study in the Development of Word Form and Word Function*. Bloomington, IN: Indiana University Linguistic Club.

Menn, L. (1983). Development of articulatory, phonetic and phonological capabilities. In B. Butterworth (ed.), *Language Production* (vol. 2). London: Academic Press.

Merriman, W. E., and Schuster, J. M. (1991). Young children's disambiguation of object name reference. *Child Development*, 62, 1288–1301.

Mitani, J. C., and Nishida, T. (1993). Contexts and social correlates of long-distance calling by male chimpanzees. *Animal Behaviour*, 45(4), 735–46. doi: 10.1006/anbe.1993.1088.

Miyamoto, R. T., Kirk, K. I., Svirsky, M. A., and Sehgal, S. T. (1999). Communication skills in pediatric cochlear implant recipients. *Acta Otolaryngologica,* 119(2), 219–24.

Moeller, M. P., Tomblin, J. B., Yoshinaga-Itano, C., Connor, C. M., and Jerger, S. (2007). Current state of knowledge: Language and literacy of children with hearing impairment. *Ear and Hearing* 28(6), 740–53. doi: 10.1097/AUD.0b013e318157f07f.

Moeller, M. P., Hoover, B., Putman, C., Arbataitis, K., Bohnenkamp, G., and Peterson, B. (2007). Vocalizations of infants with hearing loss compared with infants with normal hearing: I. Phonetic development. *Ear and Hearing,* 28, 605–27.

Molfese, D. L., Molfese, V. J., and Pratt, N. L. (2007). The use of event-related evoked potentials to predict development outcomes. In M. de Haan (ed.), *Infant EEG and Event-Related Potentials.* Hove: Psychology Press.

Moon, C., Cooper, B. P., and Fifer, W. P. (1993). Two day old infants prefer their native language. *Infant Behavior and Development,* 16, 495–500.

Moore, C., and Dunham, P. J. (eds) (1995). *Joint Attention: Its Origin and Role in Development.* Hillsdale, NJ: Lawrence Erlbaum.

Moore, C. A., and Ruark, J. L. (1996). Does speech emerge from earlier appearing oral motor behaviors? *Journal of Speech and Hearing Research,* 39(5), 1034–47.

Moore, C. A., Caulfield, T. J., and Green, J. R. (2001). Relative kinematics of the rib cage and abdomen during speech and nonspeech behaviors of 15-month-old children. *Journal of Speech, Language, and Hearing Research,* 44, 80–94.

Moore, J. (2002). Maturation of human auditory cortex: Implications for speech perception. *Annals of Otology, Rhinology, and Laryngology,* 111, 7–10.

Moore, J. K., and Guan, Y. L. (2001). Cytoarchitectural and axonal maturation in human auditory cortex. *Journal of the Association of Research in Otolaryngology,* 2(4), 297–311.

Moore, J. K., and Linthicum, F. H., Jr. (2007). The human auditory system: A timeline of development. *International Journal of Audiology,* 46(9), 460–78. doi: 10.1080/14992020701383019.

Moore, J. K., Perazzo, L. M., and Braun, A. (1995). Time course of axonal maturation in the human brainstem pathway. *Hearing Research,* 87, 21–31.

Morton, J. (1993). Mechanisms in infant face processing. In B. de Boysson-Bardies, S. de Schonen, P. W. Jusczyk, P. McNeilage and J. Morton (eds), *Developmental Neurocognition: Speech and Face Processing in the First Year of Life* (pp. 93–102). New York: Kluwer Academic/Plenum Publishers.

Munson, B. (2001). Phonological pattern frequency and speech production in adults and children. *Journal of Speech, Language, and Hearing Research,* 44(4), 778–92.

Munson, B., and Soloman, N. (2004). The effect of phonological neighborhood density on vowel articulation. *Journal of Speech Language and Hearing Research,* 47, 1048–58.

Narayan, C. R., Werker, J. F., and Beddor, P. S. (2010). The interaction between acoustic salience and language experience in developmental speech perception: Evidence from nasal place discrimination. *Developmental Science,* 13(3), 407–20. doi: 10.1111/j.1467-7687.2009.00898.x.

Nathani, S., Ertmer, D. J., and Stark, R. E. (2006). Assessing vocal development in infants and toddlers. *Clinical Linguistics and Phonetics,* 20(5), 351–69. doi: 10.1080/02699200500211451.

Newmeyer, F. J. (1998). *Language Form and Language Function.* Cambridge, MA: MIT Press.

Newport, E. L. (1976). Motherese: The speech of mothers to young children. In N. J. Castellan, D. B. Pisoni and G. R. Potts (eds), *Cognitive Theory* (vol. 2). Hillsdale, NJ: Erlbaum.

Newport, E. L., and Aslin, R. N. (2004). Learning at a distance: I. Statistical learning of non-adjacent dependencies. *Cognitive Psychology,* 48, 127–62.

Nielsen, M. (2006). Copying actions and copying outcomes: Social learning through the second year. *Developmental Psychology,* 42(3), 555–65. doi: 10.1037/0012-1649.42.3.555.

Nittrouer, S. (1993). The emergence of mature gestural patterns is not uniform: Evidence from an acoustic study. *Journal of Speech and Hearing Research,* 36(5), 959–72.

Noad, M. J., Cato, D. H., Bryden, M. M., Jenner, M. N., and Jenner, K. C. (2000). Cultural revolution in whale songs. *Nature,* 408(6812), 537. doi: 10.1038/35046199.

O'Brien, E. K., Zhang, X., Nishimura, C., Tomblin, J. B., and Murray, J. C. (2003). Association of specific language impairment (SLI) to the region of 7q31. *American Journal of Human Genetics,* 72(6), 1536–43.

O'Grady, W. (2008). The emergentist program. *Lingua,* 118, 447–64.

Oller, D. K. (1980). The emergence of the sounds of speech in infancy. In G. H. Yeni-Komshian, J. F. Kavanagh and C. A. Ferguson (eds), *Child Phonology,* vol. 1. *Production* (pp. 21–35). New York: Academic Press.

Oller, D. K. (2000). *The Emergence of the Speech Capacity.* Mahwah, NJ: Lawrence Erlbaum Associates.

Oller, D. K., and Eilers, R. E. (1982). Similarity of babbling in Spanish- and English-learning babies. *Journal of Child Language,* 9(3), 565–77.

Oller, D. K., and Griebel, U. (2008a). *Evolution of Communicative Flexibility: Complexity, Creativity, and Adaptability in Human and Animal Communication.* Cambridge, MA: MIT Press.

Oller, D. K., and Griebel, U. (2008b). The origins of syllabification in human infancy and in human evolution. In B. L. Davis and K. Zajdo (eds), *The Syllable in Speech Production* (pp. 29–62). New York: Routledge/Taylor & Francis.

Oller, D. K., Eilers, R. E., Urbano, R., and Cobo-Lewis, A. B. (1997). Development of precursors to speech in infants exposed to two languages. *Journal of Child Language,* 24(2), 407–25.

Oller, D. K., Niyogi, P., Gray, S., Richards, J. A., Gilkerson, J., Xu, D., and Warren, S. F. (2010). Automated vocal analysis of naturalistic recordings from children with autism, language delay, and typical development. *Proceeding of the National Academy of Science USA,* 107(30), 13354–9. doi: 1003882107.

Ortega-Llebaria, M., Davis, B. L., and Yang, J. (in revision). Prosody in canonical babbling: Biomechanical constraints and ambient language effects in Mandarin and English infants. *Infant Behavior and Development.*

Ostry, D. J., Vatikiotis-Bateson, E., and Gribble, P. L. (1997). An examination of the degrees of freedom of human jaw motion in speech and mastication. *Journal of Speech Language and Hearing Research,* 40(6), 1341–51.

Oyama, S. (2000). *Evolution's Eye: A System's View of the Biology–Culture Divide.* Durham, SC: Duke University Press.

Ozcaliskan, S., and Goldin-Meadow, S. (2009). When gesture-speech combinations do and do not index linguistic change. *Language Cognitive Process*, 24(2), 190. doi: 10.1080/01690960801956911.

Paatsch, L. E., Blamey, P. J., Sarant, J. Z., Martin, L. F., and Bow, C. P. (2004). Separating contributions of hearing, lexical knowledge, and speech production to speech-perception scores in children with hearing impairments. *Journal of Speech Language and Hearing Research,* 47(4), 738–50. doi: 10.1044/1092-4388(2004/056).

Pack, A. A., and Herman, L. M. (2004). Bottlenosed dolphins (Tursiops truncatus) comprehend the referent of both static and dynamic human gazing and pointing in an object-choice task. *Journal of Comparative Psychology,* 118(2), 160–71. doi: 10.1037/0735-7036.118.2.160.

Paradis, J., and Nicoladis, E. (2007). The influence of dominance and sociolinguistic context on bilingual preschoolers' language choice. *International Journal of Bilingual Education and Bilingualism,* 10(3), 277–97. doi: 10.2167/beb444.0.

Paradis, J., Nicoladis, E., and Genesee, F. (2000). Early emergence of structural constraints on code-mixing: Evidence from French-English bilingual children. *Bilingualism: Language and Cognition,* 3(3), 245–61.

Parham, D. F., Buder, E. H., Oller, D. K., and Boliek, C. A. (2011). Syllable-related breathing in infants in the second year of life. *Journal of Speech Language and Hearing Research,* 54(4), 1039–50. doi: 10.1044/1092-4388(2010/09-0106).

Pater, J., Stager, C., and Werker, J. F. (2004). The perceptual acquisition of phonological contrasts. *Language*, 80(3), 384–402.

Paterson, S. J., Heim, S., Friedman, J. T., Choudhury, N., and Benasich, A. A. (2006). Development of structure and function in the infant brain: Implications for cognition, language and social behaviour. *Neuroscience and Biobehavioral Reviews,* 30(8), 1087–105.

Paus, T., Zijdenbos, A., Worsley, K., Collins, D. L., Blumenthal, J., Giedd, J. N., . . . Evans, A. C. (1999). Structural maturation of neural pathways in children and adolescents: In vivo study. *Science,* 283, 1908–11.

Pele, M., Dufour, V., Thierry, B., and Call, J. (2009). Token transfers among great apes (Gorilla gorilla, Pongo pygmaeus, Pan paniscus, and Pan troglodytes): Species differences, gestural requests, and reciprocal exchange. *Journal of Comparative Psychology,* 123(4), 375–84.

Penfield, W., and Roberts, L. (1959). *Speech and Brain Mechanisms.* Princeton, NJ: Princeton University Press.

Peng, S. C., Spencer, L. J., and Tomblin, J. B. (2004). Speech intelligibility of pediatric cochlear implant recipients with 7 years of device experience. *Journal of Speech Language and Hearing Research,* 47(6), 1227–36.

Peters, A. M. (1985). Language segmentation: Operating principles for the perception and analysis of language. In D. Slobin (ed.), *The Crosslinguistic Study of Language Acquisition* (vol. 2, pp. 1029–68). Hillsdale, NJ: Lawrence Erlbaum.

Peterson-Falzone, S. J., Hardin-Jones, M. A., and Karnell, M. P. (2001). *Cleft Palate Speech* (3rd edn). St Louis, MO: Mosby, Inc.

Petrides, M., Cadoret, G., and Mackey, S. (2005). Orofacial somatomotor responses in the macaque monkey homologue of Broca's area. *Nature,* 435, 1235–8.

Piaget, J., and Inhelder, B. (1958). *The Growth of Logical Thinking from Childhood to Adolescence*. New York: Basic Books.

Pierrehumbert, J. (2000). The phonetic grounding of phonology. *Bulletin de la Communication Parlée*, 5, 7–23.

Pierrehumbert, J. (2003). Phonetic diversity, statistical learning, and acquisition of phonology. *Language and Speech*, 46(2–3), 115–54.

Pierrehumbert, J. (2012). The dynamic lexicon. In A. Cohn, M. Huffman and C. Fougeron (eds), *Handbook of Laboratory Phonology* (pp. 173–83). Oxford: Oxford University Press.

Pinker, S. (1994). *The Language Instinct: How the Mind Creates Language*. New York: Morrow.

Pinker, S. (2009). *How the Mind Works* (pbk edn). New York: Norton.

Plunkett, K., and Marchman, V. (1991). U-shaped learning and frequency effects in a multi-layered perception: Implications for child language acquisition. *Cognition*, 48, 43–102.

Polka, L., and Werker, J. F. (1994). Developmental changes in perception of nonnative vowel contrasts. *Journal of Experimental Psychology: Human Perception and Performance*, 20(2), 421–35.

Port, R. F., and van Gelder, T. (1995). *Mind as Motion: Explorations in the Dynamics of Cognition*. Cambridge, MA: MIT Press.

Price, D. J., and Willshaw, D. J. (2000). *Mechanisms of Cortical Development*. New York: Oxford University Press.

Prigogine, I., and Glandorf, P. (1971). *Thermodynamic Theory of Structure, Stability and Fluctuations*. New York: Wiley & Sons.

Prigogine, I., and Stengers, I. (1984). *Order Out of Chaos: Man's New Dialogue with Nature*. New York: Bantam.

Prince, A., and Smolensky, P. (2004). *Optimality Theory: Constraint Interaction in Generative Grammar*. Malden, MA: Blackwell Publishing.

Quam, C., and Swingley, D. (2010). Phonological knowledge guides two-year-olds' and adults' interpretation of salient pitch contours in word learning. *Journal of Memory and Language*, 62(2), 135–50. doi: 10.1016/j.jml.2009.09.003.

Reiss, D., and McCowan, B. (1993). Spontaneous vocal mimicry and production by bottlenose dolphins (Tursiops truncatus): Evidence for vocal learning. *Journal of Comparative Psychology*, 107(3), 301–12.

Reuterskiold-Wagner, C., Sahlen, B., and Nyman, A. (2005). Non-word repetition and non-word discrimination in Swedish preschool children. *Clinical Linguistics and Phonetics*, 19(8), 681–99. doi: 10.1080/02699200400000343.

Rice, M. L. (ed.) (1996). *Toward a Genetics of Language*. Mahwah, NJ: Lawrence Erlbaum Associates.

Rice, M. L., and Smolik, F. (2007). Genetics of language disorders: Clinical conditions, phenotypes, and genes. *Oxford Handbook of Psycholinguistics* (pp. 685–700). Oxford: Oxford University Press.

Riely, R. R., and Smith, A. (2003). Speech movements do not scale by orofacial structure size. *Journal of Applied Physiology*, 94(6), 2119–26. doi: 10.1152/japplphysiol.00502.2002.

Rizzolatti, G., and Arbib, M. A. (1998). Language within our grasp. *Trends in Neurosciences*, 21(5), 188–94.

Rizzolatti, G., Fadiga, L., Gallese, V., and Fogassi, L. (1996). Premotor cortex and the recognition of motor actions. *Cognitive Brain Research*, 3, 131–41.

Rome-Flanders, T., Cronk, C., and Gourde, C. (1995). Maternal scaffolding in mother–infant games and its relationship to language development: A longitudinal study. *First Language*, 15(45), 339–55.

Rose, Y. (2009). Internal and external influences on child language productions. In I. Chirotan, C. Coupé, E. Marsico and F. Pellegrino (eds), *Approaches to Phonological Complexity* (pp. 329–52). Berlin: Mouton de Gruyter.

Roug, L., Landberg, I., and Lundberg, L. J. (1989). Phonetic development in early infancy: A study of four Swedish children during the first eighteen months of life. *Journal of Child Language*, 16, 19–40.

Rousset, I. (2004). Structures syllabiques et lexicales des langues du monde: Donnees, typologies, tendances universalles et constraintes substantielles. Doctoral dissertation, University of Grenoble, Grenoble.

Ruiz-Felter, R., Bedore, L. M., and Peña, E. D. (unpublished manuscript). The influence of language experience on phonological acquisition in bilingual English-Spanish speaking Kindergarteners.

Rumelhart, D. E., and McClelland, J. L. (1986). *Parallel Distributed Processing: Explorations in the Microstructure of Cognition* (vol. 1). Cambridge, MA: MIT Press.

Sachs, J. (1977). The adaptive significance of linguistic input to prelinguistic infants. In C. E. Snow and C. A. Ferguson (eds), *Talking to Children: Language Input and Acquisition* (pp. 51–61). Cambridge: Cambridge University Press.

Saffran, J. (2003). Statistical language learning: Mechanisms and constraints. *Current Directions in Psychological Science*, 12(4), 110.

Saffran, J., Aslin, R. N., and Newport, E. L. (1996). Statistical learning by 8 month old infants. *Science*, 274, 1926–8.

Saffran, J., Newport, E. L., and Aslin, R. N. (1996). Word segmentation: The role of distributional cues. *Journal of Memory and Language*, 35, 606–62.

Saffran, J., Colombo, J., McCardle, P., and Freund, L. (2009). Acquiring grammatical patterns: Constraints on learning. In *Infant Pathways to Language: Methods, Models, and Research Disorders* (pp. 31–47). New York: Psychology Press.

Saffran, J., Hauser, M., Seibel, R., Kapfhamer, J., Tsao, F., and Cushman, F. (2008). Grammatical pattern learning by human infants and cotton-top tamarin monkeys. *Cognition*, 107(2), 479–500. doi: S0010-0277(07)00269-7.

Saltzman, E., and Kelso, J. A. (1987). Skilled actions: A task-dynamic approach. *Psychology Review*, 94(1), 84–106.

Sanders, L. D., Weber-Fox, C. M., and Neville, H. J. (2008). Varying degress of plasticity in different subsystems within language. In J. R. Pomerantz (ed.), *Topics in Integrative Neuroscience: From Cells to Cognition* (pp. 125–53). New York: Cambridge University Press.

Santos, F. H., and Bueno, O. F. (2003). Validation of the Brazilian children's test of pseudoword repetition in Portuguese speakers aged 4 to 10 years. *Brazilian Journal of Medicine and Biological Research*, 36(11), 1533–47. doi: S0100-879X2003001100012.

Sarant, J. Z., Blamey, P. J., Dowell, R. C., Clark, G. M., and Gibson, W. P. (2001). Variation in speech perception scores among children with cochlear implants. *Ear and Hearing*, 22(1), 18–28.

Sarid, M., and Breznitz, Z. (1997). Developmental aspects of sustained attention among 2- to 6-year-old children. *International Journal of Behavioral Development,* 21(2), 303–12. doi: 10.1080/016502597384884.

Savage-Rumbaugh, E. S., Shanker, S. G., and Taylor, T. J. (2001). *Apes, Language, and the Human Mind.* Oxford: Oxford University Press.

Schauwers, K., Gillis, S., and Govaerts, P. J. (2008). The characteristics of prelexical babbling after cochlear implantation between 5 and 20 months of age. *Ear and Hearing,* 29(4), 627–37. doi: 10.1097/AUD.0b013e318174f03c.

Scheer, T. (2010). What OT is, and what it is not. *Journal of Linguistics,* 46, 193–218.

Scherer, N. J., Williams, A. L., and Proctor-Williams, K. (2008). Early and later vocalization skills in children with and without cleft palate. *International Journal of Pediatric Otorhinolaryngology,* 72(6), 827–40. doi: S0165-5876(08)00084-0.

Schwartz, R. G., and Leonard, L. B. (1982). Do children pick and choose? An examination of phonological selection and avoidance in early lexical acquisition. *Journal of Child Language,* 9(2), 319–36. doi: 10.1017/S0305000900004748.

Schwartz, R. G., Leonard, L. B., Loeb, D. M. F., and Swanson, L. A. (1987). Attempted sounds are sometimes not: An expanded view of phonological selection and avoidance. *Journal of Child Language,* 14(3), 411–18. doi: 10.1017/S0305000900010205.

Scott-Phillips, T. (2010). Evolutionary psychology and the origins of language. *Journal of Evolutionary Psychology,* 8(4), 289–307. doi: 10.1556/JEP.8.2010.4.7.

Seidl, A., Cristia, A., Bernard, A., and Onishi, K. (2009). Allophones and phonemes in infants' phonotactic learning. *Language, Learning, and Development,* 5, 191–202.

Serry, T. A., and Blamey, P. J. (1999). A four-year investigation into phonetic inventory development in young cochlear implant users. *Journal of Speech, Language, and Hearing Research,* 42(1), 141–54.

Service, E. (1992). Phonology, working memory, and foreign-language learning. *The Quarterly Journal of Experimental Psychology,* 45(1), 21–50.

Shannon, C. E., and Weaver, W. (1949). *The Mathematical Theory of Communication.* Urbana, IL: University of Illinois Press.

Sharma, A., Nash, A. A., and Dorman, M. (2009). Cortical development, plasticity and re-organization in children with cochlear implants. *Journal of Communication Disorders,* 42(4), 272–9.

Sharma, A., Gilley, P. M., Martin, K., Roland, P., Bauer, P., and Dorman, M. (2007). Simultaneous versus sequential bilateral implantation in young children: Effects on central auditory system development and plasticity. *Audiological Medicine,* 5(4), 218–23.

Shriberg, L. D., Jakielski, K. J., and El-Shanti, H. (2008). Breakpoint localization using array-CGH in three siblings with an unbalanced 4q;16q translocation and childhood apraxia of speech (CAS). *American Journal of Medical Genetics A,* 146A(17), 2227–33. doi: 10.1002/ajmg.a.32363.

Shriberg, L. D., Tomblin, J. B., and McSweeny, J. L. (1999). Prevalence of speech delay in 6-year-old children and comorbidity with language impairment. *Journal of Speech, Language, and Hearing Research,* 42(6), 1461–81.

Shriberg, L. D., Paul, R., Black, L. M., and van Santen, J. P. (2011). The hypothesis of apraxia of speech in children with autism spectrum disorder. *Journal of Autism Development Disorders,* 41(4), 405–26. doi: 10.1007/s10803-010-1117-5.

Shriberg, L. D., Austin, D., Lewis, B. A., McSweeny, J. L., and Wilson, D. L. (1997). The speech disorders classification system (SDCS): Extensions and lifespan reference data. *Journal of Speech Language and Hearing Research,* 40(4), 723–40.

Shriberg, L. D., Lewis, B. A., Tomblin, J. B., McSweeny, J. L., Karlsson, H. B., and Scheer, A. R. (2005). Toward diagnostic and phenotype markers for genetically transmitted speech delay. *Journal of Speech, Language, and Hearing Research,* 48(4), 834–52.

Sices, L., Taylor, H. G., Freebairn, L., Hansen, A., and Lewis, B. (2007). Relationship between speech-sound disorders and early literacy skills in preschool-age children: Impact of comorbid language impairment. *Journal of Development Behavior Pediatrics,* 28(6), 438–47. doi: 10.1097/DBP.0b013e31811ff8ca.

Singer, J. (1998). Using SAS PROC MIXED to fit multilevel models, hierarchical models, and individual growth models. *Journal of Educational and Behavioral Statistics,* 24(4), 323–55.

Singer, W. (1995). Development and plasticity of cortical processing architectures. *Science,* 270, 758–64.

Slobin, D. I. (1985). Crosslinguistic evidence for the language-making capacity. In D. I. Slobin (ed.), *The Crosslinguistic Study of Language Acquisition,* vol. 2. *Theoretical Issues* (pp. 1157–256). Hillsdale, NJ: Lawrence Erlbaum Associates.

Smit, A. B., Hand, L., Freilinger, J. J., Bernthal, J. E., and Bird, A. (1990). The Iowa articulation norms project and its Nebraska replication. *Journal of Speech and Hearing Disorders,* 55(4), 779–98.

Smith, A. (2010). Development of neural control of orofacial movements for speech. In W. J. Hardcastle, J. Laver and F. Gibbon (eds), *Handbook of Phonetic Sciences* (2nd edn). Oxford: Blackwell.

Smith, A., and Goffman, L. (1998). Stability and patterning of speech movement sequences in children and adults. *Journal of Speech, Language, and Hearing Research,* 41, 18–30.

Smith, L. B., and Breazeal, C. (2007). The dynamic lift of developmental processes. *Developmental Science,* 10(1), 61–8.

Smith, L. B., and Gasser, M. (2005). The development of embodied cognition: Six lessons from babies. *Artificial Life,* 11, 11–30.

Smith, L. B., and Katz, D. B. (1996). Activity-dependent processes in perceptual and cognitive development. In R. Gelman and T.K.F. Au (ed.), *Perceptual and Cognitive Development* (pp. 413–45). San Diego, CA: Academic Press.

Smith, R., Michael, J., and Sundberg, M. L. (1995). Automatic reinforcement and automatic punishment in infant vocal behavior. *Analysis of Verbal Behavior,* 13, 39–48.

Smith, W. C., Johnson, S. C., and Spelke, E. S. (2003). Motion and edge sensitivity in perception of object unity. *Cognitive Psychology,* 46, 31–64.

Smolensky, P. (1996). The initial state and 'richness of the base' in optimality theory technical report. *JHU Cognitive Science,* 96(4), 1–31.

Snow, C. E., and Ferguson, C. A. (1977). *Talking to Children.* Cambridge, MA: Cambridge University Press.

Snowdon, C. T. (2004). Social processes in the evolution of complex cognition and communication. In K. Oller and E. Griebels (eds), *Evolution of Communication Systems: A Comparative Approach.* Cambridge, MA: MIT Press.

Stark, R. E. (1980). Stages of speech development in the first year of life. In G. H. Yeni-Komshian, J. Kavanagh and C. A. Ferguson (eds), *Child Phonology: Production* (vol. 1, pp. 73–91). New York: Academic Press.

Stark, R. E. (1981). Infant vocalization: A comprehensive view. *Infant Mental Health Journal*, 2(2), 118–28.

Stark, R. E. (1989). Temporal patterning of cry and non-cry sounds in the first eight months of life. *First Language*, 9(26/2), 107–36.

Steeles, L. (2006). Experiments on the emergence of human communication. *Trends in Cognitive Sciences*, 10(8), 347–9.

Steeve, R. W. (2010). Babbling and chewing: Jaw kinematics from 8 to 22 months. *Journal of Phonology*, 38(3), 445–58. doi: 10.1016/j.wocn.2010.05.001.

Steeve, R. W., and Moore, C. A. (2009). Mandibular motor control during the early development of speech and nonspeech behaviors. *Journal of Speech Language and Hearing Research*, 52(6), 1530–54. doi: 10.1044/1092-4388(2009/08-0020).

Steeve, R. W., Moore, C. A., Green, J. R., Reilly, K. J., and Ruark McMurtrey, J. (2008). Babbling, chewing, and sucking: Oromandibular coordination at 9-months. *Journal of Speech, Language, and Hearing Research*, 51, 1390–1404.

Steinberg, A. G., and Knightly, C. A. (1997). Hearing: Sounds and silences. In M. L. Batshaw (ed.), *Children with Disabilities* (4th edn, pp. 241–74). Baltimore, MD: Brooks.

Stemberger, J. P., and Bernhardt, B. H. (1999). The emergence of faithfulness. In B. MacWhinney (ed.), *The Emergence of Language* (pp. 417–46). Mahweh, NJ: Erlbaum.

Stevens, K., and House, A. (1963). Perturbation of vowel articulations by consonantal context: An acoustical study. *Journal of Speech and Hearing Research*, 6, 111–28.

Stivers, T., Enfield, N. J., Brown, P., Englert, C., Hayashi, M., Heinemann, T., Levinson, S. C. (2009). Universals and cultural variation in turn-taking in conversation. *Proceedings of the National Academy of Science USA*, 106(26), 10587–92. doi: 10.1073/pnas.0903616106.

Stoel-Gammon, C. (1989). Prespeech and early speech development of two late talkers. *First Language*, 9(6), 207–23. doi: 10.1177/014272378900900607.

Stoel-Gammon, C. (2004). Variability in the productions of young, typically developing children. Paper presented at the International Clinical Phonetics and Linguistics Association, Lafayette, LA.

Stoel-Gammon, C. (2007). Variability in speech acquisition. In S. McLeod and K. Bliehle (eds), *The International Guide to Speech Acquisition* (pp. 55–60). Clifton Park, NY: Delmar-Thompson Learning.

Stoel-Gammon, C. and Sosa, A. (2012). Lexical and phonological effects in early word production, *Journal of Speech Language and Hearing Research*, April, 55(2), 596–608.

Storkel, H. L. (2001). Learning new words: Phonotactic probability in language development. *Journal of Speech Language and Hearing Research*, 44(6), 1321–37. doi: 10.1044/1092-4388(2001/103).

Storkel, H. L. (2002). Restructuring of similarity neighbourhoods in the developing mental lexicon. *Journal of Child Language*, 29(2), 251–74.

Storkel, H. L. (2006). Do children still pick and choose? The relationship between phonological knowledge and lexical acquisition beyond 50 words. *Clinical Linguistics and Phonetics*, 20(7), 523–9.

Storkel, H. L. (2009). Developmental differences in the effects of phonological, lexical and semantic variables on word learning by infants. *Journal of Child Language,* 36(2), 291–321.

Storkel, H. L., and Hoover, J. R. (2011). The influence of part-word phonotactic probability/neighborhood density on word learning by preschool children varying in expressive vocabulary. *Journal of Child Language,* 38(3), 628–43. doi: 10.1017/s0305000910000176.

Storkel, H. L., and Morrisette, M. L. (2002). The lexicon and phonology: Interactions in language acquisition. *Language, Speech, and Hearing Services in the Schools,* 33, 22–35.

Striano, T., and Stahl, D. (2005). Sensitivity to triadic attention in early infancy. *Developmental Science,* 8(4), 333–43. doi: 10.1111/j.1467-7687.2005.00421.x.

Stromswold, K. (2001). The heritability of language: A review and metaanalysis of twin, adoption and linkage studies. *Language,* 77, 647–723.

Studdert-Kennedy, M. (1998). The particulate origins of language generativity: From syllable to gesture. In J. R. Hurford, M. Studdert-Kennedy and C. Knight (eds), *Approaches to the Evolution of Language: Social and Cognitive Bases* (pp. 202–21). Cambridge: Cambridge University Press.

Studdert-Kennedy, M. (2005). How did language go discrete? *Language Origins: Perspectives on Language* (pp. 48–67). Oxford: Oxford University Press.

Studdert-Kennedy, M., and Goodell, E. W. (1995). Gestures, features, and segments in early child speech. In B. De Gelder and J. Morais (eds), *Speech and Reading: A Comparative Approach* (pp. 65–88). London: Erlbaum, Taylor, & Francis.

Summers, C., Bohman, T. M., Gillam, R. B., Pena, E. D., and Bedore, L. M. (2010). Bilingual performance on nonword repetition in Spanish and English. *International Journal of Language and Communication Disorders,* 45(4), 480–93.

Sundara, M., Polka, L., and Molnar, M. (2008). Development of coronal stop perception: Bilingual infants keep pace with their monolingual peers. *Cognition,* 108(1), 232–42.

Svirsky, M. A., Teoh, S. W., and Neuburger, H. (2004). Development of language and speech perception in congenitally, profoundly deaf children as a function of age at cochlear implantation. *Audiology and Neurotology,* 9(4), 224–33. doi: 10.1159/000078392.

Swingley, D. (2005). Statistical clustering and the contents of the infant vocabulary. *Cognitive Psychology,* 50(1), 86–132.

Swingley, D. (2008). The roots of the early vocabulary in infants' learning from speech. *Current Directions in Psychological Science,* 17(5), 308–12.

Swingley, D. (2009a). Contributions of infant word learning to language development. *Philosophical Transactions of the Royal Society of London Bulletin of Biological Science,* 364(1536), 3617–32. doi: 10.1098/rstb.2009.0107.

Swingley, D. (2009b). Onsets and codas in 1.5-year-olds' word recognition. *Journal of Memory and Language,* 60(2), 252–69. doi: 10.1016/j.jml.2008.11.003.

Tam, H., Jarrold, C., Baddeley, A. D., and Sabatos-DeVito, M. (2010). The development of memory maintenance: Children's use of phonological rehearsal and attentional refreshment in working memory tasks. *Journal of Experimental Child Psychology,* 107(3), 306–24.

Teixeira, E. R., and Davis, B. L. (2002). Early sound patterns in the speech of two Brazilian Portuguese speakers. *Language and Speech,* 45(2), 179–204.

Tenenbaum, J. B., Griffiths, T. L., and Kemp, C. (2006). Theory-based Bayesian models of inductive learning and reasoning. *Trends in Cognitive Science,* 10(7), 309–18. doi: S1364-6613(06)00134-3.

Thelen, E. (1991). Motor aspects of emergent speech: A dynamic approach. In N. Krasnegor, D. Rumbaugh and M. Studdert-Kennedy (eds), *Biological and Behavioral Determinants of Language Development* (pp. 339–62). Hillsdale, NJ: Lawrence Erlbaum.

Thelen, E. (1995). Motor development: A new synthesis. *American Psychologist,* 50(2), 79–95.

Thelen, E. (ed.) (1984). *Learning to Walk: Ecological Demands and Phylogenic Constraints* (vol. 3). Norwood, NJ: Ablex.

Thelen, E., and Smith, L. B. (1994). *A Dynamic Systems Approach to the Development of Cognition and Action.* Cambridge, MA: MIT Press.

Thevenin, D. M., Eilers, R. E., Oller, D. K., and Lavoie, L. (1985). Where's the drift in babbling drift? A cross-linguistic study. *Applied Psycholinguistics,* 6, 3–15.

Thorndike, E. L. (1911). *Animal Intelligence: Experimental Studies.* New York: Macmillan.

Tinbergen, N. (1963). On aims and methods of ethology. *Zeitschrift für Tierpsychologie,* 20, 410–33.

Tobey, E. A., Wiessner, N., Lane, J., and Sullivan, J. (2008). Phoneme accuracy as a function of mode of communication in pediatric cochlear implants. *Audiological Medicine,* 6, 283–92.

Tobey, E. A., Geers, A., Brenner, C., Altuna, D., and Gabbert, G. (2003). Factors associated with development of speech production skills in children implanted by age five. *Ear and Hearing,* 24(1 suppl.), 36S–45S. doi: 10.1097/01. AUD.0000051688.48224.A6.

Tobey, E. A., Devous, M. D., Sr., Buckley, K., Cooper, W. B., Harris, T. S., Ringe, W., and Roland, P. S. (2004). Functional brain imaging as an objective measure of speech perception performance in adult cochlear implant users. *International Journal of Audiology,* 43(suppl. 1), S52–S56.

Tobey, E. A., Geers, A., Douek, B. M., Perrin, J., Skellet, R., Brenner, C., and Toretta, G. (2000). Factors associated with speech intelligibility in children with cochlear implants. *Annual Otology Rhinology Laryngology Supplement,* 185, 28–30.

Toda, S., Fogel, A., and Kawai, M. (1990). Maternal speech to three-month-old infants in the United States and Japan. *Journal of Child Language* 17, 279–294.

Tomasello, M. (2003). *Constructing a Language: A Usage-Based Theory of Language Acquisition.* Cambridge, MA: Harvard University Press.

Tomasello, M. (2008). *Origins of Human Communication.* Cambridge, MA: MIT Press.

Tomasello, M., and Carpenter, M. (2005). Intention reading and imitative learning. In S. Hurley and N. Chater (eds), *Perspectives on Imitation: From Neuroscience to Social Science,* vol. 2, *Imitation, Human Development, and Culture* (pp. 143–8). Cambridge, MA: MIT Press.

Tomasello, M., Carpenter, M., and Liszkowski, U. (2007). A new look at infant pointing. *Child Development,* 78(3), 705–22.

Tomblin, B., and Hebbeler, K. (2007). Current state of knowledge: Outcomes research in children with mild to severe hearing impairment. Approaches and methodological considerations. *Ear and Hearing*, 28(6), 715–28. doi: 10.1097/AUD.0b013e318157f093.

Tomblin, J. B. (2003). Language and genes. In D. N. Cooper (ed.), *Nature Encyclopedia of the Human Genome* (vol. 3, pp. 646–9). London: Nature Publishing Group.

Tomblin, J. B., Hafeman, L. L., and O'Brien, M. (2003). Autism and autism risk in siblings of children with specific language impairment. *International Journal of Language and Communication Disorders*, 38(3), 235–50. doi: 10.1080/1368282031000086363.

Tomblin, J. B., O'Brien, M., Shriberg, L. D., Williams, C., Murray, J., Patil, S., and Ballard, K. (2009). Language features in a mother and daughter of a chromosome 7;13 translocation involving FOXP2. *Journal of Speech Language and Hearing Research*, 52(5), 1157–74. doi: 10.1044/1092-4388(2009/07-0162).

Trehub, S. E., and Shenfield, T. (2007). Acquisition of early words from single-word and sentential contexts. *Developmental Science*, 10(2), 190–8. doi: 10.1111/j.1467-7687.2007.00545.x.

Tremblay, H., and Rovira, K. (2007). Joint visual attention and social triangular engagement at 3 and 6 months. *Infant Behavior and Development*, 30(2), 366–79.

Trevarthen, C. (1998). The concept and foundations of infant intersubjectivity. In S. Braten (ed.), *Intersubjective Communication and Emotion in Early Ontogeny* (pp. 15–46). Cambridge: Cambridge University Press.

Trost, J. E. (1981). Articulatory additions to the classical description of the speech of persons with cleft palate. *Cleft Palate Journal*, 18(3), 193–203.

Trubetzkoy, N. (1939). *Grundzüge der Phonologie*. Travaux du cercle linguistique de Prague, 7.

Tyack, P. L. (2008). Convergence of calls as animals form social bonds, active compensation for noisy communication channels, and the evolution of vocal learning in mammals. *Journal of Comparative Psychology*, 122(3), 319–31.

Tye-Murray, N., Spencer, L., and Gilbert-Bedia, E. (1995). Relationships between speech production and speech perception skills in young cochlear-implant users. *Journal of the Acoustical Society of America*, 98(5/1), 2454–60.

Tye-Murray, N., Spencer, L., and Woodworth, G. (1995). Acquisition of speech by children who have prolonged cochlear implant experience. *Journal of Speech and Hearing Research*, 38(2), 327–37.

vanKleeck, A. (1994). Potential cultural bias in training parents as conversational partners with their children who have delays in language development. *American Journal of Speech Language Pathology*, 72–81.

Varela, F. J., Thompson, E., and Rosch, E. (1991). *The Embodied Mind*. Cambridge, MA: MIT Press.

Vihman, M. M. (1993). Vocal motor schemes, variation and the production–perception link. *Journal of Phonetics*, 21(1–2), 163–9.

Vihman, M. M. (1996). *Phonological Development: The Origins of Language in the Child*. Oxford: Basil Blackwell.

Vihman, M. M. (2004). Input-based phonological acquisition. *First Language*, 24(72), 373–6.

Vihman, M. M. (2009). Word learning and the origins of phonological system. In S. Foster-Cohen (ed.), *Advances in Language Acquisition* (pp.15–39). London: Palgrave Macmillan.

Vihman, M. M., and Croft, W. (2007). Phonological development: Toward a 'radical' templatic phonology. *Linguistics,* 45(4), 683–725.

Vihman, M. M., and Keren-Portnoy, T. (2011). The role of production practice in lexical and phonological development. *Journal of Child Language,* 38(1), 41–5.

Vihman, M. M., and McCune, L. (1994). When is a word a word? *Journal of Child Language,* 21(3), 517–42. doi: 10.1017/S0305000900009442.

Vihman, M. M., DePaolis, R. A., and Keren-Portnoy, T. (2009). Babbling and words: A dynamic systems perspective on phonological development. In E. Bavin (ed.), *The Cambridge Handbook of Child Language* (pp. 163–82). New York: Cambridge University Press.

Vihman, M. M., Ferguson, C. E., and Elbert, M. (1986). Phonological development from babbling to speech: Common tendencies and individual differences. *Applied Psycholinguistics,* 7, 3–40.

Vihman, M. M., Nakai, S., DePaolis, R. A., and Halle, P. (2004). The role of accentual pattern in early lexical representation. *Journal of Memory and Language,* 50(3), 336–53.

Vihman, M. M., Kay, E., Boysson-Bardies, B. de, Durand, C., and Sundberg, U. (1994). External sources of individual differences? A cross-linguistic analysis of the phonetics of mothers' speech to 1-year-old children. *Experimental Psychology,* 30(5), 651–62.

Vihman, M. M., Thierry, G., Lum, J., Keren-Portnoy, T., and Martin, P. (2007). Onset of word form recognition in English, Welsh, and English-Welsh bilingual infants. *Applied Psycholinguistics,* 28(3), 475–93.

Vitevitch, M. S., and Luce, P. A. (2005). Increases in phonotactic probability facilitate spoken nonword repetition. *Journal of Memory and Language,* 52, 193–204.

Vitevitch, M. S., Luce, P. A., Pisoni, D. B., and Auer, E. T. (1999). Phonotactics, neighborhood activation, and lexical access for spoken words. *Brain and Language,* 68, 306–11.

Vogel Sosa, A., and Stoel-Gammon, C. (2006). Patterns of intra-word phonological variability during the second year of life. *Journal of Child Language,* 33(1), 31–50.

von Hapsburg, D., and Davis, B. L. (2006). Auditory sensitivity and the prelinguistic vocalizations of early-amplified infants. *Journal of Speech, Language, and Hearing Research,* 49(4), 809–22.

von Hapsburg, D., Davis, B. L., and MacNeilage, P. F. (2008). Frame dominance in infants with hearing loss. *Journal of Speech, Language, and Hearing Research,* 51(2), 306–20.

von Hofsten, C., Vishton, P., Spelke, E. S., Feng, Q., and Rosander, K. (1998). Predictive action in infancy: Tracking and reaching for moving objects. *Cognition,* 76(3), 255–85.

Vorperian, H. K., Kent, R. D., Lindstrom, M. J., Kalina, C. M., Gentry, L. R., and Yandell, B. S. (2005). Development of vocal tract length during early childhood: A magnetic resonance imaging study. *Journal of the Acoustical Society of America,* 117(1), 338–50.

Vygotsky, L. (1962). *Thought and Language.* Cambridge, MA: MIT Press.

Vygotsky, L. (1978). *Mind and Society: The Development of Higher Psychological Processes.* Cambridge, MA: Harvard University Press.

Waddington, C. (1962). *New Patterns in Genetics and Development*. New York: Columbia University Press.

Walley, A. C., and Metsala, J. L. (1990). The growth of lexical constraints on spoken word recognition. *Perception and Psychophysics*, 47(3), 267–80. doi: 10.3758/bf03205001.

Walley, A. C., Sloane, M. E., and Columbus, F. (2001). The perceptual magnet effect: A review of empirical findings and theoretical implications. *Advances in Psychology Research* (vol. 4, pp. 65–92). Hauppauge, NY: Nova Science Publishers.

Walsh, B., and Smith, A. (2002). Articulatory movements in adolescents: Evidence for protracted development of speech motor control process. *Journal of Speech, Language, and Hearing Research*, 45(6), 1119–33.

Warner-Czyz, A. D., and Davis, B. L. (2008). The emergence of segmental accuracy in young cochlear implant recipients. *Cochlear Implants International*, 9(3), 143–66. doi: 10.1002/cii.364.

Watson-Gegeo, K., and Gegeo, D. W. (1986). Calling-out and repeating routines in Kwara'ae children's language socialization. In B. Schieffelin and E. Ochs (eds), *Language Socialization across Cultures* (pp. 17–50). New York: Cambridge University Press.

Weir, R. H. (1962). *Language in the Crib* (vol. 14). The Hague: Mouton and Co.

Werker, J. F., and Curtin, S. (2005). PRIMIR: A developmental framework of infant speech processing. *Language Learning and Development*, 1(2), 197–234. doi: citeulike-article-id:3937582.

Werker, J. F., and Fennell, C. T. (2008). Infant speech perception and later language acquisition: Methodological underpinnings. In J. Colombo and P. McCardle (eds), *The Measurement of Language in Infancy* (pp. 85–98). Hillsdale, NJ: Lawrence Erlbaum Associates.

Werker, J. F., and Tees, R. C. (1984). Cross-language speech perception: Evidence for perceptual reorganization during the first year of life. *Infant Behavior and Development*, 7, 49–63.

Westermann, G., and Mareschal, D. (2002). Models of atypical development must also be models of normal development. *Behavioral and Brain Sciences*, 25, 771–2.

Westerman, G., and Miranda, E. R. (2002). Modelling the development of mirror neurons for auditory-motor integration. *Journal of New Music Research*, 31(4), 367–75.

Williams, P., and Stackhouse, J. (1998). Diadochokinetic skills: Normal and atypical performance in children aged 3–5 years. *International Journal of Language Communication Disorders*, 33 suppl., 481–6.

Wilson, E. O., and Holldöbler, B. (1988). Dense heterarchies and mass communication as the basis of organization in ant colonies. *Trends in Ecology and Evolution*, 3, 65–8.

Woolhouse, R. S. (1988). *The Empiricists*. Oxford: Oxford University Press.

Wyatt, R., Sell, D., Russell, J., Harding, A., Harland, K., and Albery, E. (1996). Cleft palate speech dissected: A review of current knowledge and analysis. *British Journal of Plastic Surgery*, 49(3), 143–9.

Yu, C., Ballard, D. H., and Aslin, R. N. (2005). The role of embodied intention in early lexical acquisition. *Cognitive Science*, 29, 961–1005.

Zamuner, T. S. (2003). *Input-Based Phonological Acquisition*. New York: Routledge.

Zamuner, T. S., Gerken, L. A., and Hammond, M. (2005). The acquisition of phonology based on input: A closer look at the relation of cross-linguistic and child language data. *Lingua,* 10, 1403–26.

Zeger, S. L., Liang, K. Y., and Albert, P. S. (1988). Models for longitudinal data: A generalized estimating equation approach. *Biometrics,* 44(4), 1049–60.

Zhang, X., and Tomblin, J. B. (2000). The association of intervention receipt with speech-language profiles and social-demographic variables. *American Journal of Speech-Language Pathology,* 9(4), 345–57.

Zlatic, L., MacNeilage, P. F., Matyear, C. L., and Davis, B. L. (1997). Babbling of twins in a bilingual environment. *Applied Psycholinguistics,* 18(4), 453–69.

Zubrick, S. R., Taylor, C. L., Rice, M. L., and Slegers, D. W. (2007). Late language emergence at 24 months: An epidemiological study of prevalence, predictors, and covariates. *Journal of Speech, Language, and Hearing Research,* 50, 1562–92.

Index

Page references in *italic* indicate Figures

boundary values for phonology and human language 171–2
brain-based learning, neural net modeling studies 25, 145–6, 148
brain-based machine modeling 25
Browman, K. and Goldstein, L. 140
Bruner, J. S. 58, 62
Bybee, J. L. 104

C

Camazine, S. 30
canonical babbling 10, 31, 33, 49, 53, 73–4, 78, 80, 82, 89–90, 91, 97–8, 102, 105, 141–2, 158 see also babbling
caregiver input 59, 60, 61–2, 66, 70, 72, 73, 74, 81, 86, 96, 157 see also mother–child interactions
Cartesian philosophy 21, 123–4
central nervous system 155
Chapman, K. L. et al. 89
CHILDES database 127, 172
child-internal capacities 2–3, 43, 46, 48–54, 132, 154, 156–7; altricial 42, 57, 72; cognitive see cognitive system; neural cognition; social cognition; general-purpose see general-purpose scaffolding/capacities; mutual influences with environmental partners 46, 51, 66–7; neural-cognitive 1, 2–3, 47, 53–7, 60, 69–70, 173; perception see speech perception: capacities; precocial 42; production see speech production: capacities; social capacities see social capacities
Chinese (Putonghua) 107, 108, 165
Chomsky, N. 23, 128, 155; and Halle, M. 47, 124
Clark, A. 21, 51
cleft lip/palate (CLP) 88–90
clicks 77
CLP (cleft lip/palate) 88–90
cochlear 75; implants 87, 118–19
cognitive development 57–8, 60, 102, 148; refining and increasing

complexity stage see refining pattern complexity; sensing and moving stage see sensing and moving
cognitive processing 78–9, 112–14 see also psycholinguistics; speed 114; top–down 9, 10, 21, 99
cognitive/psycholinguistic approaches to acquisition of phonology 23–4, 143–51, 147, 160–1 see also psycholinguistics; neighborhood density 145, 150–1; perceptual-neural modeling 150
cognitive science 21, 121–2, 152; approach to phonological acquisition see cognitive/psycholinguistic approaches to acquisition of phonology; cognitive processing see cognitive processing; neural cognition see neural cognition; psycholinguistics see psycholinguistics; social cognition 57–9, 61, 143, 147
cognitive system 52–4; long-term cognitive storage 53, 100, 104
Colman, A. M. 6
communication disorders 114, 166–7; hearing loss/impairment 5–6, 87–8, 118–20; of speech see speech disorders
compensatory articulation patterns 89
competence–performance dichotomy 140
complexity theory 12–14, 67; and patterns 14
computer modeling 25, 133, 138
connectionist neural net models 25, 143, 145–6, 148
constructivist interaction 19
context dependence 14–15
convex region targets 149, 150
cortex: cortical structures underlying memory 32–3, 55; maturation of connections to higher cortical structures 76–7; maturation of the auditory cortex 76; and neural maturation 56